CATHOLIC BISHOPS IN AMERICAN POLITICS

CATHOLIC BISHOPS
IN
AMERICAN POLITICS

Timothy A. Byrnes

PRINCETON UNIVERSITY PRESS   PRINCETON, NEW JERSEY

Library of Congress Cataloging-in-Publication Data
Byrnes, Timothy A., 1958–
Catholic bishops in American politics / Timothy A. Byrnes.
p.   cm.
Includes bibliographical references and index.
ISBN 0-691-07876-9 (alk. paper)
1. Catholic Church—United States—Bishops—History—20th century.
2. Catholic Church—United States—Political activity.   3. United
States—Church history—20th century.   4. United States—Politics
and government—1977–   5. United States—Politics and
government—1945–   I. Title.
BX1407.B57B85   1991
261.8—dc20   90-23098

This book has been composed in Linotron Times Roman

Princeton University Press books are printed
on acid-free paper, and meet the guidelines
for permanence and durability of the Committee
on Production Guidelines for Book Longevity
of the Council on Library Resources

Printed in the United States of America by
Princeton University Press, Princeton, New Jersey

1   3   5   7   9   10   8   6   4   2

DEDICATED TO THE MEMORY OF

——————— Sheila Mary Byrnes (1960–1986) ———————
and Randall Bruce Dull (1964–1989)

Contents

Acknowledgments

I HAVE ACCUMULATED many debts during the years I worked on this book. I owe the most thanks to Benjamin Ginsberg and Theodore Lowi of the Government Department at Cornell University. This book quite literally would not have been written or published without their help. They aided and encouraged me from beginning to end, and I hope that my own students will benefit from the example that Ginsberg and Lowi have set for me. Martin Shefter and Jeremy Rabkin also read an earlier draft of the manuscript, and they each offered a number of helpful comments and suggestions. Michael Busch helped in ways too numerous to list.

George Kahin and Walter LaFeber were there at the very beginning, although neither they nor I realized it at the time. William Barnett, Michael Himes, and Joseph McShane also provided suggestions and much needed encouragement in the early stages. Patrick Arnold, Jamie Gangel, Gerald McMurray, Thomas Reese, Rick Rolf, and Warren Willis were among the many people who offered their time and resources in order to make my task easier. A number of bishops, church officials, and political professionals sat down with me for formal interviews. Most of these people are listed in the bibliography, but a small number of them did request anonymity. Whether acknowledged or not, however, each of the interviewees was gracious and responsive.

Throughout my efforts, I was lucky to have the generous support of other scholars who have turned their attention to the political activities of the American Catholic hierarchy. In particular, Jim Castelli, John Tracy Ellis, Michael Novak, and A. James Reichley offered me their encouragement and, I am proud to say, their friendship. I am happy to have this chance to express my gratitude to them. I am also grateful to Gail Ullman at Princeton University Press. I appreciate both her interest in my work specifically, and her support for the study of religion and politics more generally. I also appreciate the stylistic help offered by Maria denBoer.

I wrote most of this book while I was on the staff of the Cornell-in-Washington Public Policy Program in Washington, D.C. K. C. Parsons, Linda Johnson, and Carol Hagen ran an efficient and very human program that allowed me to research and write while I also fulfilled my teaching duties. Jack Moran, Larry Weil, and Dan Wirls were friends as well as colleagues. I completed the book as a member of the Political Science Department at the City College of the City University of New York. Everyone in the department was unfailingly supportive, but my office neighbors, David Garrow and Diana Gordan, were particularly so. Their levelheadedness, gained from experience, was a great help in the last stages of this project.

At a more personal level, I also owe thanks to my parents, Robert and Helen Byrnes, for their encouragement over the years. They have been loving and challenging parents, and without knowing it they played an important and fundamental role in my writing this particular book. Many years ago they introduced me to the Catholic Church, to politics, and to the notion that the two might be related in interesting and significant ways. Finally, I want to thank my wife, Dolores Byrnes. She read, edited, and indexed the manuscript, and led me through innumerable word processing crises. But most important, she consistently yet gently reminded me, through her vitality, her balance, and her love, that there is a good deal more to life than Catholic bishops, political parties, and writing deadlines.

CATHOLIC BISHOPS IN AMERICAN POLITICS

CHAPTER ONE

Introduction

RELIGIOUS LEADERS have played a very prominent role in American politics over the last fifteen years. They have articulated positions on various public policies, formed coalitions with other leaders and groups, and lent support, both implicitly and explicitly, to particular candidates and parties. As a result of their political activities, these religious leaders have encountered considerable criticism. They have been accused of breaching the wall of separation between church and state, and of imposing their own sectarian values and convictions on American politics. These accusations, however, have been based on a fundamental misunderstanding of the way that religion and politics actually mix in the United States. Critics of these church leaders have failed to take into account the role that political developments and factors have played in establishing the dynamic contemporary relationship between religion and politics in the United States. Religious leaders have not imposed themselves on American politics in recent years. Rather, they have been actively sought out and drawn into the political process by politicians and party leaders anxious to emphasize new issues and build new electoral coalitions.

In political terms, the key to the modern role of American religion has been a shift in the partisan alignment of the national party system. According to V. O. Key, a critical election is a "type of election in which there occurs a sharp and durable electoral realignment between the parties."[1] No election since the 1930s has completely satisfied this definition, and so no true critical realignment has taken place since then. Nevertheless, the stable alignment that characterized American politics from the New Deal to the 1960s has given way to a more fluid and volatile competition between the parties. The once-dominant Democratic coalition, first brought together by Franklin Roosevelt, has decayed and splintered. And both major parties have sought policies and strategies that would allow them to replace that coalition with a new and equally durable electoral majority.

A byproduct of this new uncertainty has been the parties' discovery of religion as a tool of political mobilization and coalition building. Candidates for national office, seeking to shift a tenuous partisan alignment in their favor, have appealed to voters on religious grounds, focused the media's and the public's attention on religious issues, and debated among themselves the proper role that religion should play in American politics and public policy.

Along the way, these political leaders have also expanded and deepened the role religious leaders play in the national political process.

This book is an examination of the relationship between political change and the activities of the American Catholic hierarchy. In recent years, of course, the Catholic bishops have been deeply involved in American politics. They have been leaders of the antiabortion movement; they have published highly detailed pastoral letters on nuclear weapons and the U.S. economy; and they have participated, both individually and collectively, in the national electoral process. In one sense, these activities have been shaped by internal Catholic developments like the enhanced social status of American Catholicism and the reformed organizational structure of the hierarchy itself. Freed from the responsibility to defend a persecuted, immigrant church, the bishops have strengthened their national conference and addressed a number of important items on the agenda of national politics. These internal matters, however, do not, on their own, satisfactorily explain the bishops' role in the contemporary political process. As I will illustrate in this book, that role has also been shaped by political change, by an expansion of the federal government's authority and initiative, and by rumblings in the party system that have led politicians to associate themselves with the bishops or with segments of the bishops' moral agenda.

The uncertain nature of the partisan alignment, for example, has attached renewed political significance to the hierarchy's relationship with Catholic voters. Catholics, an important component of the Democratic party's New Deal coalition, have emerged as volatile swing voters at the presidential level.[2] As a result, they have been coveted and actively sought by both Democratic and Republican candidates. The bishops cannot deliver these Catholic voters to either party; they do not have that kind of authority. But what they do have is access to these voters, access that is highly prized by politicians. In fact, I have discovered in conversations with leaders from both political parties that politicians tend to believe that the bishops' access to Catholic voters is tantamount to influence over Catholic votes.

At one level, I suppose, this perception is based on solid tactical considerations. Politicians, after all, cannot afford to dismiss the leadership of America's largest church. At another level, however, this belief is based on simple ignorance of the way that the modern Catholic Church conducts its business. As I will document in later chapters, American political leaders, as a rule, have not had a particularly sophisticated understanding of either Catholics or Catholicism.[3] Regardless of what it is based on, however, a perception that the bishops can influence votes has been enough to make candidates sensitive to the bishops and anxious to identify areas of agreement with them.

The bishops have more than just access to Catholic voters, of course. They also have virtually unparalleled institutional resources at their disposal. "If you are a bishop," Walter Mondale's 1984 campaign manager said to me, "you've got some pretty substantial organizational capabilities. . . . You've got a lot of people, you've got money, places to meet. . . . You've got a lot of things that any good politician would like to have at his disposal."[4] You also have the ability, if you are the Catholic hierarchy collectively, to create or fortify social movements in support of your preferred policy positions.

The clearest example of the bishops' use of their resources for political purposes has been their role in the right-to-life movement. They gave the movement a great deal of money and other forms of institutional support that were indispensable to its initial formation and early development. And the bishops are still important guarantors of the right-to-life movement's financial and organizational viability. But the Catholic Church's resources can be applied to issues other than abortion. One of the reasons that politicians took seriously the bishops' pastoral letter on nuclear weapons, for example, was that the bishops had the wherewithal to offer substantial support to the nuclear freeze movement and its political allies.

Candidates and party leaders prefer to maintain cordial relations with anyone who can marshall these kinds of national resources. But candidates and party leaders are especially solicitous of resourceful community leaders who are also identified with religion, one of the most powerful forces in American life. The United States of America is quite simply one of the most religious nations in the world. In 1985, fully 95 percent of Americans believed in God, 68 percent belonged to an organized religious body, and 40 percent claimed that they attended church services on a weekly basis. In addition, the significance of religion in American life goes well beyond individual conviction and practice. According to *The Gallup Report*, Americans placed a higher degree of confidence in their churches than in any other institution, and 61 percent of them believed that religion could solve all or most of the problems facing the United States.[5]

During the 1970s and 1980s, the Catholic bishops came to be seen as responsible and effective spokesmen for these religious values and sensibilities that are so pervasive among the American public. The National Conference of Catholic Bishops (NCCB) demonstrated an ability to articulate morally grounded positions on a wide range of national issues. And a number of individual bishops exhibited a willingness to lend their moral authority, and that of their church, to politically sensitive issues and movements. Unlike their predecessors, these bishops have not been branded un-American or dismissed as antidemocratic threats to constitutional government. To the contrary, the bishops' visible religious identity and unapologetic moral assertiveness have made them attractive potential allies to a wide range of political forces. Anxious to attract Catholic voters, exploit Catholic resources, and apply a religious gloss to their own partisan programs, candidates and party leaders have sought the bishops out, engaged the bishops in political discussion, and highlighted the bishops' moral agenda. In short, the Catholic hierarchy has been enthusiastically welcomed into a political process in which the axis of political debate has shifted toward greater emphasis on religious issues and moral discourse.

This is not to suggest that the bishops have been entirely passive in regard to their role in the political process. To be sure, the bishops have established their own policy agenda and decided to pursue that agenda through concerted political action. In fact, I will closely examine the formulation of the bishops' policy positions, and I will point to several developments, particularly within the church, that have led the bishops to substantially alter their approach to the national political process.

Nevertheless, I will argue throughout the chapters that follow that the bishops' specific political activities, particularly in terms of their participation in the electoral process, cannot be understood without reference to the instability and renewed competitiveness that have characterized the American party system over the last twenty years. The bishops' political role, over that period of time, has been shaped by a series of particular intersections of their own policy agenda with the platforms and strategies of the major American political parties. In fact, even the content of the moral and political debate *within* the American hierarchy, a debate that has led to many of the bishops' most celebrated activities, has itself been determined by political developments.

There are essentially two camps within the National Conference of Catholic Bishops when it comes to public policy and political priorities. The first camp is made up of bishops who emphasize a whole series of modern threats to human life. These bishops approach issues such as abortion, nuclear weapons, poverty, and capital punishment in a more or less even-handed way. They argue that paying too much attention to abortion unnecessarily narrows the church's prolife concerns and blunts the potential political effectiveness of what they call the consistent ethic of life or seamless garment of human dignity. This group also points out that an exclusive emphasis on abortion inappropriately places the NCCB in political alliance with right-to-life forces whose views conflict with the church's official position on virtually every other issue.

Opposed to this camp is a group of bishops who believe that abortion should be the American church's first political priority. These bishops do not necessarily deny the validity of other prolife concerns, or even the need to respond to them. But they believe it is fatuous and dangerous to equate merely potential threats to human life, such as nuclear war, with the actual destruction of millions of fetuses every year. They argue that a diffuse, so-called consistent, approach dilutes the bishops' commitment to the protection of the unborn and undercuts the potential effectiveness of the bishops' antiabortion activities. In response to the concerns expressed by supporters of the consistent ethic, these bishops minimize the costs of an alliance with political forces who disagree with the bishops on other issues. They point out that these disagreements tend to be over the most appropriate means to agreed upon ends. Very few people, for example, actually advocate nuclear war or increased poverty, but millions of people, many of whom agree with the NCCB on other issues, do indeed strongly support legal abortion.

This debate should not be construed as a dispute over the substance of the Catholic hierarchy's policy positions. On the whole, there is a remarkable degree of consensus among the bishops over the content of their agenda. All of the bishops support their church's condemnation of abortion, and the pastoral letters on nuclear weapons and the U.S. economy, although the product of compromise, nevertheless were endorsed by overwhelming majorities of the bishops' conference. What the bishops *do* disagree about is the way their agenda should be pursued in circumstances where its major components (proarms control, prosocial spending, and antiabortion) cut across the prevailing cleavage of American national politics.

This crucial debate within the Catholic hierarchy over its political priorities has been influenced by politics in two fundamental ways. First of all, the debate is not merely over two different formulations of the Catholic Church's moral teachings. It is also over the way those teachings will intersect with the platforms and strategies of various political forces. To a great extent, in other words, the debate is quite straightforwardly a political one. Formulations and public presentations of the church's teachings that emphasize abortion over and above all other issues lend support to candidates and parties who agree with the bishops on that one issue. The consistent ethic of life, to say the least, does not.

Moreover, the bishops' debate itself has been framed and set in motion by developments that have taken place in the political process rather than in the bishops' conference. The two sides of the debate are two conflicting reactions to the fact that candidates have sought to identify themselves with limited segments of the bishops' moral agenda. The choice between the seamless garment and a more abortion-centered approach is really a political choice concerning the bishops' reaction to the use of their moral authority and policy agenda for partisan purposes.

An appreciation for the part that political developments and factors have played in shaping the bishops' activities in recent years affords us a much clearer and fuller understanding of those activities.

The bishops' opposition to legal abortion, for example, was not, at first, a partisan position. It became one, however, once the Republican party, seeking to effect a realignment and build what it called a "new majority," adopted the prolife banner and began to present itself as the party of religious and moral values.

The bishops' pastoral letters on nuclear weapons and the U.S. economy were politically significant not because they influenced public policy (they did not), but rather because they distanced the bishops from a Republican coalition and a conservative political agenda that had been linked to religion and religious values during the presidential campaign of 1980.

Cardinal Joseph Bernardin's seamless garment or consistent ethic of life was in part a political strategy designed to emphasize the fact that the bishops' agenda cut across the major cleavages of contemporary American politics. It was an attempt, in other words, to prevent candidates from identifying themselves with bits and pieces of the bishops' prolife agenda.

Cardinal O'Connor's criticism of Geraldine Ferraro in 1984, on the other hand, was an effort to redirect the media's and the public's attention away from the pastoral letters and Bernardin's consistent ethic and back onto the bishops' opposition to legal abortion. It was an invitation of sorts for antiabortion candidates to claim that the church supported their policy platforms.

In subsequent chapters I will examine this relationship between the American Catholic hierarchy and the American political process in much greater detail. I will dissect several of the bishops' policy positions, and analyze the roles that these positions played in the mobilization strategies of various political forces. I will also examine the bishops' involvement in several national election campaigns. We will see that in each and every instance the specific nature of that involvement was as much a function of the strategic maneuvering of politicians and party leaders as it was of the actions and statements of the bishops themselves.

I wrote this book with several related purposes in mind. I wanted to fill a substantial gap in the literature on the American Catholic hierarchy, suggest a more politics-centered approach to the study of religion and politics in general, and contribute to the discussion of realignment theory and its applicability to contemporary American politics.

First of all, despite widespread journalistic interest in the Catholic Church, the bishops have received relatively little attention from political scientists. A few general works on religion and politics have examined the political behavior of the Catholic hierarchy, but all of them have been limited by their very broad approach to the subject matter.[6] Mary Hanna, in *Catholics and American Politics*, did look exclusively at American Catholicism, but she concentrated more on the question of whether Catholics constitute a meaningfully distinct political entity than on the political activities of the hierarchy.[7] J. Brian Benestad, on the other hand, studied the bishops specifically, but he was more interested in criticizing the content of the hierarchy's agenda than in analyzing the bishops as political actors.[8]

I have limited the scope of my inquiry to the activities of the Catholic hierarchy alone, and I have examined those activities through the use of concepts and categories derived from contemporary political science. My aim has not been to offer a normative assessment of the bishops' agenda. Rather, it has been to offer an account of how that agenda was developed, and an analysis of how that agenda has been related to changes in the American political process. I have quite deliberately chosen, in other words, to emphasize the political side of the relationship between the bishops and politics. Furthermore, I believe that such an emphasis could bring a greater sense of balance to more broadly based studies of religion and politics as well.

Most analysis of the recent political activities of American religious leaders has focused on the extent to which those leaders have influenced the political process. Such analysis is entirely appropriate, of course, but my examination of the Catholic bishops suggests that students of religion and politics must begin to look more closely and carefully at the expressly political aspects of their subject. The relationship between religion and politics in the United States is a very dynamic one, and the political role of religion and religious leaders has been determined, in part, by developments that in themselves have had virtually nothing to do with religion.

One of these developments, as I have already indicated, has been the decline of the Democratic party's New Deal coalition. This decline has not been followed by a durable realignment of the party system, but it has sparked renewed scholarly interest in critical realignment as both a process and a theory. Traditional theory holds that realignments are primarily the results of growing tensions in society. Walter Dean Burnham, a leading student of these matters, wrote that "realignments arise from emergent tensions in society, which not adequately controlled by the organization or outputs of party politics as usual, escalate to a flashpoint."[9] James Sundquist, writing after Burnham, devised a complex model of realignment based on a review of American political history.[10] Sundquist also emphasized tensions in society, and he described how those tensions have periodically cut across, and then eradicated, the prevailing cleavages of an existing party system.

Recently, students of electoral politics have given greater weight to the role that politicians and political strategies play in causing and directing critical realignments. John Chubb and Paul Peterson, for example, have written that "the main drawback of [the traditional realignment approach] is that it overlooks the way in which political leaders, the policies they formulate, and the institutions they create also shape and reshape political life, turning it in new directions that the electorate then endorses."[11] I would add to this, that in the contemporary period, political leaders have formulated policies and adopted strategies for the express purpose of setting a realignment in motion. Realignment, in other words, is now more than an analytical theory of political change; it is also a political strategy designed to cause that change. Today's conservative leaders, for example, have read V. O. Key, Walter Dean Burnham, and the other leading scholars of realignment theory and electoral history. These conservatives believe that a realignment should have occurred by now, and they are doing everything in their power to see that it does occur sooner or later.

In this book I will be looking at the ways that these conservatives and other political strategists have tried to use religion and religious leaders to redraw the cleavages and alignments of American politics. However, I think the theoretical point holds true in a more general sense as well. Explanations of shifts in the partisan alignment of the modern party system have to credit the degree to which politicians purposefully create new issues, identify new voters, destroy old cleavages, and forge new coalitions out of a disparate mass electorate.[12]

Up to this point, I have been discussing the Catholic hierarchy's involvement in the American political process as though it were a new phenomenon. Of course, the bishops have been involved in American politics for a very long time. It is the form that their involvement now takes and the factors that influence it that have changed in recent years. Chapter 2, by way of highlighting these changes, will examine the history of the bishops' political activities and identify two consistent themes that characterized the bishops' traditional political role.

Chapter 3 will address the factors, both ecclesiastical and political, that undermined this traditional role, and it will point to several ways in which the bishops redesigned their approach to a rapidly changing political process. The history of the bishops' antiabortion activities will be presented in chapter 4, as will a discussion of the close relationship between those activities and the conservative attempt to form a "new majority" in the 1970s. Chapter 5 will carry that discussion forward by detailing the bishops' involvement in the presidential campaign of 1976. That campaign was probably the clearest case of the bishops' role and activities being determined by political developments taking place outside of the bishops' conference. Chapter 6, with its account of the bishops' more indirect role in the election of 1980, will document the ways that the bishops and their agenda can play a political role even when the bishops themselves have opted out of a particular campaign.

In chapter 7, I will turn to the bishops' expansion of their agenda through the release of their pastoral letter on nuclear weapons. I will describe the contents of the letter in detail, analyze the motivations behind the writing of it, and discuss the reception the letter received from various political forces. Chapter 8, then, will deal with the presidential campaign of 1984, during which the bishops' internal debate over the articulation and presentation of their church's teachings became public, and paralleled a central political debate between the major presidential candidates.

In chapter 9 I will assess the significance of the bishops' pastoral letter on the American economy in terms of the letter's relationship to the partisan competition between Democrats and Republicans. I will attribute the bishops' relatively marginal role in the 1988 election to political circumstances and conditions. And I will point to a number of ways in which party platforms, electoral strategies, and other political factors will continue to affect the American Catholic hierarchy. In the future, as in the past, the bishops' political role will be shaped by the intersection of their own teachings and priorities with the partisan alignment of American national politics.

CHAPTER TWO

A Political History

IT WOULD BE a mistake to view the Catholic hierarchy's participation in the American political process as a recent development. In fact, the relationship between the bishops and American politics began in 1790 when, within a few months of each other, George Washington was inaugurated as the first president of the United States and John Carroll was installed in Baltimore as America's first bishop. American Catholic bishops have always played a political role; it is the character of that role which has changed in recent years and which is in need of explication.

The first step in this explication is to place the bishops' contemporary activities within their proper historical context. In this chapter, I will present an overview of the history of the Catholic hierarchy's involvement in American politics during what I will call the traditional era, from 1790 to the Second Vatican Council of the 1960s. This review will not only provide background for analysis of the contemporary period, it will also lead to a discussion of the various political and ecclesiastical developments that have reshaped the role the bishops play in the political process. It is difficult to generalize about the character of the bishops' political role during the traditional era. Any attempt to categorize 170 years of complex history must be cautious. Nevertheless, in comparison with the contemporary era, two fundamental themes do stand out as being characteristic of the traditional period.

First of all, the bishops' political role was a function of their authoritative leadership of an embattled minority. The bishops were involved in politics insofar as they led, spoke for, or represented identifiable constituencies. American Catholics, during most of the traditional era, were an insulated minority. They were immigrants, or children of immigrants, who lived in their own neighborhoods, attended parochial schools, and suffered the various effects of anti-Catholicism. This "immigrant church" looked to its bishops for leadership, protection, and help in assimilating into a hostile American culture. And the bishops responded with political actions designed to defend the interests of their church and its members.

Second, the political activities of the American Catholic bishops were overwhelmingly local in nature. Although the bishops did make efforts at collectivization and nationalization from time to time, those efforts generally took a subordinate position to the decisions and actions of individual local bishops. In terms of the church's own law, those local bishops, by virtue of their direct relationship with the pope, exercised autonomous authority in their own dioceses. The hierarchy was not a collective authoritative entity. Rather, its authority was embodied in each bishop in each locality. At the same time, American politics itself was focused more on the local level than it is today. The better part of actual governing, particularly on so-called Catholic issues like education and public morality, was carried out by state and local officials. As a result, most of the hierarchy's salient political activities during the traditional era involved the relationships between individual bishops and these local politicians and officials.

Together, this local focus and this authoritative leadership of an important constituency formed a substantial political role for the Catholic hierarchy. Bishops were called on to defend the interests of their people and to ensure the viability of their church's institutions. Mayors, party bosses, and other political leaders had to respect the institutional resources that Catholic bishops represented. In fact, as Catholics came to comprise a larger and larger percentage of America's urban population, several cardinals and archbishops became legendary power brokers. In addition, the bishops served as apologists for the compatibility of Catholic doctrine with American political principles. Convinced that good Catholics could also be good Americans, the bishops defended the separation of church and state, announced their political independence from Rome, and vouched for the patriotic loyalties of their people. This effort often took the form of the hierarchy's main involvement with national politics during the traditional era—boosterism. From the Revolution through most of the Vietnam War, the Catholic hierarchy asserted the patriotism of American Catholics by offering enthusiastic support of U.S. foreign policy and American war efforts.

For the purposes of clarity and organization, I have divided this chapter into three subperiods. I did not set these parameters arbitrarily. Each period represents a set of distinctive emphases concerning the hierarchy's political role. These emphases and their significance will become clear as the chapter progresses.

1790–1865

Any discussion of the history of the American Catholic hierarchy must begin with John Carroll, America's first bishop. "As the new Republic was unified around the figure of George Washington, so the new American church was drawn together around John Carroll, its first bishop."[1] Furthermore, Bishop Carroll set several powerful precedents for the scope and character of the hierarchy's political role. He actively defended the interests of church institutions, argued that Catholicism and Americanism were not mutually exclusive, and vocally proclaimed his own patriotism.

The first political precedent set by America's first Catholic bishop was that the hierarchy would not involve itself in the partisan political struggles of the day. "I have observed," Carroll said, "that when ministers of Religion leave the duties of their profession to take a busy part in political matters they generally fall into contempt."[2] Nevertheless, Carroll was willing to enter the political arena to defend Catholic interests when he felt they were under attack.

This willingness manifested itself in the trustee crisis that faced the church in the early years of the Republic. Following widespread disestablishment of favored religious groups after the Revolution, the laws of most states recognized only groups of lay church members as rightful owners of church property. Although these policies were inconsistent with Catholic practice of clerical authority, they did not present a pressing problem until individual Catholic groups, known as trustees, claimed the right to name their own pastors. This was a direct challenge to episcopal authority, and Carroll demanded obedience from recalcitrant trustees. He also fought in civil courts to establish the Catholic clergy's right to mandate the internal authority structures of its own church.[3]

Trusteeism continued to plague the American church for decades, but in his initial response Carroll showed that, if necessary, the Catholic hierarchy would wage political and legal battles to protect the church's interests. He was also sensitive to the need of Catholics to portray an American image. To that end, he admonished his priests to form "not Irish, nor English, nor French congregations and churches, but Catholic-American congregations and churches."[4] Moreover, Carroll himself "came to personify the desire for complete compatibility of the ancient church with the new state."[5] Specifically, "Carroll's unstinting devotion to religious freedom put the Catholic Church squarely on the side of justice and civil liberty in the public mind."[6]

He set still another precedent through his equally unstinting devotion to American war aims. This pattern of patriotism had been set even before Carroll became a bishop through his enthusiastic support of the revolutionary cause. More importantly, Carroll displayed a patriotism that was willing to stifle personal dissent in order to assert the Americanism of his church. Although there is evidence that he "deprecated some of the policies" that led to the War of 1812, once hostilities began, he was unswerving in his defense of the American cause.[7] America's first Catholic bishop understood, as so many of his successors would also understand, that nothing was as effective in establishing the loyalty of American Catholics to their country than enthusiastic patriotism among the hierarchy at time of war.

Through its subsequent split into five dioceses and Carroll's death in 1815, the American church lost not only its actual unity, but also its revered leader and symbol of that unity. These developments inaugurated the long era of local episcopal authority and local political activity in the history of the American hierarchy. The main political problem facing the individual bishops following Carroll's death was the issue of trustees. Not only did the bishops have the internal problem of establishing absolute control of their dioceses, they also faced the problem that this effort at control itself caused for their image in the American democratic environment. Ray Billington, a historian of anti-Catholicism in America, wrote that "the impression which the whole struggle [over trusteeism] left on the average American mind was that Catholicism was a sworn enemy to democratic institutions and thus a dangerous influence in the United States."[8]

This dual problem of potential fragmentation and an antidemocratic image pushed Bishop John England of Charleston, South Carolina, into the limelight. England argued that the leaders of the Catholic Church in the United States should meet often to recapture the unity of the Carroll era. He thought the bishops needed to set national policy concerning internal authority structures, and collectively assert, loudly and clearly, the compatibility of Catholicism and Americanism.

His biographer characterized England as the "first apologist of the Catholic faith" in the United States, and as a man "who worked to clearly communicate the harmony between Catholic principles and the constitutional bases of American government."[9] There was no doubt that such communication was sorely needed in the 1820s and 1830s as anti-Catholicism was fueled by the advent of foreign Catholic immigration. England responded to this mood, and to the plethora of periodicals that expressed and encouraged it, by founding the *Catholic Miscellany* of Charleston in 1822. The stated aim of the paper was the "simple explanation and temperate maintenance of the doctrines of the Roman Catholic Church."[10] As a sign that these doctrines posed no threat to non-Catholic America, England placed the First Amendment to the U.S. Constitution at the head of the first issue.

Bishop England was aware that his personal efforts were not enough. He believed that although anti-Catholicism manifested itself in local flare-ups, episcopal councils were "the best mode of counteracting the pernicious influence of our adversaries in their publications, schools, and societies directed against us."[11] He finally succeeded in having the bishops called together in the Provincial Council of 1829. This council released a pastoral letter, written by England, that protested "misrepresentation of the tenets, the principles, and the practices of the church."[12]

Rather than abating in 1829, however, anti-Catholic agitation only got more virulent and widespread. Lyman Beecher opened the 1830s with his campaign against the dangers "popery" represented to American principles, and *The Protestant*, founded in 1832, proposed local organizations throughout the country "for the purposes of exposing the evils of popery and defending the principles of the Reformation."[13] That the Catholic Church in America was not only on the defensive but in fact under violent attack was proved by the sacking and burning of the Ursuline Convent of Charlestown, Massachusetts, in 1834.

Meeting in 1837, the hierarchy again responded through the pen of John England. The *Pastoral Letter of 1837* offered a clear statement of the relationship between American Catholics and their government. It began with a denunciation of the "misrepresentation and persecution" to which the church had been subjected "since the last council."[14] Then England directly addressed the charges of split loyalties being leveled against American Catholics:

> We owe no religious allegiance to any state in this Union, nor to its central government. No one of them claims any supremacy or any dominion over us in our spiritual or ecclesiastical concerns. . . . Nor do we acknowledge any civil or political supremacy or power over us in any foreign potentate, though that potentate might be the chief pastor of our church.[15]

England was the chief architect of a collective policy of defense adopted and proclaimed by the American bishops in the 1830s. Exhortations and pastoral letters, however, were not nearly sufficient to resist anti-Catholicism. Implementation of this defense of the church's interests through involvement in the political process was clearly the local bishops' job. They were the leaders of the Catholic people, and they had access to the local and state governments whose actions affected the church and its institutions. This local focus manifested itself in events that followed the 1840 collective statement that the hierarchy "disclaim[ed] all right to interfere with [Catholics'] judgment in . . . political affairs."[16]

Only one year later, in 1841, Bishop John Hughes of New York entered a "Catholic ticket" in the New York State legislative election and strongly urged all New York Catholics to vote for it over both the Democrats and the Whigs.[17] The issues were local ones involving the proper education of Catholic children. It was school policy in New York, as in many other states, to read the Protestant King James Version of the Bible every day in the public schools. When Hughes failed to have this process halted through protest, he called for state funding of Catholic schools where Catholic children could be educated according to their own tradition. Hughes thought he was asking no more than equal treatment from a state that was, in effect, already supporting Protestant education, but the non-Catholic public reacted sharply to the sight of a high Catholic churchman campaigning openly for public funds. Hughes was rebuffed by both major parties because of this reaction, so the bishop entered his own slate of candidates who supported state aid to Catholic as well as public schools.

In the end, the Catholic candidates were defeated, the King James Bible continued to be read in the schools, and Hughes moved to build an alternative Catholic school system without the aid of state funds. These events, however, clearly illustrate the character of the hierarchy's political role during this period. Hughes stepped with both feet into the political process in order to defend Catholic interests he perceived to be under attack. The issue was local, his authority was local, and he acted at his own discretion and not in concert with the other bishops.

Events surrounding nativist riots in Philadelphia and New York during the 1840s also highlighted the discretion afforded each individual bishop, and the fact that defense of the church was the responsibility of local bishops rather than national councils. When these riots began in Philadelphia with the burning of one church and the threat to burn others, Bishop Francis Patrick Kenrick left the city in order to diffuse a very volatile situation. "I have placed my churches," he announced, "under the care of the Municipal authorities; it is their duty to protect them. Rather let every church burn than shed one drop of blood, or imperil one precious soul."[18] John Hughes did not share his brother bishop's view of the situation. When similar riots appeared on the verge of erupting in New York, Hughes did not exit the city nor entrust the care of his churches to the municipal authorities. Rather, he marched into city hall and warned those authorities that New York's Catholics would retaliate and burn the city if a single Catholic church was harmed. "I come to warn you for your own good," Hughes confidently told New York's mayor.[19]

First in Philadelphia, and then in New York, the local church came under attack. The very different reactions of the individual leaders of those two churches are clear indicators of John Tracy Ellis's general assertion that bishops of this period became politically involved and defended their dioceses "according to their own lights and temperaments."[20]

In the years leading up to the Civil War the emphasis of the bishops' political activities shifted back to the defense of their people's Americanism through the hierarchy's own expressions of patriotism and support for American principles. The most salient features of American Catholicism during the 1850s were the large influx of Irish Catholic immigrants and the reaction to this increasingly "foreign" church in the form of the Know Nothing party. Although the relationship between these two developments was not quite one of direct cause and effect, American Catholicism nevertheless was bitterly opposed during these years by an organized political party that wielded considerable power in several states and at the national level.

As the 1850s wore on, however, the nation concerned itself less with Catholicism as it became more and more occupied with slavery. Nothing illustrates more clearly the change that has taken place in the Catholic hierarchy's political role over the last century or so than the bishops' reaction to the issue of slavery in the 1850s. Modern Americans, used to a Catholic hierarchy that takes clear positions on a whole range of public policy issues, may be surprised to learn that not a single Catholic bishop spoke out in favor of abolition preceding the war. Rather than stir up their congregations on this controversy, most bishops merely assented to their church's cautious acceptance of slavery and advised their people, in the words of Bishop Kenrick, that "nothing should be attempted against the law."[21]

This timidity with regard to slavery did not carry over to the hierarchy's response to the war once it began, however. In fact, individual bishops defended their status as loyal patriots, and by inference the status of all American Catholics, through support of their local government, be it Union or Confederate. One Northern bishop said it best: "There is but one rule for a Catholic, wherever he is . . . to do his duty there as a citizen."[22] The hierarchy enthusiastically performed that duty, and bishops such as Josue Young in the North and Patrick Lynch in the South pleaded the political and moral causes of their respective regions.[23]

The period 1790 to 1865 began with Carroll's attempt to "personify the desire for complete compatibility of the ancient church with the new state," and ended with this compatibility being expressed for both the Union and the Confederacy during the Civil War.[24] In between, men such as Hughes and England pursued a two-sided strategy that combined active defense of particular church interests with assertions of support for American principles and war aims. These activities fit well into the general proposition that the hierarchy's political role was primarily a local one. Although the bishops sometimes collectively argued the compatibility of Catholic doctrine and American principles, the actual political battles were left for individual bishops to fight at local and state levels where the issues were most often decided. The debating, negotiating, and struggling among contending forces, the stuff of American politics, was the job of the local bishop in his role as authoritative leader of the Catholics in his diocese.

1865–1917

The most important feature of American Catholic history between the Civil War and World War I was immigration. During these years the American Catholic population grew quickly as large numbers of Germans, then Eastern Europeans, and finally Italians joined their Irish co-religionists in American urban centers. This massive growth of the American church had two somewhat conflicting effects on the political role of the hierarchy.

The expansion of the Catholic population made urban Catholics a more significant constituency and made local bishops, as leaders of those constituencies, more significant political actors. The relationship between local bishops and local governments was further enhanced in several cities when Catholics, particularly Irish-Catholics, took over urban political machines. On the other hand, the growth in population presented a challenge, if not a threat, to the hierarchy's political role. With more populous and ethnically diverse dioceses the bishops' job of retaining authority became an arduous one. Given that the vast majority of immigrant Catholics belonged to the working class, this job came to require episcopal support of organized labor.

No bishop understood this institutional need to identify the church with the interests of its members more clearly than Cardinal James Gibbons of Baltimore. When a papal condemnation of the Canadian Knights of Labor was proposed for the United States as well, Gibbons recognized the threat such an action posed to the American Catholic Church.[25] The cardinal viewed a condemnation of the Knights in the United States as "a threat to the church's right in popular estimation to be called a friend of the people . . . and [a risk] of having the church regarded as un-American."[26] Moreover, Gibbons believed that the union would fail of its own accord. For the church to be perceived as hurrying its demise would risk losing the loyalty of the working-class Catholic immigrants. In a "memorial" to the Vatican opposing a papal condemnation, Gibbons warned that "to lose the heart of the people would be a misfortune for which the friendship of the few rich and powerful would be no compensation."[27]

The memorial, which succeeded in averting a papal condemnation, highlighted important aspects of the hierarchy's role during this second period of the traditional era. First of all, Gibbons' actions showed that at least some bishops were aware of their need for the loyalty of their people and were willing to take action to ensure it. In fact, Gibbons' personal support of organized labor was cautious at best.[28] His image, however, of rising to the defense of the right to organize gave his church the reputation of friendship toward the labor movement and secured the continued church membership and loyalty of the immigrant Catholic workers.

Gibbons' efforts were not limited to proving that Catholics could be good Americans. He was also trying to convince the pope and Vatican leaders that Americans—even Americans who belonged to labor unions—could also be good Catholics. Gibbons had to defend the interests of the American immigrant church from successors to the Know Nothing party, *and* from a distrustful Vatican. In the final years of the nineteenth century, this situation led to a pitched battle between two warring factions of the hierarchy over how to advance and defend the interests of the American church.

These interests were, indeed, in need of protection. The great waves of Catholic immigration in the late nineteenth and early twentieth centuries gave the American church an increasingly "foreign" character. The immigrant church of these decades was a subculture, or series of subcultures, with its own social and educational systems. The hierarchical structure and devotional practices of the church, coupled with the foreign customs and languages of its membership, made American Catholicism quite distinctive. Nativists responded to this distinctiveness with arguments that Catholics were inherently disloyal to American democratic principles. Foremost among nativist groups in this period was the American Protective Association (APA), founded in 1887. The APA was an explicitly anti-Catholic organization whose members publicly denounced the pope and the Roman Catholic Church, and whose constitution opposed the "holding of office in national, state, or municipal government by any subject or supporter of ecclesiastical power."[29]

Two factions within the hierarchy offered contending strategies for the defense of church interests in the face of this type of opposition. The first of these factions was called the liberals or Americanists and was led by Archbishop John Ireland of St. Paul, Minnesota, and supported by Cardinal Gibbons. Ireland, known as the "consecrated blizzard of the Northwest," clearly stated the liberals' point of view in a speech to the 1884 Plenary Council:

> There is no conflict between the Catholic Church and America. I could not utter one syllable that would belie, however remotely, either the Church or the Republic, and when I assert, as I now solemnly do, that the principles of the Church are in thorough harmony with the interests of the Republic, I know in the depths of my soul that I speak the truth.[30]

The liberals felt that the best way for the Catholic Church to prosper in America was for it to become more American. In that effort, they went a step beyond bishops like Carroll and England who had argued that Catholics were loyal Americans. "To overcome anti-Catholic prejudice," Gerald Fogarty wrote, "[the liberals] worked to slough off unessential Roman traditions and to rid the church of its foreign taint by rapidly Americanizing the Immigrants."[31]

This liberal strategy may have been effective in refuting the APA, but it encountered serious opposition within the Catholic hierarchy itself. The opposing faction, known as the conservatives, was led by Archbishop Michael Corrigan of New York and Bishop Bernard McQuaid of Rochester, but it was made up largely of German-American prelates who wanted to retain German culture and resented the increasing dominance of the so-called Irish hibernarchy.[32] The conservatives distrusted their liberal colleagues and worked to establish closer relations with the Vatican. The struggle between these two factions grew into a very serious crisis for the American church.

Among the great battles of this conflict were the school crisis of 1891 and the McGlynn affair of 1886/87. In both instances the conservatives and liberals disagreed over how to defend the long-term interests of the church in the American context. Should the church adopt the liberal strategy of accommodating itself to American society, and defending itself from attack by asserting that accommodation? Or should the church follow the conservative line and remain aloof from mainstream American culture, retain its "foreign" character, and defend itself through insulation and internal solidarity?

We have already seen how in the New York school controversy of 1841 the church had moved toward independent educational systems in individual dioceses. The liberal bishops thought that such separation and confrontation led to Catholic criticism of the public schools, which in turn needlessly invited nativist agitation. These bishops preferred to encourage and assert Catholic support of the public schools as a symbol of Catholic commitment to American values in general. Cardinal Gibbons, for example, framed the question not as whether Catholic schools could effectively compete with public schools, but rather as "whether the church is to be honored as a bulwark of liberty and order, or is to be despised and suspected as an enemy of [American] institutions."[33]

Archbishop Ireland clearly had this question in mind when he spoke of the public schools as "our pride and glory" and declared: "The free schools of America! Withered be the hand raised in sign of its destruction."[34] These alleged hands of destruction were, of course, Catholic hands—German-Catholic hands in particular. The bishops of Wisconsin, for example, had just successfully waged a battle to defend the Catholic schools against the Bennett Law of 1889. This statute, which called for compulsory attendance at schools that taught in English, was a direct attack on the German-speaking Catholic schools of the state. The local bishops had mustered all the political influence at their disposal to reverse the law, and they did not appreciate Ireland's implied criticism of their efforts.

The issue reached the Vatican when the conservative bishops asked the pope to disallow an accommodation in Ireland's diocese whereby the state rented Catholic facilities for secular education, and religion was taught on the same premises after regular school hours. Although the liberals won a victory when the Vatican granted its cautious consent for Ireland's school plan, the long-term effect of the crisis was to involve the Vatican more directly in determining the character and strategies of the American Catholic Church. The liberals and conservatives petitioned the Vatican, as it were, for support of their respective views.

Similar dynamics were involved in the McGlynn affair in New York. Many authors have addressed this case, but none have presented the facts as succinctly as Thomas McAvoy:

> Father Edward McGlynn was a successful pulpit orator and a leader in popular causes in New York. He did not believe in a separate Catholic school system but desired rather to support programs of social reform. . . . His chief critic was the coadjutor Archbishop Corrigan. In 1886 Henry George ran for Mayor of New York against Abram S. Hewitt. George had elaborated in his books and speeches his theory of a single tax which, according to some, denied the right of private property. When Father McGlynn supported George, Corrigan suspended him for two weeks and reinstated the suspension when Father McGlynn resumed his polit-

ical speaking during the very heated campaign. George lost the election to Hewitt. Archbishop Corrigan's pastoral on religious matters shortly after contained an implied condemnation of Henry George's proposals. McGlynn publicly criticized the pastoral, and his suspension was continued. In the meantime the Sacred Congregation of Propaganda summoned "alumnus McGlynn" to Rome. He refused to go and, when he continued his refusal, was excommunicated on July 3, 1887.[35]

The conflict did not end with McGlynn's excommunication. While Corrigan had acted as the local bishop defending the church in his diocese from what he viewed as the creeping socialism of George's thesis, other bishops outside of New York were concerned about what the denunciation of McGlynn would do to the church's image in the United States. The liberals feared that Corrigan's actions would be interpreted as "ecclesiastical tyranny" by non-Catholics and as an attack on a prominent friend of labor by the Catholic working class.[36] Better to avoid nativist antagonism and retain the allegiance of church membership by allowing George, like the Knights of Labor before him, to pass from the scene without a shove from the Catholic hierarchy.

The liberals once again carried the day in the short term. When the issue was forwarded to Rome for decision, the Vatican did not publicly condemn George's theory as Corrigan had requested, and more surprisingly, the pope reconciled Father McGlynn to the church and returned him to the active ministry in the New York archdiocese. These liberal victories in the school crisis and McGlynn affair proved pyrrhic for two reasons. First, the aggressive pursuit of the liberal agenda deepened the liberal-conservative rift in the American hierarchy. Conservative bishops not only disagreed with the liberals in substance, they also resented what they saw as liberal meddling in the affairs of their own dioceses. This disagreement and resentment split the hierarchy dramatically and discredited the liberals' claims to speak for the American church as a whole.

Second, these intramural conflicts caused the Vatican to become more intimately involved in the American church's affairs, and occasioned the assignment of an apostolic delegate from the pope to the United States. This delegate, Archbishop Francesco Satolli, initially supported the liberals' cause. But in time he came to distrust their attempt to Americanize the church and distance the hierarchy from Rome's influence.

Internal division and Satolli, however, were not enough to defeat the liberals. Their real stumbling block was the spread of liberal notions of accommodation and authority to Europe. The Vatican may have been willing to tolerate liberalism among the Americans because of the special relationship that pertained between church and state in the United States. This tolerance turned to condemnation, however, when the liberals "imprudently undertook to give lessons on up-to-date Catholicism to their unenlightened brethren abroad."[37]

In particular, the spread of so-called Americanist ideals to France resulted in Pope Leo XIII's condemnation in 1899 of the so-called Americanist heresy in *Testem Benevolentiae*.[38] John Tracy Ellis summarized the document:

> The errors amounted to this: that the church should adapt itself to modern civiliza-
> tion, relax its ancient rigors, show indulgence to modern theories and methods,
> de-emphasize religious vows, and give greater scope for the actions of the Holy
> Spirit on the individual soul.[39]

Gibbons and Ireland argued that no prominent American Catholics, includ-ing themselves, held such views, and there is no evidence that any Americans felt obliged to leave the church because of *Testem Benevolentiae*. Neverthe-less, the identification of the condemned heresy with the American liberal program had profound effects on the church in America and on the hierarchy's political role. "The significance of the Americanist crisis was that the conser-vative, authoritarian, monolithic stance that Corrigan symbolized became the dominant one in the American church in the first half of the twentieth cen-tury."[40] This development, of course, determined the type of strategies that bishops could adopt to protect the interests of the church in the United States. McAvoy, referring to the early years of the new century, noted that Arch-bishop Ireland's "enthusiastic promise of the future association of Catholicism and American democracy was scarcely alive. Instead there was a gradual Americanization of the Catholic immigrant without glamour."[41]

Thus far, I have discussed disagreements among the American bishops over how the interests of the Catholic Church in America should be advanced. One area where there was no disagreement, where all sides believed the role should be played vigorously, was the time-honored area of hierarchical sup-port of American war efforts. The only war to which the bishops had to react in the years 1865 to 1917 was the Spanish-American War of 1898, and their reaction to that war was reminiscent of Carroll's reaction to the War of 1812. Many bishops were skeptical of American aims before the war began, but they became wholly supportive once the shooting actually started.

One important difference between 1812 and 1898 was that the latter conflict involved the United States and Catholic Spain whereas the former was be-tween the United States and Protestant Britain. In fact, the pope was strongly opposed to the possibility of war between the United States and Spain, and enlisted Archbishop Ireland as his representative in efforts to mediate the con-flict short of war. Ireland actually came quite close to averting hostilities, but war fever in Washington was too strong. In the tradition of Catholic support of American war efforts, however, Ireland declared that he was "for war—for the Stars and Stripes" once his peace mission had failed.[42]

Nor was it only liberals like Ireland who supported the war. Virtually every American bishop lined up behind the United States against Spain, including many prominent conservatives.[43] Whatever the differing views among the hierarchy on the proper style and status of the American church, it would be another seventy-five years before a significant number of Catholic bishops would publicly dissent from an American war effort.

What of the general proposition that the political role of the American Catholic hierarchy was predominantly local? Despite attempts to set strategy at the national level, most of the specific efforts to defend church interests centered on individual prelates and their participation in state and local politics. Indeed, both of the conflicts discussed above were actually local matters with national ramifications. Ireland's school plan was limited to his own diocese and to his personal negotiations with local school boards. It became a national issue only when other bishops responded negatively to the implication that this local arrangement should serve as a model for Catholic education in other dioceses as well.

The McGlynn affair had significant national ramifications, of course. But at its heart it involved Corrigan's control over the priests in his diocese, and the local political consequences of one priest's actions. Some have argued that the whole matter illustrates how involved Corrigan was in local New York politics. Corrigan, this argument holds, silenced McGlynn and condemned George in order to defend the position of Tammany Hall officials with whom the New York archdiocese enjoyed a mutually beneficial relationship.[44]

Beyond these cases, defense of Catholic institutions and dealings with government officials remained mostly a local matter in the decades between the Civil War and World War I. The local focus had, as always, both ecclesiastical and political determinants. First, this period exhibits perhaps the least unity and collegiality among the hierarchy in all of American Catholic history. We have already seen the division and acrimony surrounding the Americanist crisis. This lack of unity was also demonstrated by the fact that there was not a single general meeting of the American bishops between the Third Plenary Council of 1884 and World War I. The archbishops did meet annually in this thirty-five-year interim, but their meetings lacked the unity and authority of earlier plenary sessions. McAvoy pointed to the persistent lack of consensus among the archbishops and commented that "even when the archbishops agreed, the carrying out of such an agreement in any diocese was, for the most part, dependent upon the will of the local bishop."[45] In general, McAvoy continued, "the individual bishop was supreme."[46]

Second, the issues that were important to the bishops, which most involved the interests of the church, were contested and decided on local and state levels. Foremost among these so-called Catholic issues was education. Individual bishops, in the tradition of John Hughes, continued to fight local elements that wanted to dismantle the Catholic school system. The education issue also illustrates that even when national church policy was set by the bishops collectively the individual local bishops still had to implement the policy and contend with its often powerful detractors. For example, the Third Plenary Council in 1884 mandated that the opportunity for a Catholic education be offered to all American Catholic children. Implementation of this mandate, however, required political battles against those bent on destruction of the Catholic schools. All over the country state legislatures and school boards deliberated legislation that would adversely affect the Catholic schools. According to McAvoy, "the chief restraint on such legislation was the threat of a loss of Catholic votes."[47] I have already mentioned the Wisconsin case where the German-American bishops mobilized that vote to defend their schools, but perhaps another example is in order.

In 1889 Republicans in the Illinois legislature passed the Edwards Law stipulating that only schools sanctioned by the local school boards could satisfy compulsory attendance requirements. The bishops of Illinois used the occasion of the 1892 election to express their anger at this attack on their schools. "We," they told their people, "denounce this law as a violation of our constitutional rights. . . . Let us use all right and honorable means to have it repealed."[48] These means, of course, were the vote, and "in a show of immigrant strength the Republicans were turned out of office and the Edwards Law repealed."[49]

The actions in Illinois were typical of the hierarchy's political role during this period. Individual bishops or groups of bishops entered the political arena as leaders of their people, either to negotiate for the defense of their church's interests or, failing that, to mobilize the Catholic vote for that purpose. The hierarchy's political activities were local, and they grew directly out of the bishops' leadership of an identifiable minority with institutions and particular interests in need of protection. This conclusion leads us back to the overriding development with which this section began—immigration. The bishops at the end of this period were faced with much the same problem that had occupied them throughout. What was the best way to advance the long-term interests of a large, growing, urban, immigrant church within a hostile American environment? McAvoy stated the problem in the following terms:

> The story of the Catholic Church in the United States during the next two decades [following 1898] is the story of the rejected Americanists hoping for changes that did not come and their opponents trying to solve the problem of getting Catholics accepted in American circumstances without adopting the policies they had condemned in their opponents.[50]

Toward the end of those two decades, World War I posed perhaps the greatest challenge to the patriotic allegiance of immigrant Catholics as hyphenated Americans. This time the bishops responded with new strategies and methods that significantly affected their future political role in the United States.

1917–1962

The final subperiod of what I have defined as the traditional era of American Catholic political history can best be seen as a transitional period. The themes of hierarchical political activity discussed above continued to be operative, but the bishops' political role developed in important ways that foreshadowed the modern era. The bishops' activities were somewhat less local than in the past, and they were also less limited to issues of particular interest to the Catholic minority. Nevertheless, these categories are still useful tools with which to examine these years. Moreover, the factors that caused change in these categories will help illuminate the developments that have brought about the contemporary political role of the American hierarchy.

World War I was the key event that set in motion the changes I will discuss in this section. As war raged in Europe between 1914 and 1917, and as the United States drifted toward active support of the Allies, the loyalty of American Catholics was once again questioned. Irish-American Catholics with their antipathy toward Britain and German-American Catholics with their ties to the fatherland were widely perceived to be unsympathetic with the emerging pro-British, anti-German American stance.

As so often before, however, once the United States was actually a belligerent, Catholic support was widespread and enthusiastic. The archbishops, meeting in Washington, expressed that support in unmistakable terms: "Our peoples, now as ever, will rise as one man to serve the nation. Our priests and consecrated women will once again, as in every former trial of our country, win by their bravery, their heroism and their service new admiration and new approval."[51]

Catholics did indeed mine their participation in the war as a source of approval of their patriotism and loyalty. American Catholics self-consciously fought "not only for the United States but also to make manifest the loyalty of all Catholics, native and foreign born."[52]

The most significant development surrounding World War I in terms of the bishops' political activities was the establishment of a national Catholic organization under the leadership of the hierarchy. Elizabeth McKeown has told the story of the founding of the National Catholic War Council.[53] Suffice it to say that in 1917 Paulist Father John Burke, aware of the nationalization trend in other American groups, realized that effective Catholic action during the war would require coordination at the national level. The bishops, under the leadership of Cardinal Gibbons, immediately brought the national Catholic body under their direct leadership. The significance of these events reached well beyond the coordination of Catholic war efforts. James Hennesey noted that "for the first time in [American Catholic] history an institutional commitment was being made to social and political action."[54]

This commitment was incalculably strengthened in 1919 when the bishops decided to continue their cooperation after the armistice. They renamed their organization the National Catholic Welfare Council (NCWC), and they called for annual meetings of all American bishops to discuss issues and developments that affected the life of the church. This institutionalization of the NCWC had two long-term effects. First, annual meetings were a powerful symbol of unity and collegiality among the American Catholic episcopate. A diverse group of church leaders that had not met since 1884 committed itself to regular annual consultations. Through annual meetings and pastoral letters the bishops could collectively respond to any Catholic interest in the expanding scope of national government action. Moreover, after 1919, the bishops had a formal organization, headquartered in Washington and staffed by professionals in a wide variety of fields. That the hierarchy, as an entity, could speak through this staff as well as through more formal pastoral letters was an important practical development.

Second, the NCWC was the vehicle for less parochial, more general political activity on the part of the hierarchy. The council could and did address national issues that were less narrowly Catholic. In fact, a somewhat less parochial focus predated the establishment of the welfare council. The administrative committee of the original war council released the *Program of Social Reconstruction* in February 1919.[55] This "bishops' program," which was closely followed by a pastoral letter under the auspices of the welfare council, was an extraordinary document. Written by Monsignor John A. Ryan, future head of the NCWC's social action department, it was the bishops' contribution to the national debate over how to structure the postwar economy and society. This far-reaching program called for public works, a national labor board, a minimum wage, public housing, social insurance, workers' participation in management, and other social and economic reforms.

It is impossible not to characterize the bishops' program of 1919 as a crucial turning point in the political activities of the American Catholic hierarchy. Flushed with the postwar tolerance afforded American Catholicism and motivated by Pope Leo XIII's encyclical *Rerum Novarum*, Ryan opened "an avenue to self-confident action in social matters through a program that was demonstrably Catholic and truly American."[56] Joseph McShane, historian of the bishops' program, argued that with the creation of the NCWC "the last great barriers to Catholic social action [the lack of hierarchical unity and leadership] were breached—and in a spectacular way."[57] To argue, however, that 1919 transformed the predominantly local and defensive political role of the bishops into something entirely new would be an overstatement. In fact, both this unity and the resulting action in the years following the bishops' program were limited by traditional factors.

The local nature of most of the hierarchy's political activities persisted for two fundamental reasons. First, individual bishops' canonical authority over church affairs in their dioceses was not affected by the establishment of the NCWC. Second, many of the issues of most interest to church leaders continued to be debated and decided on the local or state level. The NCWC staff or the bishops as a collectivity might release a statement on a matter such as education, obscenity, or divorce, but it would be decades before these issues and legislation on them were taken over by Congress and federal courts. This enduring combination of factors allowed prelates such as O'Connell of Boston, Mundelein of Chicago, Hayes of New York, and Hanna of San Francisco to parlay their authority over large urban constituencies and their relationships with urban machines into active political roles for themselves wholly independent of the NCWC and its activities.

Moreover, the NCWC itself was weakened considerably by the lukewarm support or outright opposition of some influential bishops. In 1922 a group of traditionalist bishops launched an attack on the very existence of the NCWC. Although their initially successful appeal to the Vatican to dismantle the council was quickly reversed (they ultimately succeeded only in having the name changed to the National Catholic Welfare Conference to avoid confusion of authority), the attempt itself damaged the credibility of the collective body's authority.

Short of attempts to actually destroy the NCWC, some bishops weakened the authority of the conference by dissenting from its actions or by publicly contradicting its staff. A particularly acrimonious example of the latter involved Cardinal William O'Connell's row in 1924 with John Ryan of the NCWC's social action department over the proposed Child Labor Amendment. O'Connell was staunchly opposed to the amendment and was so outraged by Ryan's support of it in the name of the conference that he prohibited Ryan from speaking publicly in the Boston archdiocese.[58] McAvoy summed up the enduring local quality of this period: "The administrative committee of the NCWC never had the backing of the whole American episcopate during these early years."[59]

The bishops also continued to derive most of their political role during this period from their leadership of an insular minority. From 1919 on, the bishops aggressively addressed the general socioeconomic conditions of postwar America. However, they by no means moved away from their traditional priority of using political action to defend and advance the interests of their church and its members. Indeed, the very establishment of the NCWC was motivated by the bishops' perception that they had to organize to effectively protect the interests of the church and to ensure the primary position of the church in the lives of its members:

When all the particular reasons for the formation of the National Catholic War Council have been reviewed and evaluated, we are led to the conclusion that those reasons were all subordinate to the desire of American Catholic leadership for an organization indicative of national Catholic strength and capable of protecting Catholic interests.[60]

Seen in this light, the bishops' program and the pastoral letter of 1919 were less a clear break from the bishops' political role of the past than they were more collective successors to Cardinal Gibbons' intervention in 1886 on behalf of the Knights of Labor. In fact, McAvoy argued that the reasons for the actions in 1886 and 1919 were "about the same; most Catholics were in the wage earning classes."[61]

If the bishops had to continue to act in order to retain the loyalty of their members, they also had to continue to refute charges that their church was un-American. A revived Ku Klux Klan, with its anti-Catholic program, and the frightened response to Al Smith's presidential campaign in 1928 were clear signs that anti-Catholic bigotry had not been eradicated by the increased social acceptance of Catholics during World War I. In short, American Catholics continued to be a persecuted minority in need of the protection of their episcopal leadership. The effect this persecution had on the potential scope of the hierarchy's political role was alluded to by historian James Hennesey. The church, Hennesey wrote, "remained prey to institutional narcissism which drained energies into narrowly focused crusades for what were deemed church interests."[62]

This narcissism was partially alleviated by the Depression of the 1930s. For the first time the bishops were faced with a national crisis for which a response was readily provided by Catholic social teaching. Moreover, the NCWC provided a platform from which to formulate and publicize that response. *Statement on Unemployment* (1930) and *Statement on Economic Rights* (1931) were the earliest attempts to apply the principles of Catholic social teaching to the Depression context.[63] The bishops also emphasized Pius XI's development of that teaching, *Quadragesimo Anno*, and its significance to the U.S. economy in their pastoral letter of 1933, *Present Crisis*.[64]

The compatibility of the bishops' message and the particular American political context was strengthened by President Franklin Roosevelt and his New Deal. Virtually the entire bishops' program of 1919 was eventually enacted into law during Roosevelt's presidency. Moreover, the president himself, aware of both the congruence of church teaching and his program, and of the number of Catholic voters and their electoral clout, purposefully cultivated Catholic support. As a candidate, Roosevelt sought the Catholic vote by declaring *Quadragesimo Anno* "one of the greatest documents of modern times."[65] And once in office, he courted and befriended influential prelates such as George Mundelein of Chicago and Francis Spellman of New York.[66] Never before had the hierarchy enjoyed such public participation in the American national political debate. The bishops led a large constituency, they seemed vindicated in their defense of their people's patriotism, and the president of the United States appealed to their church's teaching for moral authority.

Nevertheless, the bishops and the Catholic Church were not totally integrated into the New Deal. Father Charles Coughlin and his anti-New Deal diatribes on the radio offered an alternative Catholic position, and there were conflicts between the bishops' overall support of Roosevelt's agenda and their traditional priority of defending the parochial interests of their church. There were also the inevitable arguments that the New Deal was creeping socialism and a danger to the church, and many bishops became disillusioned with the extent to which the New Deal entailed nationalization of American government and politics. The following quote from David O'Brien's book on this period not only describes the bishops' attitudes toward nationalization in the 1930s, it also reinforces the general proposition on the hierarchy's predominantly local political role as leaders of the immigrant church:

> As long as relief, education, and aid to charitable endeavors were left in local hands, urban Catholic majorities might be translated, if not into direct assistance to private agencies, at least into benevolent neutrality that would protect them against secular competitors armed with public funds. The interests of the institutional church thus blended with the fears of the Catholic minority to shape a political outlook hostile to the permanent extension of national power.[67]

The bishops also broke with Roosevelt over the issue of the Spanish Civil War, and in the process rekindled latent anti-Catholicism. The bishops instinctively supported Franco in the war because of the alleged persecution of Catholic leaders by his opponents. Caught between mainstream views on foreign policy and the interests of their church, the bishops, in a rare dissent, opted for defense of the international church. The response of many non-Catholics was to accuse the bishops of supporting fascism and to ask once again whether antidemocratic Catholics could really be loyal and trustworthy Americans.

In the early 1930s the bishops seemed on the verge of establishing, finally, true compatibility between Catholic doctrine and American values. But by the end of the decade the bishops were back on the defensive, distrustful of the implications of the New Deal and suffering the bitter "taste of alienation as a result of their stand on the Spanish Civil War."[68]

The general war in Europe and the growing mood of intervention in the United States provided the opportunity for the bishops to regain some of their patriotic luster. After Pearl Harbor, of course, the patriotism of the bishops and of American Catholics in general was vociferous, and in Hennesey's descriptive term, "unalloyed."[69] In fact, during World War II new heights were reached in the identification of Catholicism and American war aims. The NCWC not only made the usual statement of support, it also offered the bishops' view that "we of America today fight not only for human values but also for those that are divine."[70]

No individual prelate was more vocal or enthusiastic in his patriotism than Francis Spellman of New York. Spellman was known for rhetorical flourishes when discussing the United States; he declared during the war that "our President and our Holy Father have combined the forces of our great country and the forces of religion in a battle for peace."[71] As Dorothy Dohen wrote of this type of rhetoric, "the symbols of the nation and the symbols of religion [had] become one."[72]

Spellman's efforts to identify his church with his nation went well beyond symbol, however. As Catholic military vicar of the United States, he enthusiastically adopted the role of unofficial head chaplain to American forces overseas. He traveled extensively, ministering to American soldiers and sailors, Catholic and non-Catholic alike. Moreover, President Roosevelt took advantage of Spellman's travels by employing him as an unofficial personal ambassador throughout the war. Spellman's close relationship with Pope Pius XII allowed him to act as mediator between pope and president. Spellman represented the views and interests of each to the other and played a key role in the delegation of a personal diplomatic emissary from the president to the Vatican. Nothing pleased Spellman more than this opportunity to simultaneously advance the interests of his church and his nation and to serve as a personification of the compatibility of the two. The wartime sacrifices of Catholics in general so illustrated this compatibility that George Flynn argued that "Catholic patriotism in the great crusade would be so shining that never again would anyone dare to question their Americanism."[73]

Be that as it may, cracks developed in the hierarchy's support of the U.S. prosecution of the war. Once again a tension developed between the American political agenda and the bishops' defense of the more narrowly defined interests of their church. Specifically, the bishops expressed their distress at Roosevelt's apparent hope to continue America's accommodation with Soviet communism after the war. The bishops had opposed recognition of the Soviet Union in 1933; and, although they reluctantly accepted the antifascist wartime alliance, they continued to view the Soviet Union and international communism as the mortal enemies of their church. As early as 1941, the bishops had declared their conviction that "there can be no compromise with Communism."[74] And by 1945 they were warning their countrymen of the threat posed by their erstwhile Soviet allies. "There is a clash of ideologies," the bishops argued. "The frank recognition of these differences is preliminary to any sincere effort in realistic world cooperation for peace."[75]

There was a crucial difference between this clash between U.S. policy and Catholic interests and the earlier clash over the Spanish Civil War. In the 1930s the bishops swam against the tide of public opinion, and they suffered for it. But in the 1940s the bishops were early participants in a growing anti-communist consensus in the United States. Flynn noted that "the way in which Catholics left the Roosevelt consensus helped ensure that they would adopt the cliches of the cold war. In fact, they had created most of them before President Truman entered office."[76] Historian David O'Brien captured the mood of the time:

> As nothing was more Catholic than Anti-Communism, so there was nothing more fully American. . . . In fighting the red peril the Catholic could dedicate himself to action which was both Catholic and American. . . . Thus would the objective of a reconciliation of the nation and the church and the attainment of a truly American Catholicism be realized at last.[77]

World War I, the Great Depression, World War II, and anticommunism—these major events of twentieth-century American history were the contexts within which the Catholic Church moved further into the mainstream of American life. They were also the contexts within which the bishops' assertion of compatibility of Americanism and Catholicism was most compelling. Questions about American patriotism, prevalent in 1917, were rarely heard in the anticommunist environment of the 1950s. In this sense, at least, the Catholic Church had come of age in the United States. Nevertheless, examination of the years between World War II and 1962 reveals that fundamental characteristics of the bishops' traditional role remained in place.

First, the bishops' political role between 1945 and 1962 continued to be a direct function of their authoritative leadership of a clearly identifiable minority. This minority was growing in size and importance as a political constituency, of course, and one of its members had even been elected to the presidency at the very end of this period. Nevertheless, the assimilation of Catholics of immigrant stock into the American mainstream was not complete in the 1940s and 1950s. By and large, Catholics continued to live in their own urban neighborhoods, attend their own schools, and submit to the authority of the local bishop. Garry Wills' "Memories of a Catholic Boyhood" in his *Bare Ruined Choirs* is a descriptive and, for those who remember, amusing account of urban American-Catholic life in the postwar period. There was no getting around it, Wills wrote, Catholics were just "different" from their non-Catholic neighbors.[78]

This difference continued to have political ramifications. Authors such as Paul Blanshard revived the argument that the Catholic Church was a threat to American democracy.[79] These arguments were less violent and less clearly bigoted than those of the Ku Klux Klan or American Protective Association. But talk of Vatican plots and criticism of undue influence of the Catholic hierarchy on American politics once again circulated. There was a good deal of irony in this latest attempt to discredit the bishops and their political activi-

ties. Objections were raised, for example, when some bishops opposed liberalization of divorce and birth control laws, and favored increased censorship
of films and literature. Blanshard and others called these activities un-American attempts to impose Catholic morality and a hierarchical authority structure
on the non-Catholic majority. The bishops, however, viewed these same activities as legitimate efforts to defend America from the debilitating effects of
secularism.

In *The Survival of American Innocence*, William Halsey argued that during
this period the bishops took very seriously their belief that Catholic values and
American values were compatible. It so happened, however, that the bishops
began to press their version of American values aggressively just as those very
values were being questioned, amended, and at times abandoned by the wider
society.[80] The bishops resisted these changes in the 1940s and 1950s, as much
as in the 1920s, not because they were trying to impose Catholic doctrine on
an unwilling majority, but because they were trying to defend what they
viewed as true Americanism. The bishops acted under the assumption that
they could advance the moral cause of their church and express their support
of their country's fundamental values at the same time. Given the breach that
had developed between traditional values and contemporary mores, however,
the bishops' defense of outmoded practices and proscriptions looked a great
deal like an imposition of parochial interests on the rest of society.

The NCWC participated in this process by raising specific issues in various
pastoral letters, and by addressing the problem of secularism directly in 1947
and 1948.[81] The social action department of the NCWC under George Higgins
was also active in trying to affect pieces of national legislation. Nevertheless,
the bulk of the hierarchy's political activity, their defense of the values mentioned above, continued to be focused on the local and state rather than federal
levels of government. The reasons for this focus in 1950 were the same they
had been throughout the traditional era.

First, the internal church authority of the individual bishops made them
important local figures. Each bishop continued to exercise a good deal of
influence on the lives and opinions of most Catholics within his diocese, and
continued to be perceived by non-Catholics as the authoritative representative
of his people. "In the popular mind the bishop not only represented the church,
he was the church."[82] Second, many, although not all, of the issues important
to the bishops continued to be decided on state and local levels. Federal power
was growing, but on the moral issues that energized the bishops the local and
state governments were often the important bodies. These traditional dynamics of local episcopal authority and local legislative initiative, coupled with
the size of the Catholic urban constituencies, granted local bishops an important political role.

James O'Toole, for example, in pointing to Cardinal Cushing's role in Boston, reported that "political figures learned that they could ignore the church's

position only at their peril, and in fact they sought to enlist at least tacit support in advance from the church's leaders for major projects."[83] In a similar vein, John Cooney argued that Cardinal Spellman had an indirect, but very tangible, influence on the shape of government in New York. "The politicians did their best," Cooney wrote, "to pick men acceptable to the cardinal, who represented such an enormous voting bloc in the city."[84]

The approaches adopted by Cushing, Spellman, and bishops like them in other American cities were entirely consistent with the traditional political role played by the American Catholic hierarchy. From John Carroll on, bishops had participated in politics for two purposes. In the tradition of John England and John Ireland, bishops had argued that there was no conflict between being a good Catholic and being a good American. By the 1960s, circumstances seemed to have proven the bishops right on this score. The patriotic allegiance of Catholic Americans, Paul Blanshard notwithstanding, had been established beyond much doubt. Second, in the tradition of John Hughes and Bernard McQuaid, bishops had participated in the political process to defend the parochial interests of their church and the viability of its institutions. And in the 1950s several urban bishops played this role with vigor as large Catholic populations and intact episcopal authority made some of them important urban power brokers.

However, these men were members of the last generation of American bishops who would live under the circumstances that had created and nurtured the hierarchy's traditional political role. In retrospect it is clear that by the early 1960s virtually all of the conditions that had supported the hierarchy's political activities for so long were eroding rapidly. Through education, economic advancement, flight to the suburbs, and the simple passage of time, Catholics by the 1960s were assimilating ever more rapidly into the American mainstream. Catholics became less different than their non-Catholic neighbors, and it was correspondingly less obvious what the parochial interests of Catholics were. This coming of age brought with it both a decrease in anti-Catholic agitation and a diminution in the authority of the bishops. Somewhat like adolescents in a family, American Catholics grew up and away from their "parents" in the hierarchy.

At about the same time, the governing authority of the local officials with whom the bishops had traditionally dealt was also diminished. The nationalization of American politics and government, given such a boost by the New Deal, continued apace in the late 1950s and early 1960s and spread to more and more areas of American public life. Local governments retained substantial responsibilities, of course, and they continued to relate to individual Catholic bishops. But the political significance of these relationships decreased markedly as the locus of American politics shifted to Washington, D.C.

Over the course of almost two centuries, the bishops had acted as apologists for the Catholic population and as defenders of that population's parochial interests. By the early 1960s, both sides of this role were acutely threatened by developments taking place both inside and outside of the church. The bishops faced the unpalatable prospect of having no one to speak for, and no one to speak to. If they wanted to remain relevant to American politics, they would have to respond and adjust to these fundamental changes.

CHAPTER THREE

Into the Modern Era

BOTH THE ASSIMILATION of Catholics into the American socioeconomic mainstream and the expansion of the federal government's role in the lives of American citizens brought the traditional era of the bishops' political activities to a close in the 1960s. This chapter will analyze these developments in greater detail and document the bishops' responses to them, responses that allowed the bishops to retain a significant role in modern American politics. In particular, I will argue that reforms adopted at the Second Vatican Council for theological and ecclesiastical reasons led the American bishops to adopt a more national, collective approach to politics and public policy. I will provide evidence, in other words, to support Eugene Kennedy's argument that the contemporary political role of the American bishops is "fundamentally a function of their practical efforts to implement the role of bishops as it was defined in Vatican II."[1]

A NEW AMERICAN CHURCH

Both the nature of the church's membership and the level of the bishops' authority over that membership changed dramatically during the 1950s and 1960s. David O'Brien has called this period, when second- and third-generation suburban Catholics succeeded their foreign-born and urban parents and grandparents, the "climax of American Catholic history."[2] Andrew Greeley and his colleagues have conducted sociological research that more specifically documents this historic change and shows that the American Catholic population, which had lagged behind the American mainstream in every measure of socioeconomic status for over a century, rapidly caught up in the years following World War II.

Greeley has published several volumes of survey data on the status of American Catholics relative to their non-Catholic counterparts.[3] The most comprehensive of these was a "composite sample," published in 1974, that combined data from several different surveys conducted by the National Opinion Research Center.[4] This composite strongly substantiated O'Brien's claim that an epochal change occurred within American Catholicism. Catholics still fell in the middle rank in terms of educational achievement, for example, but they were advancing very rapidly. With 11.50 years of schooling on average in 1974, Catholics lagged behind Jews (13.98), Episcopalians (13.47), and Presbyterians (12.66), but they had moved ahead of, or virtually even with, Lutherans (11.24) and Methodists (11.86).[5] This was a significant advance because, according to Greeley's data, the fathers of these Catholic respondents had received substantially less formal education than virtually all American Protestants. Only Baptists, with 8.17 years of education, had trailed the Catholic average of 8.58 in the generation preceding Greeley's study.

In terms of occupational prestige—a scale devised by scoring individual occupations according to the social status generally associated with them—Catholics continued to fall well below the national average in 1974. The significance of this result was counteracted, however, by the fact that Catholics had moved ahead of every single Protestant denomination when it came to average annual income. Catholics were not as prominent in the professions as Episcopalians were, for example, but on the average Catholics made a bit more money than Episcopalians did ($11,324 to $11,032).[6]

In short, Catholics left the immigrant era behind in the 1960s in what Greeley termed a "remarkable success story."[7] In fact, they emerged from their long immigrant history as one of the best paid, most highly educated population cohorts in the United States. "If parity with the national performance is a mark of acculturation," Greeley concluded, "then American Catholics are now thoroughly acculturated to American society."[8]

This acculturation, not surprisingly, had profound effects on the Catholic hierarchy's political role. As I discussed in chapter 2, the bishops had traditionally mobilized their resources and entered the political arena in order to defend the parochial interests of their beleaguered people. By the 1960s, however, it became increasingly difficult to differentiate Catholics from the general American population as the needs of Catholic Americans became far less parochial. On just this point, David O'Brien argued that the church could no longer "shape ecclesiastical policy in response to outside challenges." "Catholics," O'Brien contended, "would be forced to define their role in American society on the basis of something other than survival, the goal that a sense of being a besieged, threatened minority had always dictated."[9] In addition, the bishops had represented the political interests of their people by asserting over and over again that American and Catholic values were compatible. Once Catholics were succeeding handsomely at all levels of society, such episcopal assertions of patriotism and democratic fervor were no longer needed.

Finally, the entirety of the hierarchy's traditional political role—both the defense of Catholic interests and the assertions of Catholic patriotism and support of democracy—depended on the authority exercised by the bishops over the Catholic people. If bishops were to speak for Catholics, after all, they had to have the standing within the church to do so with authority and credibility. In addition to blurring the parameters of Catholic interests and debunking theories of Catholic un-Americanism, assimilation also was accompanied

by a precipitous decrease in episcopal authority. Eugene Kennedy has observed on this point that the "well-educated Catholics who have emerged from
the immigrant culture to participate in and shape the fate of pluralistic America no longer need to pay much attention to those who comport themselves as
father-figure ecclesiastics."[10] "A more intellectually and morally confident
generation of Catholics," Kennedy wrote, "(broke) naturally rather than rebel-
liously free of the obsessive-compulsive grip of the once organically whole
culture."[11]

Once this "morally confident generation of Catholics" had moved away
from this "organically whole culture," the bishops' political role as authoritative representatives and spokesmen for the Catholic constituency could not
endure. It is a bit ironic that the bishops themselves had worked so tirelessly
for the assimilation of American Catholics. In successfully arguing that Catholics were loyal Americans and in encouraging their subjects to succeed in all
facets of American culture, the bishops had sown the seeds of their own decreased authority and brought about the devaluation of their own political
functions.

Socioeconomic advances of the Catholic population and accompanying
changes in the stature of the hierarchy, then, presented a very real threat to the
viability of the bishops' traditional political activities. The kind of role played
by England in South Carolina, Hughes in New York, or O'Connell in Boston
would no longer be possible under these modern conditions. To be sure, bishops continued to advance "Catholic interests," such as they were, and to vigorously defend Catholic institutions. In time, however, the bishops also adopted
a much broader, but less authoritative, scope of political activity that allowed
them to reshape and expand their participation in the American political
process.

The first factor bringing about this broadening of scope was the same development that had threatened the bishops' traditional role in the first place—the
assimilation of Catholics into the American mainstream. Decreased parochial-
ism and diminished episcopal authority led to decreased anti-Catholicism and
less strident opposition to the political activities of Catholics and their clerical
leaders. Paul Blanshard and others continued to speak of the dangers bishops
posed to American democracy, but these dire warnings rang increasingly hollow in the 1960s as American Catholics established themselves as fully American. Indeed, these concerns appeared to be wholly without foundation once
a Catholic had loyally served as president of the United States.

Many observers have stressed John F. Kennedy's pivotal role in American
Catholic history.[12] He was the first Catholic president, and he remains a myth-
ical figure in American Catholicism. We should be careful, however, about
how much emphasis we place on Kennedy and his presidency as causal agents
in the assimilation and acceptance of American Catholicism. In truth, Kennedy was as much a reflection of the acculturation of American Catholicism as

he was its cause. Like Al Smith before him, Kennedy had to defend himself against charges that a Catholic could not loyally perform the duties of the presidency. But unlike Smith, Kennedy's style, worldview, and personal history all readily discredited arguments that Catholics could not simultaneously remain loyal to their church and their nation.

One observer wrote of Kennedy's "seemingly effortless loyalty to the Church and his easy assumption that the Catholic faith was in no way a strain on his character as an American fully at ease with the nation's traditions."[13] Indeed, Kennedy's importance as a Catholic symbol arose out of the discernible fact that he was both Catholic and American, comfortably loyal to his religious roots yet quintessentially American in his politics and lifestyle.

Kennedy, then, both reflected and advanced the social and political acceptance of American Catholics. This acceptance was also facilitated by the other John with whom Kennedy is often linked in American Catholic history: Pope John XXIII. Pope John's positive image and easy style went a long way toward legitimizing the church and its leadership in the eyes of non-Catholic Americans. If, the thinking went, the notorious "pope of Rome" could be such a nonthreatening, nonautocratic, and reasonable man, then perhaps his American associates, the bishops, were not that dangerous either.

John Cogley has explicitly linked the influence of the "two Johns" to a subtle, yet very real, change in the Catholic Church's image in the United States:

> At the very time when Pope John, by his pronouncements but more importantly by his public behavior, was turning ecumenism and the ecumenical attitude into a new reality on the religious scene, President Kennedy, almost inadvertently, was bringing an end to American Catholic sectarianism and withdrawal from the general culture.[14]

Image, however, can only do so much. No matter how urbane Kennedy was, or how nonthreatening John XXIII appeared, opponents of Catholic involvement, and particularly hierarchical involvement, in American politics could always point to Catholic teaching on church-state relations to justify their reservations. In 1960 the church still held that Catholicism, "the one true religion," deserved preferential treatment from civil authorities. No less an authority than John A. Ryan of the NCWC's social action department, when responding to those who feared that other religions would suffer should Catholics gain a significant majority in the United States, could only reply that such an overwhelming majority was unlikely to occur in the foreseeable future.[15] Significantly, the status of other religions in some future "Catholic America" was at the heart of both Charles Marshall's famous debate with Al Smith in 1927 in the *Atlantic Monthly* and the Houston ministerial meeting's misgivings about Kennedy in 1960.[16]

In a remarkable reversal, this obstacle to compatibility between American and Catholic values was swept away by the Second Vatican Council's *Decla-*

ration on Religious Freedom.[17] Often called the "American document" because of the vital support it received from the American hierarchy, this conciliar document declared that "the human person has a right to religious freedom."[18] This freedom, argued the council, was not dependent on the discretion of individual governments but was based on the dignity of every human person. "This right of the human person to religious freedom," the declaration continued, "is to be recognized in the constitutional law whereby society is governed."[19]

This historic declaration, a rare reversal of Catholic teaching, was a vindication of the bishops' support of the American Constitution, as well as a harbinger of improved relations between Catholics and other Americans. John Courtney Murray, a vocal supporter of religious liberty before and during the council, wrote that the American bishops supported the declaration because they had "learned the practical value of the free exercise clause of the First Amendment."[20] And one American bishop added that the declaration was "essential for fruitful dialogue with non-Catholics."[21]

The full effects of these factors—decreasing anti-Catholicism, the influence of the "two Johns," and the *Declaration on Religious Freedom*—were not felt, of course, for many years. Nearly two centuries of virulent opposition to the Catholic hierarchy's involvement in the political process was not swept away in a moment. To be sure, some of that opposition persists to this day. Nevertheless, one cannot understand the political role of the American hierarchy today without first understanding how assimilation of the Catholic population, Kennedy's status as an American hero who happened to be Catholic, John XXIII's ecumenical worldview and image, and the *Declaration on Religious Freedom* cumulatively undercut predictable opposition to such a role.

It took more than diminished resistance on the part of non-Catholic Americans to broaden the scope of the hierarchy's political concerns and activities. As we saw in the Americanist crisis of the 1890s, the scope of the bishops' political activities was also influenced, if not controlled, by the Vatican. It was not only American bigots who limited the bishops to defending the interests of their church. Official church policy also required that bishops focus their attention inward and busy themselves protecting their church from the influence and dangers of the outside world. Traditionally, the church tended to stand apart from the rest of the world to protect itself from secular forces (particularly in a hostile environment like that of the United States). The Vatican had clarified this separatist doctrine in 1864 in a *Syllabus of Errors* that rejected the notion that "the Roman Pontiff can and ought to reconcile and harmonize himself with progress, with liberalism, and with modern civilization."[22]

The Second Vatican Council and its *Pastoral Constitution on the Church in the Modern World* absolutely revolutionized this deeply rooted tradition. The pastoral constitution rejected a defensive posture and called for the church to move out into the world where it could enter into mutually respectful dialogue with non-Catholics and bring the gospel to bear on the world's problems.[23] George Higgins, who contrasted the *Syllabus of Errors* with the pastoral constitution as "dramatic symbols of their respective eras in the modern history of the church," stressed the seminal influence of the latter document:

> Whereas for generations—if not for centuries—the Church, however understandably, had been mistrustful and suspicious of the "others" who were looked upon as actual or potential enemies, and had systematically deprecated other people's values as potentially dangerous, she did an almost complete about face during the Council. In [the *Pastoral Constitution on the Church in the Modern World*] she broke the siege, took one leap across the chasm, and became open for dialogue with the contemporary world.[24]

In the very first words of the constitution, the council expressed the church's sense of solidarity with all peoples of the world. "The joys and hopes," it began, "the griefs and anxieties of the men of this age, especially those who are poor or in any way afflicted, are the joys and hopes, the griefs and anxieties of the followers of Christ."[25] The council also declared that the mission of the church was to speak to "the whole of humanity," and to engage "with [the human family] in conversation about these various problems."[26]

In the past, the Vatican had repeatedly cautioned the American bishops about poisoning the church through contact with American culture, and had required them to defend their faith by insulating the church from secular influence. In stark contrast, the pastoral constitution challenged the bishops to involve the church in the life of society. As representatives of the universal church the bishops were called on to express their solidarity with all people, to speak to all Americans about the church's salvific answers to the world's problems, and to engage in conversation with non-Catholics in an effort to build a more humane and just society.

In this way, the Vatican Council offered the bishops a path out of their traditional political role. We have seen how the insular, defensive style of the past lost relevance as Catholics assimilated into the mainstream. In these new circumstances, where parochial defense was no longer needed, Vatican II authorized the American bishops to turn their attention to the whole range of social problems facing the American people. Just as American Catholics were questioning and rejecting episcopal authority, the bishops were also encouraged to expand their potential audience to include all Americans and to move away from a style of authoritative pronouncement toward one of dialogue and persuasion. The bishops were no longer to view American culture as a force against which the church had to defend itself. Rather, they were to view that culture as the very arena in which the church would pursue its mission. To this end, post-Vatican II bishops were to "fit themselves to do their part in establishing dialogue with the world and with men of all shades of opinion."[27]

In one way this document ratified the American hierarchy's conception of the church's relationship with American society. The bishops, from Carroll to Spellman, had argued that Catholicism was compatible with American society. This argument implied that "the world" outside the church was worthy of the church's attention and concern, and that a kind of dialogue was possible between Catholic beliefs and American values. But whereas Catholic bishops traditionally understood this dialogue in terms of compatibility, understanding, and support, the Second Vatican Council envisioned the church as a challenger and critic of modern culture. The church was not to enter into dialogue with the world merely to affirm the world's values. Rather, the pastoral constitution charged the bishops with "scrutinizing the signs of the times and . . . interpreting them in the light of the Gospel."[28]

Part 2 of the pastoral constitution, "Some Problems of Special Urgency," included very specific notions of what this scrutiny and interpretation could mean. This list of problems to which the church was to turn its attention reads like a blueprint of the American hierarchy's political agenda of the 1970s and 1980s. The first of these problems was a traditional area of church concern: marriage and family in the modern world. This section offered uncompromising general support for the "nobility of marriage and family," but it also made a specific statement on an issue which was becoming politically volatile in the United States at the time—abortion:

> God, the Lord of life, has conferred on men the surpassing ministry of safeguarding life—a ministry which must be fulfilled in a manner which is worthy of man. Therefore, from the moment of conception life must be guarded with the greatest of care, while abortion and infanticide are unspeakable crimes.[29]

I will return to abortion at length in later chapters, but at this point we can see how the bishops were likely to respond to the liberalization of American abortion laws in the 1960s and 1970s. In the case of abortion, scrutinizing the signs of the times and entering into dialogue with the world about its problems surely would require some level of political action on the part of the hierarchy. This action would have to be designed not only to protect Catholics from the effects of liberalized policies, but also to provide a way for the hierarchy to speak to the "whole of humanity" in an effort to "do their part in establishing dialogue with the world and with men of all shades of opinion."[30]

The council fathers next addressed the matter of economic development. This section contained no surprises for those familiar with the history of Catholic social teaching, as the council basically affirmed papal teachings of the previous one hundred years.[31] The fact was, however, that very few Americans were familiar with this history despite the application of papal teaching to the American economy in 1919 in the *Program of Social Reconstruction*. Since the bishops had muted their criticism of the American system during the New Deal and the cold war, it was significant that the council viewed centralized socialism and laissez-faire capitalism with seemingly equal disfavor:

> Growth must not be allowed merely to follow a kind of automatic course resulting from the economic activity of individuals. Nor must it be entrusted solely to the authority of government. Hence theories which obstruct the necessary reforms in the name of a false liberty must be branded as erroneous. The same is true of those theories which subordinate the basic rights of individual persons and groups to the collective organization of production.[32]

Finally, the council took up the fostering of peace, an area where both circumstances and the church's teachings were developing rapidly. For the American bishops, with their firm tradition of superpatriotism and support of American foreign policy goals, the Vatican Council issued a disturbing challenge. The "multiplication of scientific weapons" drew the council's most focused attention in this regard. The possibility of total war involving these weapons led to the council's famous exhortation "to undertake an evaluation of war with an entirely new attitude."[33] It also led to the following declaration on the use of nuclear weapons: "Any act of war aimed indiscriminately at the destruction of entire cities or of extensive areas along with their populations is a crime against God and man. It merits unequivocal and unhesitating condemnation."[34]

The challenge this section presented to the American hierarchy can scarcely be overstated. The call for an evaluation of war with an entirely new attitude could easily be read as a repudiation of the kind of uncritical superpatriotism practiced by America's bishops. And the council actually condemned, in so many words, the foundations of American nuclear strategy. Massive retaliation, the destruction of the Soviet Union with nuclear weapons in response to a Soviet nuclear or large-scale conventional attack, was the declared policy of the United States government in the early 1960s. In the pastoral constitution, the leadership of the Catholic Church dismissed implementation of such a strategy as "a crime against God and man." In addition, that leadership characterized the arms race in which the United States was enthusiastically engaged at the time as an "utterly treacherous trap for humanity," which threatened "lethal ruin."[35]

In addressing marriage and family, economic development, and the fostering of peace, the Vatican Council touched on issues of increasing controversy in American political life. The *Pastoral Constitution on the Church in the Modern World* not only offered the bishops the opportunity to adopt a broader, less parochial scope of political activity, it also identified specific issues where these activities should be directed and suggested the general positions that the bishops should take on these issues.

In short, the pastoral constitution addressed one of the major threats to the American hierarchy's traditional political role. It authorized the bishops to be

less parochial in outlook and to consider a more general array of social problems. The change did not happen overnight, of course, but in time the American hierarchy adopted the expanded mission of the constitution and applied
the techniques of assessment and dialogue to the urgent problems alluded to
by the council. As Monsignor George Higgins, a participant and student of
these events, told me: "It was natural and inevitable that gradually the bishops
would implement the *Pastoral Constitution on the Church in the Modern
World*."[36]

The document also called on the bishops to shed the apologetic view of
American society that had served their interests so well in the past. Still, the
bishops, or at least many among them, were hesitant to adopt the critical
agenda of the council's document. The sections on conscientious objection
and nuclear weapons were particularly disquieting to some influential prelates. The American bishops had long pointed to their people's unquestioning
response to the government's call to war as evidence of the patriotic credentials of American Catholics. The council, however, declared that the church
"cannot fail to praise those who renounce the use of violence . . . and who
resort to methods of defense which are otherwise available to weaker parties."[37] Francis Spellman, the cardinal-archbishop of New York and head of
the American Military Vicariate, strongly dissented from this view of conscientious objection. "If," he asked on the floor of the council, "the leaders of a
nation decide in good faith and after mature deliberations that military service
by their citizens is absolutely necessary for the defense of peace and justice,
how can the citizens justly refuse military service?"[38]

American objections to the sections on nuclear weapons were even more
strongly articulated at the council. In fact, ten American bishops, led by
Bishop Phillip Hannan, took the unusual step of publishing a letter detailing
their objections to the views espoused in the pastoral constitution. The ten
argued "that the defense of a large part of the world against aggression
(through possession of nuclear weapons) is not a crime, but a great service,"
and they cautioned that "the Council should not make a decision on this matter
about which there is still no consensus of opinion among theologians who are
most competent in the matter."[39]

The 175-year tradition of hierarchical support of U.S. foreign and defense
policy still had its powerful proponents, and the American bishops were not
going to emerge from Vatican II as defenders of conscientious objection and
critics of American nuclear strategy. The dispute over the council's view of
acceptable military strategy also related to another obstacle to the implementation of the pastoral constitution. The American bishops were a large group
of individuals, not a collective body, and it was very difficult for them to
speak with one voice. The Vatican Council called upon the bishops to enter
into "dialogue" with the world about problems such as the morally acceptable
use of military force, but a dialogue consisting of several hundred separate

episcopal voices was not what the council fathers had in mind. For the bishops of a given nation to "play their part in dialogue with the world," they would have to learn to speak as the council itself had spoken—as a body or as a church.

The American bishops had a long way to go on this score in 1965. Bishop Gerald McDevitt publicly regretted, for example, that Hannan's letter had been "mistakenly assumed to be backed by the American hierarchy. . . . It is not backed by the American hierarchy," he countered. "It is the opinion of the individuals who signed the petition and they represent only themselves."[40] It seems from American comments on the floor of the council and from the dispute over the authority of the dissenting letter that both the attitudes of many bishops and the structures through which the hierarchy spoke and acted would have to be transformed before the Vatican Council's broader mission and agenda could be implemented in the American church.

At the beginning of this chapter I observed that both themes of the hierarchy's traditional political role had been eroded by the 1960s, that both the parochial scope and local focus of the hierarchy's political activities had been overrun by events. Thus far I have discussed only the scope of the bishops' role, and how socioeconomic changes in the Catholic population deprived the bishops of their political function of defending and advancing the interests of that population. I have shown how a series of factors, including the documents of the Second Vatican Council, offered the bishops a path out to a new, broader role in American politics. However, the hierarchy's role was also threatened by changes in the political system itself.

A NEW AMERICAN POLITICAL SYSTEM

The large, active national government that contemporary Americans take for granted is a relatively recent phenomenon. As Theodore Lowi noted, "between 1789 and the 1930s the national government was not such a significant force in the economic or social life of the citizens of the United States."[41] Specifically, Lowi had in mind the limited role that the federal government had historically played in exercising what he called the police power of government. This power, defined as "the authority and obligation of governments to provide for the health, safety, and morals of the community" was the responsibility of local and state governments.[42]

Roosevelt's New Deal was obviously a watershed in the growth of the federal government, and many cite the 1930s as the inauguration of a new nationalized system of American government. Lowi, however, while affirming the historic significance of the New Deal, did not view the 1930s as the proper focal point of this shift. He argued that the New Deal was an emergency program designed for emergency circumstances and was presented by Roosevelt and other federal officials as such. Only with the activist administration of Kennedy and the Great Society of Lyndon Johnson was the nationalization of the police power presented in the American body politic as a positive good to be pursued absent a crisis such as the Great Depression. Returning to the definition of police power, Lowi saw the 1960s as the decade when the national government adopted "the authority and obligation for the health, safety, and morals of the community."

The following partial list of congressional statutes passed between 1961 (the year after Kennedy's election) and 1966 (the year after the close of Vatican II) illustrates the expanding role of the federal government in the private lives of American citizens. It also suggests the bishops' growing need for an effective national voice with which to "scrutinize the signs of the times."

1961 *Community Health Services and Facilities Act of 1961*—Expansion of community health services through increased federal expenditures.[43]

Housing Act of 1961—Federal money for urban renewal, planning, and mass transit and loans for public housing.

Juvenile Delinquency and Youth Offender Control Act of 1961—$10 million for control and prevention of juvenile delinquency.

1962 *Drug Amendments of 1962*—Federal supervision of drug industry facilities and production.

Senior Citizen Housing Act of 1962—Federal construction of low-rent housing for urban aged.

Public Welfare Amendments of 1962—Extended Aid to Families with Dependent Children to unemployed and increased federal share in several programs designed to reduce dependency.

Gambling Devices Act of 1962—Restricted interstate passage of gambling devices.

Vaccination Assistance Act of 1962—Federal purchase of vaccine for polio, dyptheria, whooping cough, and tetanus.

1963 *Higher Education Facilities Act of 1963*—Federal grants and loans for construction and improvement of public and private higher education academic facilities.

Mental Retardation Facilities Construction Act—Federal aid for construction of community mental health centers and state and private clinics for the mentally retarded.

1964 *Food Stamp Program*—permanent congressional establishment of pilot program launched by 1961 executive order.

Economic Opportunity Act of 1964—Main "War on Poverty" bill included jobs corps, community action programs (including birth control education), work experience programs, and expanded public assistance.

Housing Act of 1964—Expansion of federal urban renewal programs.

Civil Rights Act of 1964—Desegregated public facilities, created the Equal Employment Opportunity Commission, and extended voting rights and barred discrimination in all federally funded programs.

1965 *Medicare*—Medical insurance for the aged.

Elementary and Secondary Education Act of 1965—General federal school aid including limited aid to private school children.

Higher Education Act of 1965—Federal subsidy and insurance of college loans.

Voting Rights Act of 1965—Suspended literacy tests, challenged poll tax, and ordered registration of Southern blacks.

1966 *Comprehensive Health Planning and Services Act of 1966*—Federal grants to states for health services and family planning facilities.

Demonstration Cities and Metropolitan Development Act—Consolidation of federal and local programs to combat urban blight.

Child Protection Act—Required warning labels on dangerous household items.

Economic Opportunity Amendments of 1966—Enlargement of War on Poverty programs.

This package of legislation greatly increased the federal government's "authority and obligations for the health, safety, and morals of the community." It involved national agencies and officials in areas of family life that had been left, theretofore, either to the discretion of individuals and their families or to the regulation of state and local governments. Nor was congressional action the only way that federal responsibilities were expanded. The U.S. courts and federal bureaucracy are also, of course, part of the national government. Decisions and actions of federal agencies proliferated during these years, and the federal courts generally upheld the authority of these actions when they were challenged.

Perhaps most significantly, the Supreme Court, an important instrument of national power, also expanded its own role at the expense of state and local discretion. During the early and mid-1960s, "the court undertook sweeping reforms of the electoral system and the nature of political representation, the administration of criminal justice in the states, school desegregation and race relations, the law of freedom of speech including the local regulation of obscenity, and the status of religion in public life."[44] The constitutional content of these decisions was "principally the imposition of national standards on the states."[45] The following select but representative list of Supreme Court cases during the 1961–66 period highlights this nationalization of governmental authority.

1962 *Engel v. Vitale*—Found a Judeo-Christian prayer read in New York's public schools to be in violation of the First Amendment's establishment clause. This was the watershed case of a trend of reversing "state laws recognizing or permitting Bible reading and prayer in public schools."[46]

1963 *Gideon v. Wainwright*—Sixth Amendment right to counsel in *all* criminal cases was applied to the states. This case was only one element in a sequential expansion of federal power as the "Warren Court incorporated virtually all of the criminal procedure guarantees of the Bill of Rights into the due process clause of the 14th Amendment."[47]

1965 *Griswold v. Connecticut*—Outlawed state legislation prohibiting the use of contraceptives and the dispensing of birth control information to married couples. This influential case was thought by some to have "fashion(ed) a constitutional right of privacy virtually out of whole cloth," and this right was subsequently used to limit the power of local and state authorities over the actions of their citizens.[48]

1966 *Miranda v. Arizona*—Pretrial custody enjoyed the same protection of self-incrimination and right to counsel as trial according to Fifth Amendment. This case resulted in the famous (infamous?) warning to arrestees and represented a significant introduction of federal authority into the local exercise of police power.[49]

The combined effects of these congressional and judicial trends was a marked shift in the locus of American politics to Washington, D.C. "There is no room left for doubt," Lowi argued, "that a large positive interventionist national state is finally and forever the central feature of the American political system."[50] This is not to suggest that important matters of public policy were no longer decided at local levels nor that local bishops' dealings with these levels ceased. For the most part the national government added to, rather than replaced, the governing already going on at lower levels. And some bishops continued to wield considerable local influence. Nevertheless, the national government did take on new authority and new responsibilities in a number of areas in which the Catholic hierarchy was ill-equipped to play a significant national role.

The bishops were not completely without a structure through which to speak and act on national issues. The National Catholic Welfare Conference (NCWC) was headquartered in Washington and was, at times, quite active. However, Luke Ebersole, in his *Church Lobbying in the Nation's Capital*, characterized all of the NCWC's departments as involved in defense of Catholic institutional interests, and argued that such defense was really the conference's reason for being.[51] Its education department, for example, was a vigorous advocate of parochial school interests and an important player in the school aid battles of the Kennedy years. But the conference was much less prepared to deal with the more general issues about which the bishops were to establish a dialogue with secular society.

The social action department (SAD) was perhaps the only exception to Ebersole's sweeping judgment. In the tradition of its first director, John A. Ryan, the department strenuously advocated the cause of labor, Catholic and non-Catholic alike. However, the head of the SAD in the 1950s and early 1960s, Monsignor George Higgins, told me in an interview that his department was limited by its small staff and lack of institutional support from the bishops. "We were working on a shoe-string," he said of his operation. "We were nobody's baby."[52]

Higgins' comment points to another of the NCWC's shortcomings as a potential vehicle for national political activity: it was organizationally weak. It was a voluntary coalition of the American hierarchy to which individual bishops did not have to belong; its annual meetings were often perfunctory affairs that not all bishops attended; and its statements were generally released by a particular committee or individual bishops and rarely were presented as the collective pronouncement of the entire hierarchy. The NCWC was far from the authoritative voice of the American hierarchy:

> Anything coming out of Washington [the NCWC's headquarters] was looked upon with suspicion. In fact, bishops often paid their tax to the national office in the quiet hope that their fealty ended with the mailing of a check. Important metropolitan archbishops and cardinals had such a modest opinion of the Washington operation that they rarely permitted their priests to work there.[53]

For our purposes, the point is that the American bishops had to strengthen their own organization in Washington if they were going to retain a significant role in an evolving political process in which more and more policy initiative was centered in Washington. Once again, the Second Vatican Council, with theological and ecclesiastical motivations, offered the American hierarchy a way out of its political limitations.

The *Decree on the Bishops' Pastoral Office in the Church* clarified the role of bishops in the Roman Catholic Church by going beyond Vatican I's stress on papal infallibility and elevating the episcopate's status relative to papal authority.[54] In the American context the most significant section of this document was "Synods, Councils, and especially Episcopal Conferences" in which the council mandated the establishment of national or regional conferences:

> Nowadays especially, bishops are frequently unable to fulfill their office suitably and fruitfully unless they work more harmoniously and closely everyday with other bishops. Episcopal conferences, already established in many nations, have furnished outstanding proofs of a more fruitful apostolate. Therefore, this most sacred Synod considers it supremely opportune everywhere that bishops belonging to the same nation or region form an association and meet together at fixed times.[55]

The council also decreed that decisions of these conferences, in certain limited circumstances, were to have "juridically binding force."[56] The major effect of this decree on the American bishops was the restructuring and strengthening of their national conference. The National Catholic Welfare Conference had been created and sustained by the often lukewarm consent and support of the American bishops. Its successor, the National Conference of Catholic Bishops (NCCB), was a canonical body created by the highest church authority and instituted according to universal church law. Membership in the new conference was mandatory for all American bishops, and the conference could actually exercise legitimate authority of its own, separate and apart from the authority of individual bishops. That collective authority, regardless of how circumscribed it was, significantly enhanced the status of the national conference among both the bishops and their various audiences.

This new conference would also need a more extensive staff to do its work. This staff would not only be larger and more varied in function than the staff that served the old NCWC, it would also derive a greater measure of indirect authority from its role of speaking expressly for "the bishops" as a collectivity.

All of these changes came to fruition during a meeting of the American hierarchy in November 1966. The bishops formally established the National Conference of Catholic Bishops as their official collective body and instituted the United States Catholic Conference (USCC) as their administrative arm and secretariat. The Catholic press noted at the time that these administrative re-organizations were very significant and portentous. *America*, the Jesuit weekly, editorialized that the national conference had been "converted from a confraternity into a government, from a service organization into a true society of bishops."[57] *Commonweal*, a journal published by Catholic laity, added that the "unwieldy and largely voluntary association of bishops [was] being shaped into a viable instrument with power adequate to national problems."[58]

These changes provided the American bishops with a timely opportunity to recapture a relevant political role for themselves. The NCCB's structure and status, coupled with the USCC's staffwork, gave the American hierarchy a cohesive collective voice with which to enter into a dialogue with other elements of American society about the problems facing the nation. *Commonweal* recognized the connection between the bishops' organizational structure and their ability to participate meaningfully in the political process: "In an age when more and more problems can only be dealt with adequately on a national level stronger national conferences are necessary."[59] Likewise, *America* stated that "the United States of America is a nation and it is time that the Catholic bishops think of it habitually as such. . . . There must be more and more collaboration, more and more openness to the national dimensions of local problems."[60]

It is interesting to note that the Vatican Council itself recognized the significance of the growing nationalization of social problems. The final promulgation of the *Decree on the Bishops' Pastoral Office in the Church* had a note attached to it which "mention[ed] especially those questions which concern a whole nation, e.g., schools, administration, the responsible use of civil rights, etc." as a justification for the establishment and strengthening of national episcopal conferences.[61] In a reference that clearly foreshadowed the importance of the NCCB's structure to the American hierarchy's political role in the 1980s, the council commented that "public statements might sometimes be necessary which would carry greater weight if they were made in the name of all the bishops."[62] Monsignor Higgins of the NCWC's social action department agreed that the actions of the NCCB and their staff at the USCC would carry greater weight. "We were speaking in the name of a department in a voluntary organization," he said of himself and his staff. "They are speaking now in the name of an established conference."[63]

One more important obstacle stood in the way of the bishops' participation in a broader scope of political activity at the national level: the deeply held tradition of individualism among the hierarchy that manifested itself in distrust of collective action and jealous protection of individual prerogative. Bishops could be forced to hold membership in a national conference, but that fact would not by itself alter the attitudes that had hindered truly collective action in the past. The Second Vatican Council released another important document, however, that directly addressed those attitudes.

The *Dogmatic Constitution on the Church* called for greater collegiality among the Catholic hierarchy.[64] Eugene Kennedy, who in his recent writings has most clearly outlined the importance of this concept in the American context, defined collegiality as "that method of church government that acknowledges and enlarges the role of the world's bishops, defining their authority as derived from God and not doled out by the Pope."[65] Bishops are incorporated into the authority structure of the church, not through delegation of the pope's power, as from a general to his lieutenants, but rather directly through their consecration as bishops. As part of the effort to redress the imbalance of Vatican I's stress on the papacy, the Second Vatican Council declared that "by divine institution bishops have succeeded to the place of the apostles as shepherds of the church."[66]

But this apostleship and its authority are not bestowed upon bishops individually or independently. Rather, the bishops exercise their authority collectively, in terms of "the collegial nature and meaning of the episcopal order."[67] For Karl Rahner, this notion of the collegial nature of the episcopate was "one of the central themes of the whole Council."[68] The dogmatic constitution's use of the word "college," Rahner wrote, "shows at least that the episcopate as a whole and its powers are not just the sum of individual bishops and their powers. . . . This inclusive unity precedes the individual bishop as such. . . . Hence . . . the power of the individual bishop as an individual . . . is to be regarded as coming to him insofar as he is a member of the college and shares in the power of the college as such."[69] To be a bishop, in other words, and to properly exercise the functions of that office, is to be a member of a college that, in conjunction with the pope, collectively exercises "supreme and full power over the universal church."[70]

The theology may be complex and some of the language arcane, but the effects of these sections of the dogmatic constitution on the American bishops and on their ability to act collectively on a national scale were far-reaching. This document was another exhortation to the American hierarchy to be more assertive in its assessment of the problems of the day. As full participants in the exercise of church authority, the bishops cannot content themselves with merely implementing directives from Rome. They must play an active role in the definition and implementation of the church's mission within their own cultural context, and they must do so together, as a conference. "Episcopal bodies of today," the council fathers wrote, "are in a position to render a manifold and faithful assistance, so that this collegiate sense may be put into practical application."[71]

This spirit of collegiality and the American bishops' sense of a collective identity have very real limits. In later chapters, I will refer often to a rather heated debate among the bishops over the proper role and authority of the National Conference of Catholic Bishops. Still, in the years following the Second Vatican Council, the American hierarchy embraced collegiality enthusiastically and built one of the most cohesive and active episcopal conferences in the world.

The American bishops of the 1960s and 1970s were practical men who understood their social and political circumstances; they understood the new limitations that had been placed on their traditional roles. In particular, they recognized that many of the issues in which they were interested, from education and birth control to social justice and economic conditions, had shifted more and more to the national level of government and politics; they recognized that a cohesive organization was probably necessary for meaningful participation on that level.

In addition, many of the leading figures of the previous era either retired or passed away in the years following the Second Vatican Council. Archbishop Jean Jadot, as the pope's apostolic delegate to the United States, played a very important role in deciding who would replace them. Jadot was deeply committed to the approach of the pastoral constitution and to the collegial style of the dogmatic constitution. He became known for his openness to the input of American priests and bishops and for his practice of emphasizing the pastoral qualities of the men he nominated for the episcopacy. The bishops appointed during Jadot's tenure tended to be less enamored of the imperial trappings of the traditional hierarchy, and more attuned to the pastoral, collective style of the post-Vatican II church.[72] And that style often found expression in the activities of the National Conference of Catholic Bishops.

Finally, strong early leadership was crucial to the American Catholic hierarchy's acceptance of collegial structures and processes. Particularly important in this regard were Cardinal John Dearden, the first president of the new conference, and Bishop Joseph Bernardin, Dearden's hand-picked general secretary. Eugene Kennedy was so impressed with Dearden's role in the creation of the modern hierarchy that he characterized the entire collaborative style of the NCCB, and indeed of the American church itself, as the "Dearden inheritance."[73] "The future of the American church," Kennedy wrote, "depended on transforming the conference of bishops from a loose aggregate of men who considered themselves independent colleagues into cooperators in managing a national church. . . . Combining them into a working conference would be something like reuniting the many kingdoms of Italy."[74]

Not only was Dearden successful at this enormous task he set for himself, he also was quite clear about the principles that motivated him. "The most significant note of this week," he declared on the occasion of his election to the presidency of the NCCB, "[was] the application in our discussions of the principle of episcopal collegiality."[75] Dearden also affirmed that this principle was for him the indispensable vehicle through which the bishops were to play a new role in American society:

> One of the great directions that came from the [Pastoral] Constitution is the underscoring of the fact that a Christian today is literally involved in the world and has an obligation to work toward the improvement of the world. . . . The reorganization of the conference and its secretariat makes it more likely that there will be time and inclination to thrash out social issues among the bishops nationally.[76]

Joseph Bernardin was also very committed to the conference at its founding in 1966. He was a key figure in building the NCCB originally, and since then he has held virtually every leadership position that the conference has to offer. Bernardin, who is now the cardinal-archbishop of Chicago, has been deeply involved in many of the conference's most public and politically sensitive activities, and in the chapters to follow I will have occasion to refer to him and his activities again and again.

The development of collegiality among the American Catholic hierarchy that these leaders fostered, combined with the restructuring of their national conference and the reformulation of their teaching mission, gave the American bishops the coherent national voice they had been lacking. As a result of the documents of the Second Vatican Council, in other words, the American hierarchy was well-equipped by the 1970s for active participation in national policy debates and political processes.

It is not nearly enough, however, to look at the changes that took place within the Catholic hierarchy itself. To grasp the true nature and significance of the bishops' participation in the modern political process, we must look at the political developments that have shaped and directed that participation. Over the last twenty years the national electoral process has been dominated by the breakdown of the Democratic party's New Deal coalition and by a renewed competition between two major parties trying to build and solidify new electoral majorities. Just as the bishops were turning to a more national and less parochial approach to politics and public policy, the Republican and Democratic parties were turning to new issues, new strategies, and new voting coalitions in efforts to assert dominance over American electoral politics.

The bishops' specific political activities over the last two decades have been shaped by a series of intersections between their new approach and agenda with these new political strategies. In fact, in pursuit of these strategies, party leaders and presidential candidates have, at different times on different issues, tried to use the bishops to expand their electoral bases and morally ground their policy platforms. The Catholic hierarchy's role in contemporary American politics, in short, has been determined by the strategies and tactics of secular political leaders as well as by the actions and statements of the bishops themselves.

CHAPTER FOUR

The Bishops, Abortion, and a "New Majority"

THIS CHAPTER will focus on the bishops' activities involving abortion between 1968 and 1975 and establish that these activities conformed to the model of the hierarchy's modern political activities that I outlined in the previous chapter. That is to say, on abortion the bishops acted collectively through their strengthened national forum to address a central issue of the American public policy agenda in an unapologetic and nonparochial manner.

This chapter will also establish that the bishops' decision to actively oppose abortion coincided with an attempt by conservative political operatives to realign the American party system. In search of voters and issues with which to build a "new majority" of the national electorate, the conservative movement adopted the prolife banner in the 1970s in order to draw socially conservative voters away from the Democratic party. This chapter will examine the relationship between the bishops' policy agenda and this political strategy. In the following chapter, I will discuss the ways in which this relationship directly shaped the bishops' participation in the 1976 national election.

THE BISHOPS AND ABORTION

The bishops' involvement with abortion as a political issue began in earnest shortly after the close of the Second Vatican Council when the American Law Institute's Model Penal Code called for liberalization of the various state laws governing abortion. At a series of meetings in 1967, the bishops decided to denounce the code and actively oppose legal abortion. For a number of reasons, that decision was practically a reflex reaction.

The first thing to keep in mind when assessing the motivation behind any of the bishops' publicly articulated positions is that the bishops are officials of the *Roman* Catholic Church. They are appointed by the pope, not elected by the people or the clergy, and they properly exercise their authentic authority only in conjunction with the supreme authority held by the pope; the bishops cannot contradict clearly defined teachings of the papacy.

By 1967, the Catholic Church and its leadership in Rome had a clear and lengthy record of opposition to abortion. Much has been made in recent years of arcane debates in Catholic history over ensoulment or quickening, and over distinctions between early and late abortions. These debates and distinctions,

however, had to do with gradations of evil and categories of relative criminal-
ity, not with differences between licit and illicit medical procedures.[1] And
regardless of ancient practices and policies, by 1967 the popes and the church
had unequivocally condemned *all* direct abortions for over a century. The
American bishops, quite naturally, did the same.

Moreover, the American political and legal debate over abortion reopened
less than two years after the bishops returned from the final session of the
Second Vatican Council. At that session the American bishops, along with
their colleagues from around the world, had adopted the *Pastoral Constitution
on the Church in the Modern World* calling for an active dialogue between the
church and the world and for an application of Catholic teaching to the needs
and problems of modern society. That constitution had referred specifically to
abortion as one of the issues to which the bishops should address themselves:

> For God, the Lord of life, has conferred on men the surpassing ministry of safe-
> guarding life—a ministry which must be fulfilled in a manner which is worthy of
> man. Therefore, from the moment of its conception, life must be guarded with the
> greatest of care, while abortion and infanticide are unspeakable crimes.[2]

In short, two years after Vatican II charged the bishops with the mission of
actively "reading the signs of the times" and engaging in dialogue with modern American society, they faced an effort to legalize abortion, a procedure
that they and their church had just roundly condemned as an "unspeakable
crime." Given Catholic teaching on abortion and the bishops' mission to relate that teaching to the world beyond the church, one can hardly imagine
a policy initiative more likely to capture the attention and galvanize the efforts of the American hierarchy in the mid-1960s than the liberalization of
abortion law.

The bishops assigned the job of monitoring the issue to the United States
Catholic Conference's family life bureau. Throughout the late 1960s and early
1970s, the bureau coordinated the release of a series of statements in which
the bishops declared their moral rejection of abortion and their political opposition to its legalization. The first of these statements appeared in 1968 as part
of *Human Life in Our Day*, the American bishops' response to Pope Paul VI's
condemnation of artificial birth control. "Stepped up pressure," the bishops
wrote, "for moral and legal acceptance of directly procured abortion make
necessary pointed reference to this threat of the right to life."[3] Not for the last
time, the bishops quoted Vatican II's characterization of abortion as an "unspeakable crime," and they stressed the church's doctrine that human life
should be inviolable from the moment of conception. The bishops did not
limit their arguments to Catholic doctrine and values, however. They also
took a broader view and stated that abortion was "contrary to Judeo-Christian
traditions inspired by love for life, and Anglo-Saxon legal traditions protective of life and the person."[4]

This initial statement was followed, in rapid succession, by *Statement on Abortion* in 1969, *Statement on Abortion* and *Declaration on Abortion* in 1970, and *Population and the American Future: A Response* in 1972.[5] Each of these documents followed the precedent the bishops had set in *Human Life in Our Day* in that each of them cited both Catholic doctrine and American legal principles as the bishops' reasons for opposing the liberalization of abortion law. None of them, however, included any discussion of specific strategies for making that opposition politically effective.

The only hint of the role that the bishops would come to play in the political struggle over abortion was the increasingly aggressive tone of their statements. As the effort to legalize abortion gained ground in state after state, the bishops became ever more pointed in their criticism. In April 1970, for example, they noted "regrettably" that "there has been a radical turn of events during this past year, and a new effort has been directed to the total repeal of all laws [prohibiting abortion]."[6] In the same document, they also expressed regret that "an effort has been mounted in the courts to have such laws declared unconstitutional."[7]

In chapter 2 I described a traditional political role in which the bishops acted individually on the local level to defend the parochial interests of their church and people. In chapter 3, I contrasted that traditional approach with a modern role in which the hierarchy collectively participates in national policy debates by articulating and advocating their preferred positions on the general public policy questions facing American society. One could argue, I suppose, that abortion is a Catholic issue, and that the bishops' opposition to it was consistent with their traditional defense of Catholic values and practices. However, both the substance of the bishops' opposition to abortion and the form that their subsequent political activities took were essentially modern as I define the term.

As they were instructed to do at the Second Vatican Council, the bishops consistently looked beyond their own church and declared their intention to address "all [their] fellow citizens" on abortion.[8] They did so, they said, "in fulfillment of [their] teaching responsibility as bishops."[9] But they also did so out of a "conviction that whatever is opposed to life is a violation of man's inherent rights, a position that has a strong basis in the history of American law."[10] These statements were not traditional defenses of Catholic rights or prerogatives; they were self-confident declarations of the hierarchy's interpretation of American law and tradition. In fact, the bishops assured their readers that "we do not urge one ethical conviction as the sole basis of public policy, but we articulate the concerns that are also held by persons of other faiths and by specialists in the fields of medicine, law, and the social sciences."[11]

The bishops used this inclusive language, of course, to deflect charges that abortion was merely a Catholic issue and to broaden the base of support for their position. They realized that to effectively fight the legalization of abortion they would have to reach out beyond their church to communicate and cooperate with other segments of society, both religious and secular. But this more inclusive style is a central component of the bishops' modern approach to the political process. In the case of abortion, that style, including the explicit references to American legal principles and the great founding documents of the American political system, facilitated the addition of the "right-to-life" to the political agenda of powerful secular forces.

Through 1972, the bishops' opposition to abortion could not conform to the more national character of their modern approach to public policy. Statutes and regulations having to do with abortion, and therefore mobilization and lobbying having to do with that issue, remained on the state level. In recognition of these facts, James McHugh, then a monsignor and the staff director of the family life bureau but now a bishop himself, described the role of his bureau before 1973 as "advisory."[12] There was little he and his colleagues could do except monitor the national situation from Washington and coordinate national statements in support of efforts at the state and diocesan level. The Supreme Court changed all that in 1973, of course, with its decision in Roe v. Wade. That decision thrust abortion onto the *national* political stage, and in time, gave rise to political developments that brought the Catholic hierarchy more actively into national electoral politics.

The bishops' reaction to Roe v. Wade was immediate and condemnatory. Cardinal John Krol, president of the NCCB, denounced the decision as "bad logic and bad law," and called it "an unspeakable tragedy for this nation."[13] By coincidence, the NCCB's newly formed ad hoc committee on pro-life activities held its inaugural session the day after the court handed down its decision. Expressly speaking for the whole hierarchy, this committee of bishops refused to "accept the court's judgment," and advised people "not to follow its reasoning or conclusions."[14]

The committee also recommended that "every legal possibility . . . be explored to challenge the opinion of the United States Supreme Court decision which withdraws all legal safeguards for the right to life of the unborn child."[15] According to McHugh, who was the staff director of this committee as well, the bishops realized "within twenty-four hours" of the court's action that exploring every legal possibility meant, in practice, mounting a campaign in favor of a constitutional amendment prohibiting abortion.[16] Indeed, by November 1973 the bishops had explicitly declared that they wished "to make it clear beyond a doubt to our fellow citizens that we consider the passage of a prolife constitutional amendment a priority of the highest order."[17]

As these statements were being released in their name, the bishops were engaged in a debate behind the scenes over how specific they should be concerning the form that a constitutional amendment should take. Many bishops opposed offering specific amendment language because they did not want to lend credence to arguments that abortion was an exclusively Catholic issue. In addition, the amendment with the best chance of passing, a plan to return responsibility for abortion back to the individual states, was unacceptably lenient for many bishops because it acquiesced, however reluctantly, in some legal abortion. Despite this discussion, the bishops did take two steps to enhance the prospect of an amendment—any amendment—being adopted.

First, they established the National Committee for a Human Life Amendment (NCHLA) as a lobby group to work for passage of an amendment. To protect the church's tax exemption and to broaden the base of the antiabortion movement, the bishops made the NCHLA a separate entity outside of the church's official bureaucracy. The separation was more formal than real, however. The NCHLA's funding came exclusively from the bishops, and unlike the National Right to Life Committee, which was also initially launched by the bishops, it never severed its ties to the church in favor of real independence. In 1975, for example, the bishops called for more direct communication between the NCHLA and the ad hoc committee on pro-life activities "to secure greater guidance for the NCHLA and also to demonstrate to the bishops the closer cooperation of the two Committees."[18]

Second, the National Conference of Catholic Bishops sent Cardinals John Krol of Philadelphia, Timothy Manning of Los Angeles, Humberto Medeiros of Boston, and John Cody of Chicago to testify on its behalf before a Senate subcommittee on constitutional amendments.[19] The cardinals stated the hierarchy's strong opposition to abortion, and repeated the assertion that these views were based as much on the bishops' understanding of American law and tradition as they were on Catholic doctrine and moral values. They also argued that "the only feasible way to reverse the decision of the Court and to provide some constitutional base for the legal protection of the unborn child is by amending the Constitution." On "the advice of political and legal advisors," however, they declined to offer an opinion on the specific form that such an amendment should take.[20]

In 1973 and 1974, the American Catholic hierarchy committed its energies and resources to the task of reversing Roe v. Wade through a constitutional amendment. They repeatedly stated their support of an amendment, and generously funded organizations devoted to passing one. Looking ahead to the election year of 1976, however, the bishops realized that getting a constitutional amendment passed would require more than releasing statements, testifying on Capitol Hill, and founding right-to-life organizations. It would require focused and coordinated political action.

The *Pastoral Plan for Pro-life Activities*, released in November 1975, has been called the most "focused and aggressive political leadership" ever exerted by the American Catholic hierarchy.[21] It consisted of a call for a "public information/education program," a promise of "pastoral care" for women and families facing difficult child-bearing circumstances, and a detailed blueprint for a "legislative/public policy effort":

> Accomplishment of this [legal/public policy effort] will undoubtedly require well-planned and coordinated political action by citizens at the national, state and local levels. This activity is not simply the responsibility of Catholics, nor should it be limited to Catholic groups or agencies. It calls for widespread cooperation and collaboration. As citizens of this democracy, we encourage the appropriate political action to achieve these legislative goals. As leaders of a religious institution in this society, we see a moral imperative for such political activity.[22]

The debate within the NCCB over the pastoral plan centered on the degree of involvement the bishops could afford in the specifics of these political activities. Some bishops and members of their national staff feared that an expressly political approach risked both the loss of the church's tax exemption and a rekindling of anti-Catholicism. These fears were particularly acute concerning the hierarchy's call for the creation of prolife lobby groups in every congressional district across the country.

"It is absolutely necessary," the plan stated, "to encourage the development in each congressional district of an identifiable, tightly knit and well organized prolife unit. This unit can be described as a public interest group or a citizen's lobby."[23] How, some conference members asked, could the bishops credibly claim that these groups were not expressly subordinate to the NCCB? McHugh, who actually drafted the plan, told me that the NCCB's administrative board (which first passed the plan and authorized its presentation to a plenary session for adoption by the conference as a whole) debated this section of the document for "several hours," searching for a way to formally distance these politically charged advocacy groups from the tax-exempt church.[24]

As finally adopted, the pastoral plan defined a "congressional district prolife group" as "an agency of citizens operated, controlled, and financed by these same citizens" and added that "*it is not an agency of the church, nor is it operated, controlled or financed by the church.*"[25] Some observers nevertheless pointed out that the actual as opposed to formal independence of the lobby groups was belied by the highly detailed list of objectives and guidelines that directly followed this disclaimer.[26]

More fundamentally, the great detail of the pastoral plan led some within the conference to question the wisdom of emphasizing abortion over all other issues. Bishop Thomas Gumbleton, a noted peace activist from Detroit, for example, remarked in the course of the discussion that "elaborate procedures had not been developed in dealing with such issues as penal reform, world hunger," and other matters to which the conference had recently addressed itself.[27] Gumbleton's concern about the limitations and political dangers of an emphasis on a single issue did not have much of an effect on the bishops' conference in 1975; it passed the *Pastoral Plan for Pro-Life Activities* by an overwhelming margin. But the events surrounding the bishops' involvement in the presidential campaign the following year occasioned a reopening of this question and a reinvigoration of the debate within the hierarchy over its political priorities. This debate has had a significant impact on the bishops' political activities since 1976, and I will return to it in detail in later chapters.

The pastoral plan of 1975 was emblematic of the hierarchy's approach to political activism in the modern era. The bishops, through their national collective organization, offered their moral judgment on an important public policy issue. They devised a strategy for turning that judgment into legislative action, and they communicated that strategy through a document that, in Paul Weber's descriptive phrase, "crackle[d] with political idiom."[28]

The pastoral plan and the bishops' commitment to the antiabortion cause were taken seriously by politicians for a number of reasons. Some of these politicians, as we will see, apparently believed that the bishops' conference could collectively play the kind of political role that individual local bishops had played in an earlier era. The available data, of course, suggests that this was not the case. Despite the bishops' very clearly expressed opposition to abortion, American Catholics are still only slightly more likely to oppose "abortion on demand" than are Protestants (65 percent to 62 percent). In fact, Catholics and Protestants do not differ at all on whether abortion should be legally available in cases of rape, incest, or threat to the mother's life.[29] Nevertheless, the possibility that the bishops could mobilize or influence large numbers of right-to-life voters in 1976 was enough to capture the interest of politicians who were particularly interested in Catholic votes.

The significance of the bishops' opposition to abortion was not limited to its effect on Catholic voters, however. The bishops also presented themselves and their church as the center of a broad, grass-roots movement opposed to legal abortion. By 1976, "right-to-life" was much more than a term in one of the NCCB's official statements. It was also the name of a growing social movement, supported and funded by the Catholic bishops, that was organized nationwide to engage in single-issue political action to achieve its goals.

Once again, however, the political significance of the bishops' actions was also fundamentally affected by the political context in which they took place. The bishops' perceived influence on Catholic voters and their role in the development of the right-to-life movement did not exist in a political vacuum. To the contrary, the bishops' identification of themselves and their church with the antiabortion cause took place within an American political system characterized by an unusual degree of volatility. The New Deal Democratic coalition was coming apart, and Catholics were drifting away from the Democratic party. Emerging political forces were seeking new issues with which they might be able to build a new electoral majority.

One of these forces, the conservative movement, attempted to capitalize on the bishops' effort to stop abortion by adopting the right-to-life cause and launching a direct appeal to Catholic voters. This appeal, part of a broader political strategy designed to build what conservatives referred to as a "new majority" of the American electorate, raised the political profile of the Catholic bishops and drew them into active participation in the national electoral process.

BUILDING A "NEW MAJORITY"

Walter Dean Burnham has noted that "historically speaking, at least, national critical realignments have not occurred at random. Instead," he wrote, "there has been a remarkably uniform periodicity in their appearance."[30] Indeed, the elections of 1800, 1828, 1860, 1896, and 1932 are widely recognized as the five critical elections in American political history, and they followed each other with remarkable regularity. There were twenty-eight years between 1800 and 1828, thirty-two years between 1828 and 1860, and thirty-six years between both 1860 and 1896, and 1896 and 1932, respectively. Based on this progression the Republicans had every reason to look to the 1960s with great hope. After more than thirty years of Democratic dominance, the political tide, if history was a reliable guide, should have been ready to turn.

Republicans, especially conservative Republicans, did more than hope. They tried to harness the political tide, hasten its effect, and ride it to control of a realigned party system. To that end, they set out to capture national leadership of their party and to redefine it as a truly conservative alternative to Democratic liberalism. The long-term strategy was to shift the parameters of the American political debate sharply to the right, build a new broad-based Republican coalition, and, finally, enact conservative principles into law.

This strategy first manifested itself in the movement to draft Barry Goldwater for the Republican presidential nomination in 1964.[31] Conservatives succeeded in taking over the official leadership of the Republican party that year, but that success came at a very high price. Goldwater's nomination amounted to a bloody coup at the convention, and he emerged from San Francisco with a remarkably narrow base of support. Alienated by the insurgency on their right wing, moderate Republicans sat on their hands during the general election and Goldwater was clobbered by Lyndon Johnson. Despite their defeat, however, conservatives learned two very important lessons from their experiences in 1964: (1) ideological conservatism enjoyed limited support among the American electorate at large; and (2) a conservative realignment would require more than simply wresting temporary and tenuous control of the Republican party's national apparatus; it would require a new, mass-based coalition.

In this connection, the presidential campaign of 1964 revealed that the dislocation that usually precedes realignment, the kind of dislocation that would facilitate the formation of a new Republican coalition, was quite advanced by the mid-1960s. Issues traditionally left to local or individual initiative had been taken over by the federal government under the Democratic Kennedy–Johnson administration, and some of these issues had cut directly across the base of Democratic support. The national Democratic party's support for civil rights, in particular, had alienated millions of white Southerners and taken a serious toll on the health of the New Deal coalition. A party built on a coalition including Southern whites and Northern blacks could be held together only as long as economic "class" issues dominated the political agenda. Once racial conflicts moved from the state to the national level in the late 1950s and early 1960s, the underlying split in the Democratic coalition was revealed. And the "Solid South" went solidly for Goldwater in 1964.

The year 1968, then, was a pivotal year. Realignment history with its consistent periodicity suggested that it could be a year of fundamental political upheaval; it was exactly thirty-six years since the last critical election of 1932. In addition, the fissures revealed in 1964 appeared to be consistent with realignment theory. E. E. Schattschneider, in his seminal book *The Semi-Sovereign People*, noted the tensions and stresses that build up in the American political system as an electoral alignment and political regime designed to address one set of issues is confronted with another. As these tensions escalate, he argued, a kind of macrolevel change occurs in the parameters of political debate. There is, in time, "a substitution of one conflict for another" and a "profound change in the agenda of American politics."[32]

James Sundquist applied these insights across the breadth of American political history in *Dynamics of the Party System*, and found that the tensions alluded to by Schattschneider have arisen specifically when "the line of cleavage between the parties cut[s] across the electorate in a new direction." As a result of this new cleavage, Sundquist concluded, "the party system shift[s] on its axis."[33] Sundquist also noted that "if both major parties persist in their straddle [of new issues] . . . supporters of the new issue at some point form a third party."[34]

By 1968 a potentially realigning issue had apparently arrived on the American political scene. Race, or the issue of civil rights for blacks, in terms of realignment theory, looked like it might well "shift the axis" of the existing party system. It had already produced a "profound change in the agenda of American politics" that had led to a third party movement. And George Wallace based his presidential bid on the notion that there was not a dime's worth of difference between the two major parties on the crucial issues of the day.

In the end, however, race and Wallace's candidacy, as possible agents of a critical realignment, suffered from the same fundamental weakness as Goldwater's campaign had. Just as 1964 had revealed the limited constituency of ideological conservatism, so 1968 showed that segregation, at least in national terms, had limited electoral appeal. Wallace carried his native South, to be sure, but a deep and lasting realignment of the national electorate did not take place. "The new [cross-cutting] issue," according to Sundquist, "must also be one powerful enough to dominate political debate and polarize the community."[35] Race could not dominate the national political debate in 1968, nor could it polarize the entire national community. What it could do was dominate *Southern* politics and effect a rather dramatic regional polarization of the Democratic party.

Still, that was enough to deny the presidency to Hubert Humphrey. Richard Nixon won in 1968 because he was able to hold his party's base together while his Democratic opponent lost a large portion of his to George Wallace. In terms of the future alignment of the American electorate, the electoral results of 1968 were extremely portentous. If the Republicans could build a coalition made up of their traditional base and those Democrats and independents who had voted for Wallace, then they might be able to replace the Democratic New Deal party as the dominant force in American electoral politics for, say, the next thirty-six years.

These long-term implications of the 1968 vote were noted at the time by Kevin Phillips, a Republican strategist. In *The Emerging Republican Majority*, Phillips examined Nixon's victory state by state and concluded that it "bespoke the end of the New Deal Democratic hegemony and the beginning of a New Era in American politics."[36] According to Phillips's analysis, this era would be dominated by a new conservative coalition made up of Republican economic conservatives and theretofore Democratic social conservatives. A reformulated Republican party designed to appeal to this potential majority would no longer be dominated by the "establishmentarian Northeast," Phillips predicted, but by "the rising insurgency of the South, the West, the New York City Irish, and middle-class suburbia."[37]

The Emerging Republican Majority was more than a dispassionate analysis of electoral trends; it was also a partisan tract calling for swift capitalization on new political opportunities. Conservatives, frustrated by decades of Democratic dominance and disappointed by the defeat of their candidate in 1964, saw Phillips's vision of an emerging majority as the bright hope of a conservative future. William Rusher, for example, a veteran of Goldwater's campaign and the publisher of *National Review* magazine, called Phillips's book a "dazzling display of erudition and statistics" that "laid bare and greatly developed the foundations of the political strategy that has dominated the modern conservative movement in the United States."[38]

Rusher and others like him realized, however, that a concerted appeal to disaffected social conservatives within the Democratic party could not be based merely on race and segregation. A new political agenda, including but not limited to race, would have to be formulated in order to respond to the social concerns of Northerners as well as Southerners. Rusher himself offered one such formulation. "The issue," he maintained, "was no longer segregation or any other formulation of the race question, but the much larger problem of federal intrusion into the lives of individuals and the prerogatives of the several states."[39] Conservative strategists knew that the introduction of federal police power into ever more areas of political and social life had triggered widespread resentment, and they recognized that this resentment, if skillfully channeled, could be turned against the Democratic party. The Democrats, after all, had been in charge in Washington all those years; they had implemented, and up to that point benefited from, the fantastic growth in federal initiative and power.

Richard Scammon and Ben Wattenberg also recognized the critical importance of so-called social conservatives and of the danger their festering resentment posed for the Democratic party. In *The Real Majority*, Scammon and Wattenberg called on the national Democratic party to address itself directly to what they termed the "social issue": (1) fears concerning race and crime; (2) anger concerning the decay of traditional values and sexual mores; and (3) outrage concerning the anti-American tone of opposition to the war in Vietnam.[40] In fact, Scammon and Wattenberg referred explicitly to the potentially realigning power of this cluster of issues. The social issue, they argued, was "so powerful that it may rival bimetallism and depression in America's political history, an issue powerful enough that under certain circumstances it can compete in political potency with the older economic issues."[41] For Scammon, Wattenberg, and many others it seemed entirely possible that the social issue, to use Schattschneider's terms, could cause a substitution of one conflict for another and a profound change in the agenda of American politics. Or to use Sundquist's terms, that it could dominate debate and polarize the political community.[42]

Phillips's argument and the strategies derived from it focused most pointedly on capturing Republican votes in the previously Democratic South. However, the prospective new majority was to include another segment of the old Democratic coalition as well—Catholics. Note the four elements of the emerging majority envisioned by Phillips. The first two were the South and West, but the second two—the "New York City Irish" and "middle-class suburbia"—were made up, in the first place exclusively and in the second place largely, by Catholics. In fact, Phillips was quite explicit that much of the support a socially conservative Republican party could expect in the Northeast and Midwest would come from "the sons and daughters of Al Smith supporters."[43] Middle-class Catholics had supported Eisenhower in large numbers before returning home to the Democrats in droves to vote for Kennedy. Phillips and other conservatives hoped that with the "status quest" of electing a Catholic president fulfilled, these Catholics would be willing to once again drift away from the Democratic party.[44]

In this very specific context, the Catholic bishops' most significant political act in the late 1960s and early 1970s was their identification of themselves and their church with the movement to ban abortion. With the help of the bishops' attention and resources, abortion became a prominent item on the conservative social agenda, and in time conservatives made abortion the centerpiece of their effort to draw socially conservative Catholics away from the Democratic party. As early as 1970, Republican registrars in California gathered outside Catholic churches to accommodate any parishioners who might want to switch their partisan affiliation in response to the California Democratic party's support of legal abortion. This registration drive, according to *Commonweal*, was a "political experiment engineered by the Republican State Central Committee to see if the abortion issue could be used to cause a mass defection of Catholics from the Democratic Party."[45]

If such a thing as a meaningfully unified "Catholic vote" still existed in the 1970s, it was not possible for the bishops to deliver it to the Republican party, or to anyone else for that matter. But political activists and electoral strategists interested in winning Catholics to their side still had good reasons to consider the bishops significant political actors. First of all, as leaders of both the Catholic Church and the antiabortion movement, the bishops enjoyed access to millions of voters. Catholics were the largest single religious denomination in the country, and the bishops could and did communicate with them regularly. Second, through their traditional relationships with urban machines across the country, the bishops had come to embody the strong, traditional ties that bound the Catholic Church and the Democratic party together. Conservatives, and other Republicans, set out to break that link by emphasizing the widening rift that had opened between the bishops and the Democratic leadership over abortion.

President Nixon offered an early example of how the bishops could be used to facilitate political appeals to Catholic voters. Hoping to attract Catholics to his reelection campaign, Nixon publicly disavowed the prochoice findings of his own presidential commission on population in 1972. He communicated that disavowal in an equally public letter to Cardinal Terence Cooke, a leading spokesman for the bishops' opposition to abortion.[46]

In fact, Nixon did succeed in attracting social conservatives to his candidacy in 1972. George McGovern, stressing the New Politics themes of progressivism and peace, alienated large elements of the Democratic base and lost every state but Massachusetts. As Phillips had predicted and many conservatives had hoped, Nixon captured every Southern state and won a comfortable majority of the Catholic vote. For some observers, Nixon's landslide reelection, and the role that the social issue apparently played in it, heralded the arrival of a critical realignment and a new Republican majority.

The Catholic vote was especially important to Nixon and his publicists in 1972. They referred to Catholic support of the Republican ticket in order to refute the notion that Nixon had formed his new coalition by cynically appealing to the baser motives of Southern whites. They relied on Catholic participation in the new majority, in other words, as proof that the "social issue" was much more than repackaged racial prejudice. As one of these publicists, Patrick Buchanan, put it: "Though his critics were crying 'Southern Strategy,' the President's politics and policy decisions were not going unnoticed in the Catholic and ethnic communities of the North, East, and Midwest."[47]

V. O. Key and other realignment theorists have consistently held that a legitimate reordering of the American electorate cannot be inferred from a single election. True critical elections effect *enduring* shifts in the partisan alignment. For that reason, conservatives looked to 1976 with both a great deal of trepidation and a great deal of hope. The election in 1976 was an important challenge to the staying power of the new Republican coalition. If this coalition was to be more than an aberration brought on by Democratic ineptitude in 1972, then the Republican presidential candidate had to carry Southern whites and Northern Catholics again. If he could do so, of course, then a lasting realignment of the national party system might occur at last.

The Watergate scandal, however, intervened and dashed the new majority hopes raised in 1972. Nixon, to be sure, was never the darling of the Republican right wing. But while conservatives had come to accept Nixon as the standard-bearer of their "emerging Republican majority," they were openly distrustful of Nixon's successor, Gerald Ford. Ford's succession to the presidency and, perhaps even more importantly, his choice of the conservatives' hated enemy, Nelson Rockefeller, as his vice-president, substantially widened the ideological rift in the Republican party. "The historic opportunity," Buchanan wrote, "first presented to the Republicans in 1968 to become the party of the emerging majority in American politics—seemingly realized in 1972—may finally have passed away."[48]

Realignment as a political *development* was set back by Watergate, but realignment as a political *strategy* was not abandoned. The magnitude of the victory in 1972 had impressed upon the Republican establishment the necessity of broadening the party's base by appealing to vulnerable elements of the Democratic coalition. Ford and his supporters did not want to use their party as the vehicle of ideological conservative change, but they were politicians willing to hunt, as the expression goes, where the ducks were. Although they did not share Pat Buchanan's conservative zeal, they did agree with his analysis that "for Republicans the Democratic ducks are in South Boston, and they are roosting all over Dixie. There are next to none in Manhattan and Harlem, but hundreds of thousands in Queens and the North Bronx."[49] Once the Democrats had nominated Jimmy Carter of Georgia, of course, the Southern ducks returned to the Democratic roost, and Ford was left to search for votes in areas such as South Boston, Queens, and the North Bronx. He was left to search, in other words, among Catholics. In short order, Nixon's Southern strategy of 1972 gave way to Ford's Catholic strategy in 1976.

This chapter has examined the simultaneous progress of two related developments: the bishops' decision to oppose the legalization of abortion, and the Republican strategy to divide the Democratic party's New Deal coalition against itself with the social issue. The intersection of these two developments, more than any other factor, shaped the bishops' controversial participation in the presidential campaign of 1976.

CHAPTER FIVE

The Bishops and Electoral Politics: 1976

THE PRESIDENTIAL ELECTION of 1976 was the key episode in the development of a relationship between the bishops' own publicly articulated policy agenda and the platforms and electoral strategies of the two major political parties. Other events such as the pastoral letters on nuclear war and the American economy and John O'Connor's criticism of Geraldine Ferraro in 1984 have received more attention, and they will be dealt with in detail in later chapters. None of these events, however, can rival the seminal and lasting influence that 1976 has had on the bishops' involvement in American politics. In fact, all of the bishops' activities since 1976 can be characterized, to some extent, as responses to, or consequences of, the controversial events of that year.

POLITICAL RESPONSIBILITY

In chapter 4 we saw that the bishops had prepared themselves to push for an antiabortion amendment to the U.S. Constitution during the political campaign in 1976. The *Pastoral Plan for Pro-Life Activities*, calling for "well planned [antiabortion] political action," had established the bishops' commitment to an effort to heighten the significance of abortion as a political and electoral issue in 1976.[1] Not everyone within the bishops' conference was pleased with the tone and implications of this effort, however. Some bishops and staff members were concerned that the plan's strong and expressly political language would limit the hierarchy's political role in 1976 to abortion alone. They wanted to avoid creating an impression that the NCCB would judge candidates and parties solely on the basis of abortion.

Monsignor George Higgins, the "eminence gris" of the so-called social justice staff at the United States Catholic Conference, said of the plan:

> I was afraid it was too much of a one shot, one issue affair, and it might involve [the bishops] in one issue politics. I think in the minds of some of the people who were responsible for it it was a one issue thing. They were going to move on that one issue and they were going to use whatever political clout they could muster. That was particularly true of Monsignor McHugh; we disagreed completely on what I thought was a very heavy handed approach to one issue.[2]

McHugh, not surprisingly, saw the situation quite differently:

> I was the director of the pro-life committee and my job was to do everything that was humanly possible to forestall any more liberalization of abortion law or any more social acceptance of abortion. Now, I presume that if somebody else was responsible for something else that they would be working as hard on that as I was working on what I was doing and in the end the conference would be perceived as being interested in all of these issues. So anybody who ever threw the one issue church thing up to me, I'd say don't tell me about that. We'll be a one issue church if everybody else sits around and does nothing. But if everybody else goes out and does their job we're not going to be a one issue church.[3]

The truth of the matter was that the bishops *had* publicly articulated positions on a whole range of public matters other than abortion. At the same meeting in November 1975 at which the bishops had adopted the antiabortion plan, they had also approved *The Economy: Human Dimensions*, *The Right to a Decent Home: A Pastoral Response to the Crisis in Housing*, *Resolution on Farm Labor*, and *Resolution on New York City*.[4] The problem, for Higgins and others, was not that the bishops were not addressing issues other than abortion. The problem was that none of the bishops' applications of the church's teachings to these other contemporary problems contained the detailed blueprint for legislative action or call for organized political activity that were at the heart of the *Pastoral Plan for Pro-Life Activities*.

In response to this disparity, Bishop James Rausch, secretary of the bishops' conference and general secretary of the bishops' national secretariat, developed, along with his staff, a document called *Political Responsibility: Reflections on an Election Year*.[5] Rausch and his colleagues designed this statement to affirm the bishops' right and responsibility to speak out on contemporary issues, and to publicize and codify the conference's positions on a long list of issues, a list that included, but was not limited to, abortion.

Approved by the full NCCB in May 1976, the statement conveyed the bishops' intention to "call attention to the moral and religious dimensions of secular issues, to keep alive the values of the Gospel as a norm for social and political life, and to point out the demands of Christian faith for a just transformation of society."[6] The statement also emphasized that the bishops "specifically do not seek the formation of a religious voting bloc," and that they would not "instruct persons on how they should vote by endorsing candidates."[7]

This statement shifted ground from the pastoral plan in that the latter document stated that "the church's concern for human rights and social justice should be comprehensive and consistent," and it listed "a broad range of topics on which the bishops of the United States have already expressed themselves." In addition to abortion, this list also included the economy, education, food policy, housing, human rights, U.S. foreign policy, military expenditures, and the role of the mass media in the political process.[8]

In 1984, the press and the political community paid a great deal of attention to an apparent split within the bishops' conference between supporters of Bernard Law's designation of abortion as the "critical" issue of the day, and supporters of Joseph Bernardin's broader "consistent ethic of life." It is clear from the above, however, that official episcopal documents had already articulated both these positions in 1975 and 1976. It is clear, in other words, that by 1976 a debate had begun among the American bishops concerning the priority they should collectively give to various issues. This debate was politically significant then, as it still is today, because the bishops' priorities determine the way their agenda intersects the platforms and strategies of the political parties at any given time. In 1976, the bishops' priorities were particularly significant because each of the presidential candidates tried to associate himself with the Catholic hierarchy and with limited aspects of the hierarchy's moral agenda.

Both Carter and Ford considered Catholic voters crucial to the outcome of their campaign. Four years earlier a majority of Catholics had broken traditional ties to the Democratic party and had rejected McGovern in favor of Nixon.[9] This defection, along with the defection of white Southerners, had dismantled the Democratic coalition that had dominated presidential politics since Roosevelt and the New Deal. Carter, as a former governor of Georgia, was sure to return one group of defectors, white Southerners, to the Democratic column. But Catholics were seen as swing voters, and they were actively courted by both candidates. As part of that courting process, each of the candidates also sought to establish a positive and, if possible, supportive relationship with the Catholic bishops.

Carter was concerned that the cultural gap between a "born again" Southern Baptist candidate and northern ethnic voters would create a "Catholic problem" for his campaign. In the hope of ameliorating such a problem, Carter went out of his way to assure Catholics at every opportunity that he was personally sensitive to their particular concerns. He also worked diligently throughout the campaign to establish a positive relationship with the Catholic hierarchy. Carter and his advisers hoped that cordiality between the candidate and the bishops would symbolically downplay Carter's cultural distance from Catholics, and at the same time defuse any active opposition to his candidacy by the bishops themselves. Carter "needed desperately to win the northern blue collar vote," recalled one of his top aides. "The bishops could affect that vote at the margin, and it is at the margin, after all, that elections are won and lost."[10]

Ford had even more compelling reasons for seeking a friendly relationship with the Catholic hierarchy. Resigned to losing the South to his Georgian opponent, Ford's only chance for victory was to carry the heavily Catholic states of the Northeast and upper Midwest. As a result, Ford launched a concerted, direct appeal to Catholic voters, and made an effort, in the words of an aide, to "exploit the cultural combativeness between Baptists and Catholics."[11] One way to do this was to associate with the Catholic bishops and their policy positions. Friendly bishops, after all, could provide Ford with valuable opportunities to speak directly to Catholic audiences, and public agreement between Ford and the bishops could highlight and exacerbate Carter's potentially troublesome "Catholic problem."

As it turned out, both candidates overestimated the political influence, either direct or indirect, that the hierarchy could exert on Catholic voters. The bishops' authority over Catholic citizens and their influence on Catholic political attitudes had undergone a fundamental change during the two decades or so preceding 1976. In terms of their actual involvement in the 1976 presidential campaign, however, the true extent of the bishops' influence on Catholic voters did not really matter that much. The fact that Ford and Carter both *believed* that the bishops influenced the Catholic vote meant that the candidates were sensitive to the bishops' views and attentive to the bishops' statements and actions. The candidates' shared perception drew the bishops into the center of a closely fought national election campaign and granted the bishops an opportunity to advance their moral agenda in the public arena of presidential politics.

As we have seen, however, the official public policy agenda of the National Conference of Catholic Bishops, as articulated in late 1975 and early 1976, contained an apparent contradiction. On the one hand, the pastoral plan called for a political mobilization for the purpose of electing candidates who supported a constitutional amendment outlawing abortion. On the other, the political responsibility statement declared that "the church's concern for human rights and social justice should be comprehensive and consistent." In abstract principle, of course, these two positions may not be completely incompatible. But in 1976 the bishops agreed with the Republican party on abortion, and with the Democratic party on virtually everything else. Given these political circumstances, it is difficult to see how the bishops' conference could encourage the election of antiabortion candidates and at the same time maintain a consistent concern for other issues related to social justice. In practical political terms, in terms of publicly articulated political priorities, the bishops would have to choose in 1976 between the *Pastoral Plan for Pro-Life Activities* and *Political Responsibility: Reflections on an Election Year*. And in effect, this is just what their leadership did that summer when it decided to downplay other issues and strongly denounce the Democratic party's support for legal abortion.

While seeking the Democratic presidential nomination, Carter had tried, with some success, to play both sides of the abortion issue. In Iowa, for example, with its large and influential right-to-life movement, Carter had emphasized his own moral opposition to abortion. But once success in Iowa had launched his national candidacy he reassured prochoice activists within his party that his personal ethical stand did not mean that he was in favor of amending the Constitution to make abortion illegal. In fact, in an effort to solidify his support among these activists Carter lent strong support to an unequivocally prochoice plank in his party's platform. "We fully recognize," the plank read, "the religious and ethical nature of the concerns which many Americans have on the subject of abortion. We feel, however, it is undesirable to attempt to amend the Constitution to overturn the Supreme Court decision in this area."[12]

Archbishop Joseph L. Bernardin, by that time President of the National Conference of Catholic Bishops, reacted strongly to this section of the Democratic platform. "Though this may be someone's idea of compromising an issue," Bernardin said, "the compromise here amounts to opposing protection of the life of the unborn and endorsing permissive abortion." Setting aside the fact that the platform at hand agreed with the bishops on virtually every issue that followed abortion in the political responsibility statement, Bernardin called the Democratic plank on abortion "irresponsible."[13]

Bernardin's action was a very unwelcome development for a Democratic candidate who was trying to rebuild the party's tattered coalition and who was already concerned about a potential "Catholic problem." But even more ominously for Carter, Bernardin later added that he was "deeply concerned that this action by the Democratic platform committee may have the effect of increasing feelings of frustration and alienation from the political process felt by many Americans."[14] Although rather cryptic, these words seemed to suggest that the Democratic position on abortion had the potential to create just the kind of wedge between Carter and Catholic voters that could prove disastrous to his campaign.

Carter moved quickly to "clarify" his position on abortion. In an exclusive interview with Jim Castelli of the National Catholic News Service, Carter reemphasized that he was strongly opposed to abortion on moral grounds and argued that it was only the current proposals for a constitutional amendment that he found unacceptable. Carter also tried to distance himself from some of the more uncompromising implications of a Democratic platform that, by all accounts, had been written by members of his own campaign staff. "The wording," he told Castelli, "was not in accordance with my own desires. . . . The insinuation of the plank's opposition to citizen effort to amend the Constitution as inappropriate is what I object to."[15]

If Carter thought that the bishops' conference would be mollified by this "clarification," then he was immediately disappointed. Bernardin, again speaking as president of the NCCB, promptly dismissed Carter's maneuvering:

Despite [Governor Carter's] personal opposition to abortion, we regret that he continues to be unsupportive of a constitutional amendment to protect the life of the unborn. His reiteration of this stance reveals an inconsistency that is deeply disturbing to those who hold the right to life to be sacred and inalienable. . . . The pro-abortion plank of the Democratic platform remains seriously objectionable.[16]

A shift from "irresponsible" to "deeply disturbing" and "seriously objectionable" could not have been the change in rhetoric for which Carter had hoped when he sought the interview with Castelli. Carter, it seemed, was not going to be able to sidestep the public criticism directed at him from the Catholic hierarchy. In fact, the split between the Democratic presidential candidate and the Catholic bishops' conference only widened shortly thereafter when Archbishop Bernardin publicly praised a Republican platform that diverged from the NCCB's policy on virtually every issue except abortion. Deferring discussion of "other important issues" to "the days ahead," Bernardin lauded the Republicans for their "timely and important" support of an amendment banning abortion.[17]

Not surprisingly, the bishops and staff who had devised and strongly advocated the political responsibility statement were unhappy with Bernardin's responses to the two platforms. They were distressed at what they saw as a rapid degeneration of their broad, cross-cutting policy agenda into a single-issue crusade. As we have seen, these bishops and aides had argued against such an approach within the bishops' conference itself. Now, in the heat of the campaign, they turned to their personal contacts within the Democratic party in an effort to get Carter to take the initiative in broadening his public dialogue with Bernardin and the conference. The key figure in these backchannel communications between the Catholic Conference and Carter's campaign was Bishop James Rausch.[18]

Rausch was, in effect, chief of staff of the entire NCCB/USCC bureaucracy. Unlike Bernardin and most of the members and officers of the NCCB, he lived and worked in Washington, D.C., where he directed the day-to-day operations of the conference and coordinated the hierarchy's various collective activities. He was also, according to everyone with whom I spoke about him, "fascinated by politics" and deeply committed to a broad range of social justice issues.[19] He saw his job as general secretary as one of leading the bishops' conference to more active, more broadly based participation in the national political process.

One of Rausch's many contacts in the Democratic party was a Washington lawyer named Thomas Farmer who, by his own admission, was looking for a way to "insinuate" himself into Carter's campaign.[20] Farmer saw an opportunity for himself in the rather inept way that Carter and his staff had handled the flap with Bernardin over the Democratic platform. He presented himself to Carter's staff as someone who understood the bishops, who had valuable contacts within the bishops' conference, and who could help bridge the rift between Carter and Bernardin.

As a first step in that process, Farmer arranged a meeting between Bishop Rausch and Andrew Young, a close aide to Carter. Rausch and Young met, discussed Carter's relationship with the Catholic hierarchy, and readily agreed that a way had to be found to get the political spotlight off abortion and onto the issues on which the Democratic candidate and the National Conference of Catholic Bishops held virtually identical positions. According to Farmer, Rausch's initial meeting with Young was followed by a personal phone call from Carter in which the candidate expressed his desire to resolve his difficulties with the Catholic hierarchy. Rausch assured Carter that he agreed with that objective, but added that as a bishop and an officer of the NCCB he would not be able to play an active or public role in achieving it. He encouraged Carter to continue to work through Farmer as an intermediary in establishing strategies and approaches for shifting the public dialogue with the bishops onto a broader range of issues.

Discussions concerning Carter's relationship with the bishops proceeded on several different levels over the next few weeks. Farmer, for example, traveled to Atlanta for a meeting with Carter's top advisers; Rausch sent an aide from the Catholic Conference to observe one of Carter's strategy sessions in Plains, Georgia; and Rausch personally met with the Democratic vice-presidential candidate Walter Mondale (another old friend) to discuss their mutual interest in defusing further criticism of Carter's views by the NCCB's leadership.[21] In the end, Rausch, Farmer, and their interlocutors in Carter's campaign decided that the best way to lower the decibel level of the dispute on abortion was to arrange a personal meeting between Carter and the leaders of the bishops' conference. At such a meeting, they decided, a whole range of issues could be discussed, and the disagreement on abortion could be placed within a wider context of general agreement.

Carter, who had just captured the Democratic presidential nomination through his ability to convince people of his sincerity and trustworthiness, readily agreed with the idea of a personal meeting with Archbishop Bernardin. He apparently believed that he would be able to resolve his difficulties with the bishops by establishing "an intimate personal relationship" with their leaders.[22] Once Carter had agreed, his campaign then formally approached Bernardin with a proposal for a meeting. After some initial hesitation, Bernardin announced that he and the NCCB's executive committee would be willing to meet separately with each of the presidential candidates.

MEETINGS WITH THE CANDIDATES

Carter opened his meeting with the bishops' executive committee in late August 1976 by stressing his agreement with the committee on a wide range of issues and by pointedly assuring the bishops of his strong support for parochial education.[23] Turning quickly to abortion, however, Carter then reminded the bishops that he personally shared their conviction that abortion was immoral. His only difference with them on that issue, he argued, had to do with political strategy rather than ethical principle, and he expressed the hope that they would not allow such a limited disagreement to continue to cast such a cloud over their relationship.

Carter's opening remarks at the meeting revealed that he still thought it was possible to reach an accommodation with the bishops on abortion. Despite rather clear evidence that the disagreement was intractable, he clung to the notion that "his position [on abortion] could be made minimally acceptable [to the bishops]."[24] Carter, in other words, went into the meeting not merely wanting to expand the scope of his discussions with the bishops (as he had been urged to do by Rausch and others), but also wanting somehow to resolve the dispute that had dominated the discussion to that point. The problem with this approach was that Bernardin had no intention of resolving the disagreement over abortion on any grounds other than Carter's agreement that a constitutional amendment was necessary and desirable. Bernardin was quite willing to discuss other issues with Carter at the meeting, but he was emphatically not open to compromise or accommodation on the central question of abortion.

In a statement released several weeks before his meeting with Carter, Bernardin had made quite clear how he, as president of the NCCB, felt abortion should be viewed in relation to other issues. "Human life is threatened in many ways in our society," he conceded. "Abortion, however, is a direct assault on the lives of those who are least able to defend themselves. If the church seems particularly concerned with abortion at the moment, it is for this reason: if we become insensitive to the violation of the basic right to life, our sensitivity to the entire spectrum of human rights will ultimately be eroded."[25]

At the meeting with Carter, Bernardin read a prepared statement that repeated these sentiments and that directly challenged the Democratic presidential nominee to change his position on abortion:

> We have called for a constitutional amendment that will give the maximum protection possible to the unborn. Despite contrary positions, there is no other way to correct the serious situation that now exists. If there is an agreement that abortion is a moral evil because it violates a person's most basic right, then the only logical conclusion is that something must be done to correct the evil, and the only remedy is a constitutional amendment. It is for this reason that, on behalf of the Conference of Catholic Bishops, I issued a statement on June 23 expressing strong disagreement—indeed outrage—with the abortion plank in the Democratic platform. . . . We . . . repeat, today, with all the moral force we can muster, the need for a constitutional amendment to protect the life of the unborn. Indeed, without such a remedy, the effort to promote other human life causes for individual and social betterment, about which we are all concerned, is seriously weakened.[26]

This statement should have finally made it clear to Carter that he was not going to be able to make his position on abortion palatable to the Catholic bishops. Nevertheless, he gave it one last try. Carter told the executive committee that he was not opposed to any and all constitutional amendments restricting abortion, but only to those amendments that had actually been proposed. He said that he would be willing to consider a "partial" amendment, whatever that meant, and he asked the bishops if they wanted to offer specific language for an amendment. As they had from the very beginning, they declined to do so.[27]

Like Bernardin's reaction to Carter's interview with Castelli, the exchange at the meeting indicated that the bishops were not willing to reach an accommodation with Carter on abortion. But comments that Bernardin made after the meeting also dashed the hopes of Rausch and others that the bishops' abortion dispute with Carter would be placed in a wider context of comity and agreement. Before taking any questions from reporters at a press conference that followed the meeting, Bernardin read a prepared statement reporting that abortion had been discussed "extensively," and that the bishops continued to be "disappointed" with Carter's position on that issue.[28]

This press conference, and Bernardin's prepared remarks in particular, dominated the media's coverage of Carter's meeting with the bishops. The press depicted the session as a cool rebuff of the Democratic candidate for president by the leaders of the American Catholic hierarchy. *Newsweek*, for example, reported that Carter had been "interrogated" by the executive committee.[29] *Time* spoke of "an hour's grilling" for Carter at the hands of the bishops.[30] Regardless of various characterizations, all of the major news stories emphasized one particularly descriptive word: "disappointed."

Carter's staff was angered by the outcome of the meeting. What they had seen as an opportunity to draw attention away from abortion and the dispute with the bishops, had had precisely the opposite effect. They also apparently felt that they had been misled by Rausch and others who had strongly advocated the meeting. "We were sandbagged," complained one of Carter's aides. "We had assurances beforehand that the meeting would not degenerate into an abortion debate."[31]

Gerald Ford and his campaign staff, on the other hand, were "nearly ecstatic" at the outcome of Carter's meeting with the bishops.[32] The meeting had identified Carter more closely than ever with the prochoice position on abortion, while at the same time it had drawn the media's attention to the distance between Carter and the Catholic hierarchy. Both of these outcomes fit perfectly with Ford's campaign strategy.

Ford, to be sure, was no right-to-lifer. In fact, his own relative moderation on abortion had brought him a great deal of criticism and pressure from Ronald Reagan during the campaign for the Republican nomination. However, once Ford had acquiesced in an abortion plank written by the right wing of his party, he was able to sharply distinguish himself from his opponent on an issue that could serve as the centerpiece of an updated version of the "social issue." Abortion, an issue that in the view of Ford's campaign had "made Catholics refrain at least temporarily from automatically going to Carter," could be put to use as part of an appeal to Catholic voters.[33] At a Catholic Eucharistic Congress in Philadelphia, for example, Ford drew a standing ovation from a predominantly Catholic right-to-life crowd by declaring his concern over an increasing "irreverence for life" in American society.[34]

More to the point for our purposes, the prolife Republican platform also allowed Ford to associate himself with the abortion-centered agenda that had been firmly identified with Joseph Bernardin and the National Conference of Catholic Bishops. Acting on this opportunity, Ford invited Bernardin and the other members of the executive committee to meet with him at the White House. Bernardin opened this session with Ford by once again reading from a prepared statement that featured abortion: "On August 18th I issued a statement in which I called the Republican platform plank on abortion 'timely and important.' We would welcome a statement of your position on the plank as well as clarification concerning the kind of amendment you support and are prepared to work for."[35]

Ford, like Carter, assured the bishops that he shared their moral opposition to abortion. However, unlike Carter, Ford also expressed support for the so-called local option amendment that would reverse Roe v. Wade and return responsibility for abortion to the individual state legislatures. This was not the sweeping, restrictive amendment that the bishops wanted, nor did it even go as far as Ford's own Republican platform had gone. But it was concrete support for a constitutional amendment of some kind and, as such, it clearly distinguished Ford's position from his opponent's.

After the meeting, Bernardin once again proceeded to a press conference where he made remarks that completely dominated the media's coverage of the meeting. "Relative to the abortion decision," Bernardin read from a prepared statement, "we are encouraged that the President agrees on the need for a constitutional amendment. We urged him to support an amendment that will give the maximum protection possible to the unborn."[36] Reporters, of course, pounced on "encouraged" as they had on "disappointed" ten days earlier, and Bernardin's comments made headlines across the country. This time the media explicitly concluded that the Catholic bishops had endorsed the Republican ticket. *Time*, for example, reported that "the bishops' statement was a clear signal of support for Ford."[37] The *Washington Post* claimed that Ford had won the "tacit support of the nation's Roman Catholic bishops."[38]

The bishops' participation in the presidential campaign of 1976 was a vivid example of the way their political role is shaped by the intersection of their own policy priorities with the platforms and strategies of the major political parties. In truth, the bishops did not *explicitly* endorse Gerald Ford for president in 1976. Archbishop Bernardin said he had not meant to do so, and there is no reason to doubt his word. But his responses to the parties' platforms, his statements to the candidates, and his remarks at two separate press conferences clearly established an antiabortion amendment to the Constitution as the Catholic hierarchy's top political priority in 1976. Ford favored such an amendment; Carter did not. Carter's strategy was to deemphasize his differences with the bishops; Ford's was to highlight them. It was a very short step from this relationship between the bishops' emphasis on abortion and the positions and tactics of the two candidates to a conclusion that the bishops favored the Republican ticket. Given the specific political circumstances of 1976, in other words, *Political Responsibility: Reflections on an Election Year* was routed by the *Pastoral Plan for Pro-Life Activities*.

Bernardin and other officials of the NCCB object to this formulation of their participation in the presidential contest between Carter and Ford. They argued then, and they continue to argue today, that their actions that summer and autumn were misunderstood and misrepresented. They maintain that the NCCB's spokesmen limited themselves to addressing issues only, and that it is inappropriate to infer opinions about candidates from positions on issues. They also claim that it is simply not true that abortion was their top political priority in 1976. They argue that the media distorted their agenda by concentrating exclusively on abortion and completely ignoring the NCCB's positions on other issues. Neither of these claims, however, stands up to scrutiny.

Following the executive committee's meeting with Ford at the White House, Russell Shaw, director of the bishops' office of public affairs, wrote to the *Washington Post* to complain about the media's coverage of the session. Pointing out that no reporter had asked Bernardin a question about anything but abortion at his press conference, and that the subsequent news stories focused almost exclusively on that issue, Shaw asked, "Is it the bishops who have an exclusive preoccupation with abortion or is it—at least in their coverage of the bishops—the media?"[39]

The record of the executive committee's meetings with the candidates and of the press conferences that followed, however, indicates that Bernardin, although he may not have had an "exclusive preoccupation" with abortion, had nevertheless emphasized that issue over all others in 1976. The prepared statement that Bernardin read to Carter during their meeting paid far more attention to abortion alone than it did to all of the other issues combined.[40] More to the point, Bernardin's opening statement at the press conference that followed the meeting was devoted exclusively to abortion:

> The meeting was courteous; there was a good exchange of information. The abortion issue was discussed extensively. The Governor repeated his personal opposition to abortion and his opposition to government funding for abortion. He also indicated he would not oppose an effort to obtain a constitutional amendment. However, on the crucial point of whether he would support an amendment, he did not change his position. At this time he will not commit himself to supporting an amendment. We, therefore, continue to be disappointed with the Governor's position. And we repeat our call for a constitutional amendment.[41]

It hardly seems appropriate to blame the media for concentrating on abortion during the question and answer session that followed this opening statement. It was Bernardin's own characterization of the meeting, and not the media's preoccupation, that caused abortion to dominate coverage of the bishops' session with Carter. To be fair, it is true that the prepared statement Bernardin later read to Ford was more even-handed in terms of its attention to the other issues than his earlier statements had been.[42] But Bernardin's opening remarks at his press conference again explicitly directed the reporters' attention to abortion and to the candidates' views on it:

> The meeting was courteous; there was a good exchange of information on many issues. Relative to the abortion issue, we are encouraged that the President agrees on the need for a constitutional amendment. We urged him to support an amendment that will give the maximum protection possible to the unborn. We also discussed at some length the issues of employment, food, illegal aliens, and the defense and protection of human rights as a key element in determining U.S. foreign policy. On these issues we explained our position which generally calls for sensitivity to human needs and an acknowledgement of the legitimate role of government in a free society. One final issue brought up by the President was aid to non-public schools.[43]

Bernardin was obviously making an effort, in response to the general reaction to the meeting with Carter, to indicate that abortion was not the only issue that interested the Catholic hierarchy. That said, however, his statement at the press conference still reinforced the impression that the bishops believed abortion was the most significant political issue in 1976. Abortion was the first issue mentioned in the statement, and it was the only issue on which Bernardin acknowledged and evaluated Ford's position. Bernardin said that the bishops were "encouraged" by Ford's support of a constitutional amendment, but he did not even mention what Ford's positions were on the other issues that had been discussed. Concerning the many issues on which the bishops and Ford disagreed, Bernardin limited himself to a general call for "sensitivity" and an innocuous endorsement of the "legitimate role of government." In fact, asked later if he was "disappointed" in Ford's positions on any of these other issues, Bernardin merely allowed that "there was not total agreement on the approaches that should be taken to some issues."[44] It is impossible to square this record with Shaw's claim that the media was responsible for the emphasis on abortion.

Nevertheless, Joseph Bernardin, now the cardinal-archbishop of Chicago, continues to press Shaw's interpretation of these events by depicting himself as a victim of the media's preoccupation with abortion in 1976. "They asked me what I felt about Carter's position on abortion and what I felt about Ford's," he recalled in an interview I conducted with him. "Now it so happened that Ford's position was more in accord with our position than Carter's. In candor and truth I had to indicate that, and that was what was picked up as being the signal that we were favoring Ford over Carter."[45]

As the record indicates, however, Bernardin's expression of encouragement at Ford's position was not made in response to a reporter's question concerning the two candidates' views. Instead, it was offered in a prepared statement that he and his colleagues had independently drafted ten days after the initial uproar over their disappointment in Carter's position. The members of the executive committee must have known that their characterization of Ford's views on abortion would be picked up and emphasized by the press. In fact, Cardinal Bernardin told me that he fully realized that "the media were focusing only on the abortion issue and in particular they wanted to highlight the difference between Ford and Carter on that particular issue."[46] Why, then, if he realized this at the time, did he repeatedly emphasize abortion in his public comments on the candidates and the campaign?

The answer, in my view, is that Bernardin and his colleagues believed that the 1976 presidential campaign represented a real opportunity for them to gather support for a constitutional amendment banning abortion. The political circumstances that I detail in chapter 4, and to which I refer at the beginning of this chapter, meant that the presidential candidates, particularly Jimmy Carter, were sensitive to the views, statements, and actions of the Catholic hierarchy. Bernardin, speaking for that hierarchy, repeatedly emphasized abortion because he hoped that Carter would change his position on that issue if put under enough pressure to do so.

It is unlikely that the bishops were genuinely upset at the media's emphasis on abortion. Drawing attention to abortion, after all, was the whole point behind the *Pastoral Plan for Pro-Life Activities*, the responses to the party platforms, and the statements read to the candidates during the meetings with the executive committee. What is much more likely is that Bernardin and his colleagues were genuinely upset that the media interpreted this emphasis on abortion as an endorsement of Ford's candidacy. In this regard, NCCB officials have consistently argued that the bishops' spokesmen addressed themselves to issues and not to candidates in 1976.

While more credible than the claims that the media distorted the bishops' actions, this argument is also misleading because it implies that the bishops were merely passive victims of a misunderstanding, and that they played no role in creating the impression that they favored Ford over Carter. The problem with this argument is that it neglects completely the political context within which the bishops' activities took place. Bernardin's many comments on abortion and on the candidates' views on that subject were made in the middle of a heated presidential campaign in which one candidate supported the bishops' policy views on abortion and the other did not. Moreover, Bernardin's comments were made at the same time that both candidates were actively maneuvering to maintain positive relationships with the Catholic hierarchy in order to buttress their appeals to Catholic voters. Through their statements to the candidates and to the press, the bishops' spokesmen articulated policy priorities that clearly reinforced the electoral strategy of the Republican candidate. The press then concluded that this reinforcement amounted to an endorsement of the Republican ticket.

This conclusion flies in the face of Bernardin's denials, both at the time and since. Perhaps a more benign conclusion would be that Bernardin and his colleagues sincerely but mistakenly believed that they had meaningfully distinguished between candidates and issues in 1976. Such a distinction can be made, of course, if one has spoken out on a range of issues that cuts across the platforms and policy preferences of the competing candidates. Then one can be perceived as putting forward an issues-based agenda that does not necessarily favor one candidate over the other. This distinction between issues and candidates was lost in 1976, however, when the hierarchy's spokesmen repeatedly emphasized a single issue on which the candidates sharply differed. In that case, the press and the professional politicians were not willing to recognize or accept a distinction between encouragement and endorsement.

This seems to be exactly the lesson Bernardin and many other Catholic bishops have drawn from their experiences in 1976. During the ensuing years, the leadership of the National Conference of Catholic Bishops has tried to identify itself with a broadly based policy agenda that cannot be readily interpreted as favoring one party over the other. They have taken note, in other words, of the fact that the meaning of their activities is shaped by the political context in which those activities take place. I do not want to get too far ahead of myself, however. In the following chapters I will discuss in detail both the broadening of the bishops' agenda and the attempts by various individual bishops to reorient the way this agenda intersects with American electoral politics. First, however, I want to turn in the next chapter to the more immediate implications of the bishops' activities in 1976—in particular for the bishops' participation in the national election of 1980.

_____ **CHAPTER SIX** _____

The Bishops and Electoral Politics: 1980

As in 1976, the bishops' role in the presidential election of 1980 was shaped by the relationship between, on the one hand, their own positions on the issues and, on the other, the electoral strategies of secular political forces. In 1980, the conservative movement tried to effect a lasting realignment of the national electorate by drawing together a new, mass-based coalition of social conservatives. In this chapter, I will argue that the Catholic bishops, through their emphasis on abortion as a political issue and their role in the creation of the right-to-life movement, helped to erect the political foundation on which that conservative effort was built. I will argue, in other words, that the bishops played an important, if indirect, political role in 1980. Before I move on to 1980, however, I want to assess both the impact that the bishops had on the 1976 election, and the impact that the bishops' activities in 1976 had on the future political approach and agenda of the National Conference of Catholic Bishops.

1976 REVISITED

"We address ourselves to issues only," Bernardin said in 1976. "We neither endorse nor oppose candidates or parties."[1] Nevertheless, the perception conveyed by the national media was that Bernardin and his colleagues on the executive committee had indicated a preference for Ford over Carter. And many observers both inside and outside the church felt that the bishops themselves were responsible for that perception. John Carr, for example, then an aide to Bishop Rausch and today a leading official of the uscc, left no doubt where he felt responsibility should be placed. "When someone says disappointed and encouraged," Carr told me, "that is as close as you get in American life to partisan. The only thing left is 'I endorse.'"[2]

In fact, several Catholic groups attempted, at the time, to provide a counterweight to Bernardin's emphasis on abortion by pointing to the broader agenda of issues on which the nccb had previously expressed itself. The Bishops' Advisory Council (a lay body which advised the nccb's leadership), for example, issued a statement stressing the "scope of the public policy positions" taken by the bishops in preceding years.[3] The board of the National Federation of Priests Council expressed its "deep concern that this one issue [abortion] is being stressed by the National Conference of Catholic Bishops."[4] And the National Coalition of American Nuns went so far as to publicly endorse Carter's candidacy in order to counteract what they called the "injustice" done to him by the bishops' executive committee.[5]

Even some members of the hierarchy spoke out in protest against the committee's alleged tilt toward Ford. Bishop Bernard Flanagan of Worcester, Massachusetts, for example, reminded readers of his diocesan newspaper of the breadth of the political responsibility statement. "The National Conference of Catholic Bishops," Flanagan said, "has taken a public stand on a great number of national issues."[6] Bishops like Flanagan were careful, of course, not to criticize Bernardin and the executive committee directly. They decried the "perception" of the committee's actions rather than the committee itself. But others, like Monsignor George Higgins, recognized that in politics perceptions often create their own realities. "Whatever the intention was," Higgins recalled of 1976, "the conference was being widely perceived as favoring one party over the other. I didn't think that was going to do us any good."[7]

The bishops' conference as a whole apparently agreed with Higgins because it moved rather quickly to try to undo the impression that Bernardin and his colleagues had left. The NCCB's administrative board, a larger governing body than the executive committee, held a previously scheduled meeting in Washington, D.C., one week after the executive committee's meeting with Ford. Those bishops who were distressed at the overriding emphasis on abortion and at the perception that the bishops favored the Republican ticket succeeded in placing the matter of the conference's political priorities at the top of the administrative board's agenda. In the end, the assembled bishops released a statement, *Resolution of the Administrative Committee*, that in tone and content returned to the multiissue approach that had been consistently advocated by Bishop Rausch and Monsignor Higgins, among others.

The resolution began with the collegial statement that the administrative board wished to "unite" itself with the "efforts of [the] Executive Committee to make known [the NCCB's] positions and clarify issues."[8] It then stated the posture that the conference wished to officially and formally adopt concerning the presidential election: "There are elements of agreement and disagreement between our positions and those of the major parties, their platforms and their candidates. . . . We are not supporting religious bloc voting nor are we instructing people for whom to vote."[9]

While the executive committee's actions had borne the imprint of the *Pastoral Plan for Pro-Life Activities*, the *Resolution of the Administrative Committee* explicitly referred to the political responsibility statement and strongly reaffirmed the cross-cutting, multiissue approach it had envisioned:

> Abortion and the need for a constitutional amendment to protect the unborn are among our concerns. So are the issues of unemployment, adequate educational opportunity for all, an equitable food policy both domestic and world wide, the

right to a decent home and health care, human rights across the globe, intelligent arms limitation and many other social justice issues. . . . The Catholic Bishops of the United States have often publicly stated—and we here reaffirm—deep commitment to the sanctity, dignity, and quality of human life at all stages of development, as well as to legislation and public policy which protects and promotes these values in all contemporary contexts.[10]

As a barometer of opinion in the NCCB at large and as an indicator of the conference's future political behavior, this resolution was a seminal document. But as an effort to reorient the general perception of the Catholic hierarchy's political posture during the presidential campaign of 1976, it was a failure. The responses to the platforms, the meetings with the candidates, and Bernardin's press conferences had all occurred in the glare of publicity associated with the direct participation of the presidential candidates. The effort to soften the effects of those events, in contrast, took place in the context of a rather obscure meeting of a committee of bishops. The statement was reported in the press, but the original impression created by the meetings with the candidates endured.

Regardless of that impression, however, the Catholic hierarchy's direct impact on the 1976 election was negligible. Despite all the talk of his "Catholic problem" and the bishops' obvious displeasure with his position on abortion, Carter nevertheless received 56 percent of the Catholic vote in 1976.[11] This solid majority was only 3 percent less than Hubert Humphrey had received in 1968, and fully 8 percent more than George McGovern had received in 1972.[12] Carter's reconstruction of the New Deal coalition was temporary, to be sure, but it was not significantly hampered by his conflict with the Catholic hierarchy.

Nor was Carter hurt by the bishops' efforts to expand the prolife movement and enhance the salience of abortion as an electoral issue. Abortion, in short, was not a very significant issue in 1976. Maris Vinovskis has performed a statistical analysis of the 1976 election returns which suggests that abortion cut across partisan lines and had almost no relationship to voting behavior that year.[13] He found that "voters did not divide in any consistent pattern for Carter or Ford on the basis of their own attitudes on abortion," and that "less than one half of one percent of the variation in voting can be explained by the abortion variable." In fact, Vinovskis found abortion to be the weakest of all the potential voting predictors that he included in his study.[14]

THE DEBATE CONTINUED

If in the short term the bishops' effect on the 1976 election was negligible, in the longer term their activities that year were still very significant. First of all, the experiences of 1976 had a major impact on the debate within the bishops' conference over the style and substance of the Catholic hierarchy's collective political behavior. As a result of 1976, the bishops' national leaders recognized the desire of politicians to be associated with the bishops and their positions, and they gained an appreciation of their own corresponding need to articulate their political priorities more carefully. In the ensuing years, the national officers of the NCCB sought to avoid entanglement in partisan politics by advancing a broad agenda based on the methodology and content of the political responsibility statement.

Between 1976 and 1980, for example, the American Catholic bishops continued to advocate a constitutional amendment prohibiting legal abortion, and they continued to participate in national and state efforts to eliminate public financing of abortions for poor women. But heading into the 1980 political campaign, the leadership of the NCCB quite purposefully resolved to prevent a repeat of the 1976 affair. The NCCB released *Political Responsibility: Choices for the 80's*, a recapitulation of the church's teachings on a broad range of policy issues; but this time the NCCB's spokesmen honored the scope of those teachings in practice as well as principle.[15]

When the Democratic party reaffirmed its unequivocal support for legal abortion, for example, the bishops' conference barely reacted. There were no official statements of outrage, no protracted interstaff negotiations, and, most importantly, no meetings between the candidates and the conference's executive committee. In short, the leaders of the NCCB stood aloof from the national political debate and adhered to a cross-cutting agenda that could not be exclusively identified with any party's platform or electoral strategy.

Not every American bishop agreed with the conference's official approach in 1980, however. The debate within the hierarchy over political priorities had been profoundly affected by the experiences of 1976; it had not been definitively decided. Cardinal Humberto Medeiros of Boston, for example, made clear that abortion was still the overriding consideration in his assessment of whether a candidate was worthy of Catholic votes. Medeiros wrote an open letter to his diocese one week before a Democratic primary election that involved congressional candidates who disagreed on the issue of abortion. In the letter the cardinal argued that "those who make abortion possible by law— such as legislators and those who promote, defend, and elect these same legislators—cannot separate themselves totally from the guilt which accompanies this horrendous crime and deadly sin. If," he concluded, "you are for true freedom—and for life—you will follow your conscience when you vote to save our children, born and unborn."[16]

Medeiros's letter, which was far more partisan than anything Bernardin ever said in 1976, received relatively little attention outside of Massachusetts. Unlike Bernardin in 1976, Medeiros did not speak as the elected president of the National Conference of Catholic Bishops, nor did he speak in the middle of a presidential campaign. Nevertheless, Medeiros's letter did indicate that some leading bishops did not share the conference's official approach to the political circumstances of 1980. And his letter suggested that individual bishops who remained committed to a narrower agenda dominated by abortion could, if the political circumstances allowed, compete with the NCCB's spokesmen for the right to determine the public's perception of the Catholic hierarchy's political priorities. Medeiros's voice was rather faint in 1980, but voices bearing similar messages rang considerably louder in different political circumstances four years later.

THE BISHOPS, ABORTION, AND THE RISE OF THE NEW RIGHT

The bishops' internal debate was not the only political process that was affected by the bishops' activities in 1976. Between 1976 and 1980, as the NCCB's spokesmen watched from the sidelines, the American conservative movement adopted the bishops' antiabortion agenda and tactics from 1976 and used them as tools in a major mobilization and coalition-building effort. By 1980, the bishops' right-to-life commitment and activities had been used to cloak a conservative political agenda in religious imagery and rhetoric. And as a result, the bishops themselves had become associated with a policy platform and political movement with which very few of them were in agreement.

As I mentioned earlier, the Watergate scandal and Gerald Ford's ascension to the presidency deepened the ideological rift in the Republican party. Conservatives, who distrusted Ford in the first place, were particularly outraged by his selection of Nelson Rockefeller as his vice-president.[17] In fact, William Rusher responded to Ford's choice of Rockefeller by leaving the Republican party and setting himself the task of building a "new majority party" based on a coalition of economic and social conservatives.[18]

Rusher's attempt to build a viable, conservative third party failed when Ronald Reagan refused to leave the Republican camp to head a new ticket. But Rusher's efforts succeeded in bringing together a disparate group of conservative activists who shared a desire to shift the axis of American party politics to the right during the 1980s. Richard Viguerie, the so-called direct mail wizard of the American right, was a prominent figure in Rusher's short-lived third party. Viguerie, disaffected with Republican temerity, was as ready as Rusher to bolt the Grand Old Party in order to build a reliably conservative alternative to the Democrats. And Viguerie was allied with a growing network of relatively young conservative leaders who were similarly inclined and highly motivated. This group, known collectively as the "new right," was described by the *Congressional Quarterly* in 1976 as "a new conservative leadership group . . . carefully raising money and building the organization for an effort to move Congress sharply to the right over the next several elections."[19]

In addition to Viguerie, this new right featured Paul Weyrich of the Committee for the Survival of a Free Congress, Howard Phillips of the Conservative Caucus, and Terry Dolan of the National Conservative Political Action Committee. These men, supported by veterans of Goldwater's campaign like William Rusher and publicists of the "emerging Republican majority" like Kevin Phillips and Pat Buchanan, resumed and reinvigorated the conservative effort to supplant the New Deal coalition as the dominant force in American electoral politics.

The new right was made up of ideological activists rather than party operatives. But Ford's loss to Carter in 1976 reopened the possibility that the Republican party could serve as the vehicle of a conservative ascendancy. The new right's prospects, of course, were tempered by the same liability that had plagued Goldwater's candidacy in 1964—the limited constituency of ideological conservatism. The leaders of the new right, however, were hoping for much more than a bloody coup on the floor of a convention and temporary leadership of a presidential campaign. Their plan was to identify and mobilize a new mass-based coalition that would constitute a lasting majority of the American electorate.

Abortion, as a leading element of an updated version of what Scammon and Wattenberg had called the "social issue," became a central facet of the new right's political strategy. Paul Weyrich, a man who believes that "the bedrock of political effectiveness is making coalitions," decided that abortion could be the Achilles' heel of the Democratic party in 1980.[20] If properly exploited, Weyrich argued, abortion could link disparate sources of opposition to continued Democratic dominance. Abortion was an example of judicial imposition of national standards on local communities; it was connected to a large, grassroots social movement; and it neatly captured the religious gloss that the new right sought to give its social agenda.

The potential value of abortion to conservative political strategies was first revealed in a 1978 senatorial campaign in Iowa between incumbent Democrat Dick Clark and his Republican challenger Roger Jepsen.[21] Jepsen was financed by Richard Viguerie's direct mail solicitations and organizationally and strategically advised by the new right's network of political operatives in Washington. At the same time, his opponent was shadowed throughout the campaign by the large and very vocal right-to-life movement in the state of Iowa. The movement's efforts included distributing three hundred thousand anti-Clark leaflets outside Catholic churches on the Sunday before election day.[22]

Thanks to this combination of factors, Jepsen won the Senate seat, and Weyrich, Viguerie, and their colleagues got a glimpse of the potential national clout of a new right/right-to-life political alliance. Coming out of Iowa, they set out to establish contacts with the right-to-life movement at the national level for the purpose of drawing right-to-lifers, Catholic and otherwise, into a broader conservative coalition.

Connie Paige has maintained that the "brilliant innovation" of the new right was to expand the "pro-life" agenda into a "pro-family" one.[23] This innovation, Paige argued, "allowed conservatives to broaden right-to-life concerns to cover what they saw as the proper role of government with respect to family matters, and its cost."[24] It allowed them to incorporate opposition to abortion into a broader political agenda and to channel that opposition into coordinated and conservative political action. The first step in this process was the infiltration of the right-to-life movement in order to identify its symbols and leaders with the broader social issue agenda of the new right.

The official leaders of the National Right-to-Life Committee, however, were unwilling to dilute their single-issue appeal by entering into alliances with groups advocating positions with which many of their members did not agree. As a result, Weyrich and his colleagues went out looking for dissident prolife activists who did not share these hesitations. They did not have to look very hard. Judy and Paul Brown were veterans of the prolife movement who had become frustrated by its lack of political success in actually making abortion illegal. Hoping to pursue a more aggressive political program, the Browns broke away from the National Right-to-Life Committee, formed their own antiabortion organizations, and, in time, allied those organizations with the new right's political network. Paul Weyrich became a leading adviser to Paul Brown's Life Amendment Political Action Committee (LAPAC), for example, while Richard Viguerie served as a primary fund raiser for Judy Brown's American Life Lobby.[25] As a matter of fact, Viguerie listed Mrs. Brown as among the few activists and leaders who had made the most "significant contributions" to the growth of the new right.[26]

With the help of the Browns and others like them, the new right succeeded by 1980 in associating the phrase "right-to-life" with a much broader social agenda and with a highly partisan, conservative movement. As one board member of the Life Amendment Political Action Committee put it, "We are a tool of the New Right, and (the New Right) is a tool of ours."[27] But this identification, regardless of how successfully it was accomplished, was only one part of the new right's mobilization strategy. At about the same time that they were recruiting the Browns and other prolifers to a broader political cause, Weyrich, Phillips, and the other leaders of the new right were also mobilizing a social force that Albert Menendez has called the "sleeping giant of American politics": evangelical and fundamentalist Protestantism.[28]

By the late 1970s, evangelicals and fundamentalists had begun to move toward more active participation in the political process. Many so-called born again Christians had eschewed their religious tradition of avoiding politics in order to help put one of their own, Jimmy Carter, in the White House in 1976. And many had been motivated to continue and broaden their political activity by the Internal Revenue Service's revocation of the tax exemption of racially segregated religious schools. These schools, known as Christian academies, had opened around the country in response to the Supreme Court's desegregation rulings of the 1950s. Loss of the tax exemption not only threatened the existence of these schools, it also threatened the social and religious autonomy of the local communities that supported them. The IRS ruling, in other words, was symptomatic of the increase in federal initiative and decrease in local prerogative on social and family issues discussed in chapter 3. The same type of federal police power that had spurred the Catholic leadership to more active participation in the national political process also engendered resentment and opposition in the evangelical and fundamentalist communities.

The Democratic and Republican establishments, however, had no idea how to channel the potent political energy of religious conservatives. National political leaders, on the whole, had not associated with born agains, pentecostals, and fundamentalists before, and they were confused and perhaps even a bit put off by them. Responding to the awakened political force of conservative Protestantism, one Republican national official admitted that "I don't know how to deal with it," while a Democratic leader called it "a relatively new phenomenon we haven't had to deal with before."[29]

The leaders of the new right, however, knew instinctively how to "deal with" this growing resentment of federal intrusion into local and individual prerogative. Weyrich, Viguerie, and their colleagues enthusiastically reached out to the evangelical and fundamentalist communities. They established personal relationships with important leaders of these communities, and they adopted issues and political strategies designed to incorporate these potential new voters into a broad conservative coalition. In short, the new right set out to capitalize on the religious commitment and cultural resentment of conservative Protestantism by channeling those energies into coordinated political action.[30]

Jerry Falwell, a Baptist minister and the host of the popular "Old Time Gospel Hour," served as the new right's point man in the conservative religious community.[31] In 1979, Paul Weyrich and Howard Phillips traveled to Lynchburg, Virginia, to meet with Falwell and enlist him in their mobilization effort. They told Falwell that, by their reckoning, there were between eighty and one hundred million social conservatives with deep religious convictions who were just waiting to be organized into an effective political organization. In fact, Weyrich made the memorable assertion that evangelical Protestants, right-to-life Catholics, and Orthodox Jews represented a "moral majority" of the American population that could tip the balance of national politics in favor of conservatism.

The rest, as the old cliche has it, is history. Falwell was impressed with Weyrich's and Phillips's presentation, and quickly dedicated his considerable resources to building the *religious* new right. He established an umbrella organization, named it the "Moral Majority," and closely aligned himself and his movement with the new right's conservative agenda. As Weyrich put it, "This alliance between religion and politics didn't just happen."[32] Indeed, it did not. The alliance between religious leaders and political operatives that burst on the scene in the late 1970s was the result of a carefully implemented strategy to mobilize new voters, build new political coalitions, and effect a lasting realignment of the American electorate.

The final element of the new right's strategy was the linking together of a reoriented right-to-life movement and a politically energized conservative religious community into a single political coalition. The key to this coalition-building effort was convincing Falwell and other Protestant leaders to place a greater emphasis on abortion as a moral and religious issue. At the original meeting with Falwell, Weyrich and Phillips identified abortion as the key to broadening and holding together their proposed moral majority of the electorate.[33] If Falwell would give abortion a prominent place on his list of political priorities, they argued, then abortion could be used to bring traditionally antagonistic Southern Protestants and Northern Catholics together.

Falwell responded favorably on this point as well. He gave abortion a featured place on the Moral Majority's agenda, and he personally broke with the long fundamentalist tradition of anti-Catholicism. He assured Catholic leaders who had "stood alone and fought the abortion issue that Protestant ministers . . . have joined the fight," and he spoke of Pope John Paul II, the successor to the notorious "popes of Rome," as the "best hope we Baptists ever had."[34] In short, Falwell did all he could to facilitate the creation of a political coalition that included both socially conservative Catholics and Southern conservative Protestants.

It is difficult to determine the impact that the mobilization of a new conservative coalition had on the presidential election in 1980.[35] Ronald Reagan, surely, owed his election more to inflation and the Ayatollah Khomeini than to Jerry Falwell and the profamily agenda. Nevertheless, as A. James Reichley noted, "the conventional wisdom in Washington is that the Reagan coalition is made up of Conservatives, neo-Conservatives, and the religious new right."[36] Moreover, in terms of underlying shifts in the partisan alignment of the American electorate, the new right was quite significant. It brought many voters into the political process; it moved the Republican party sharply to the right on social issues; and it strengthened the Republican hold on presidential politics.

For our purposes, the key point is that the arrival of the religious new right on the political scene between 1978 and 1980 was not the spontaneous result of religious revival or religious activism. It was, as this brief analysis has suggested, the result of various policy initiatives at the federal level, and of secular political operatives reaching out and drawing socially conservative Protestants into the political process. An adequate account of the political role of evangelicals and fundamentalists in the late 1970s and early 1980s has to include a recognition of the extent to which this role was a function of political developments that in themselves had absolutely nothing to do with religion. It also has to include a recognition of the indirect but important role that the Catholic hierarchy played in the new right's strategy.

The bishops set the groundwork for the creation of the profamily movement in the late 1970s through their role in the creation of the prolife movement during the preceding decade. From the very first rumblings of liberalization of abortion laws in the 1960s, the bishops firmly identified their church and their own moral authority with the right-to-life cause. They were also the source of critical early funding for the right-to-life movement, and they were the most consistent institutional supporters of the effort to pass a constitutional amendment banning legal abortion. The bishops did not agree with the new right on many social issues, but when the new right set out to mold the right-to-life movement to new political purposes, it was dealing with a movement whose original institutional structure and financial resources had come directly from the National Conference of Catholic Bishops, and with a movement that continued to be closely identified with the Catholic Church.

The bishops had also set an example in 1976 of how abortion could be used to highlight the differences between the parties and to place political pressure on a Democratic presidential nominee. The difference between 1976 and 1980 in this regard was that the new right had learned in 1976 that abortion and the right-to-life movement on their own were not enough to decisively split the Democratic coalition. Conservatives hoped that by associating abortion with other issues in a broader social agenda, they would be able to build a much more potent electoral force.

I do not want to put too fine a point on this matter or overemphasize the Catholic bishops' role in the rise of the religious new right. Nevertheless, the bishops' part in the creation of the prolife movement and in the introduction of abortion to American presidential politics facilitated the identification of a highly partisan political program with religious sentiment and moral values. The bishops did not seek this political role for themselves; it was established for them by the nature of the intersection of their policy agenda with the platforms and strategies of major political forces.

Reagan, due in part to his opposition to abortion, succeeded in 1980 in identifying himself as a candidate who was particularly devoted to America's religious traditions and moral values. At the same time, however, Reagan sharply disagreed with the Catholic hierarchy's positions on a long list of important issues. Faced with these two facts, several bishops concluded that it was time for their national conference to devote more of its resources and energy to some of these other issues. This conclusion, along with several other factors, led the bishops to embark on a detailed and searching study of American policy on nuclear weapons. This study and its influence on the bishops' role in the political process will be the subjects of the next chapter.

CHAPTER SEVEN.

The Bishops and Nuclear Weapons

THE AGENDA for the bishops' annual meeting in 1980 included a proposal by Auxiliary Bishop Francis P. Murphy of Baltimore that the National Conference of Catholic Bishops produce a summary of the Catholic Church's teaching on war and peace. The bishops had made several statements over the years on nuclear weapons, as had the popes, but Murphy and a handful of other bishops wanted the American hierarchy to be more pointed and more aggressive in its approach to U.S. defense policy. Over the next two and one-half years, the bishops, through an ad hoc committee on war and peace under the chairmanship of Joseph Bernardin, studied closely the matters of nuclear weapons and deterrence. The final result was *The Challenge of Peace: God's Promise and Our Response*, a pastoral letter of unprecedented length and specificity that expressed the bishops' dissent from several central features of American defense policy.[1]

Many people were surprised at the depth and extent of the bishops' criticism. Apparently, the Catholic bishops were not expected to denounce nuclear war, condemn American targeting doctrine, question the morality of nuclear deterrence, or endorse a nuclear freeze. However, as George Weigel has pointed out, "those who were surprised by the fact and content of the bishops' address to nuclear weapons issues can be said, quite simply, not to have been paying attention to American Catholicism since 1965."[2]

In this chapter I will trace an evolution in the bishops' thinking on war and peace that led to their pastoral letter on nuclear weapons. I will establish that the letter was grounded in Catholic teaching on the just war, and in a number of papal and conciliar statements on modern weaponry. I will also argue that the letter was emblematic of the bishops' modern political activities in that it was a collective, nonparochial approach to a public policy issue of central political importance. Finally, I will assess the political meaning and impact of the letter by examining its effect on the views of American Catholics, its connections to the campaign for a nuclear weapons freeze, and its relationship with the moral agenda of the religious new right and the Republican party.

SUPERPATRIOTISM

Throughout the traditional era of the American hierarchy's political history, the Catholic bishops took a back seat to no one in their expressions of patriotic fervor. Relying on the church's traditional teaching that military service in defense of one's nation is compatible with the Christian life, the bishops were unflappable supporters of American foreign and defense policy. They readily and vocally endorsed every American war effort from the Revolution up through and including most of the Vietnam War.

Dorothy Dohen, in *Nationalism and American Catholicism*, offered several reasons for the bishops' tradition of superpatriotism. First, most of these bishops were either Irish or Americans of Irish descent. Their Catholic experience of oppression at the hands of English Protestants brought these men "to identify their Irishness with their Catholicism."[3] Once in America, they transferred this identification of nation and religion to their new setting. For them, being a good Catholic and a good American came to be seen as complimentary and mutually reinforcing responsibilities. Anti-Catholic sentiment, however, held that one could not be a patriotic American and a faithful Catholic at the same time. In order to counter such claims, the bishops self-consciously and purposefully expressed their unqualified support of American foreign and defense policy. As spokesmen for an immigrant people, Dohen argued, the bishops felt a responsibility to act as apologists for the patriotism and loyalty of Catholic Americans.

By the mid-1960s, however, the Irish experience of English persecution no longer characterized the American church. Modern Catholics and their bishops were second-, third-, or even fourth-generation Americans who did not identify their country with their church as readily as their parents and grandparents had. Moreover, the anti-Catholicism that had challenged the patriotism of American Catholics had also abated by 1965. The country had elected a Catholic president and raised that president to its highest rank of heroes after his death. Suburban, middle-class Catholics had joined the American mainstream by the millions; they neither needed nor wanted hierarchical spokesmen to defend their patriotic credentials. As a matter of fact, in the context of the Vietnam War, the bishops' superpatriotism became an embarrassment rather than a comfort to at least one segment of American Catholicism.

VIETNAM

Upon his arrival in Saigon in 1965, Cardinal Francis Spellman was asked to comment on his country's Vietnam policies. "I fully support everything it does," the cardinal said. "My country, may it always be right. Right or wrong, my country."[4] Spellman had long been a superpatriot of the first order. His instinct to link his God and his country was "spontaneous," and his "acceptance of the messianic mission of America . . . [was] complete."[5] Spellman was the cardinal-archbishop of New York, and had been schooled in defending an immigrant church from nativist charges. But he was also the military vicar, or bishop to all Catholics in the armed forces. His reflexive support for

American actions in Vietnam was a logical culmination of his own personal experience and of the hierarchy's tradition of unwavering patriotism.

By 1965, however, some of the antiwar activists who later came to be known as the "Catholic left" were already calling for an end to U.S. intervention in Vietnam, and they were doing so on the basis of traditional Catholic teaching.[6] They pointed to Pope John XXIII's statement that "in an age such as ours which prides itself on its atomic energy it is contrary to reason to hold that war is now a suitable way to restore rights which have been violated."[7] They quoted the Vatican Council's call for "an evaluation of war with a whole new attitude." And they made a slogan of Pope Paul VI's declaration at the United Nations: "No more war, war never again."[8] In short, Catholic activists and journalists began to ask how their bishops could fail to see that Catholic principles and teachings required a critical moral assessment of American actions in Vietnam. In fact, these Catholics did more than ask questions; they also attacked Spellman and others like him for their patriotic boosterism, and they condemned the "scandal" of the hierarchy's "near total silence" on the morality of the war.[9]

The bishops were used to attacks, but not of this sort and not from this quarter. For almost two centuries they had been challenged by a hostile culture to demonstrate that it was possible to be a good patriotic American and remain a faithful Catholic. In the 1960s this question was turned completely on its head, and the bishops were challenged by members of their own church to consider whether one could be a faithful Catholic and still remain a blindly patriotic, uncritical American.

The Catholic Church is not a pacifist church. Not since the earliest days of the church have Catholics been required to eschew violence or military service. To the contrary, at least since St. Augustine, Catholic doctrine has supported the reasoned application of force in the pursuit of just goals. However, the just war theory, the foundation of Catholic teaching on the subject, has always set specific limits on *when* force can be used legitimately (*jus ad bellum*), and *how* force can be applied once hostilities have begun (*jus in bellum*).[10] These limits are based on two fundamental principles: proportionality and discrimination.

In terms of the decision to go to war, proportionality refers to the requirement that the good to be sought through the resort to war be proportionate to the evil of killing and destruction that will inevitably result from it. According to this principle, political leaders who resort to force must have good "reason to believe that in the end more good will be done than undone or a greater measure of evil prevented" through war than through avoidance of it.[11]

The discrimination principle, on the other hand, holds that once a war has begun noncombatants can never be the *direct* target of military operations. Attacking cities by nuclear or conventional means, therefore, is clearly disallowed. The tradition does recognize, however, that injury and death of noncombatants cannot be avoided completely in modern warfare. The acceptability of various forms of *indirect* violence against noncombatants is determined by a second, intrawar application of the proportionality principle. In each individual military operation, just as in the original decision to go to war, the good sought through an action must outweigh the evil that results from it.

It is impossible to understand the bishops' statements on war and peace over the last twenty years without understanding the just war principles of proportionality and discrimination. As we will see, these principles invariably appear in these statements as the basic justifications for the particular positions being advocated. It was not surprising, therefore, that when the bishops began cautiously and tentatively to consider the moral status of U.S. policy in Vietnam they did so from the perspective of the just war tradition.

At its inaugural meeting in November 1966, the National Conference of Catholic Bishops expressed its desire "to help magnify the moral voice of [the] nation," and "to insist that [the issues involved in the Vietnam conflict] be kept under constant moral scrutiny."[12] Given the way that the bishops had traditionally interpreted just war principles, it perhaps was also not surprising that they concluded in 1966 that "in the light of the facts as they are known to us, it is reasonable to argue that our presence in Vietnam is justified."[13]

In 1968 the bishops returned to the morality of the Vietnam War in *Human Life in Our Day*, a statement devoted primarily to birth control and the scope of church authority. Referring explicitly to the principle of proportionality, the bishops limited their comments to a series of questions about the war:

> In assessing our country's involvement in Vietnam we must ask: Have we already reached, or passed, the point where the principle of proportionality becomes decisive? How much more of our resources in men and money should we commit to this struggle, assuming an acceptable cause or intention? Has the conflict in Vietnam provoked inhuman dimensions of suffering? Would not an untimely withdrawal be equally disastrous?[14]

The bishops stopped short in 1968 of answering any of these questions affirmatively. In fact, their assumption of "an acceptable cause or intention" could be read as an endorsement of American aims in Vietnam. The only question that seemed to bother the bishops at that point was whether the destruction associated with the war had become disproportionate to the presumed good of the American cause. The bishops never reversed their acceptance of that cause, but three years later they did finally answer their own questions concerning the proportionality of the war's destruction.

In *Resolution on Southeast Asia*, released in November 1971, the bishops judged the Vietnam War to be disproportionate to the good being sought by the United States. They concluded, therefore, that the war had become immoral:

> At this point in history, it seems clear to us that whatever good we hope to achieve through continued involvement in this war is now outweighed by the destruction

of human life and of moral values which it inflicts. It is our firm conviction, therefore, that the speedy ending of this war is a moral imperative of the highest priority. Hence, we feel a moral obligation to appeal to our nation's leaders and indeed to the leaders of all the nations involved in this tragic conflict to bring the war to an end with no further delay.[15]

By 1971, of course, such a position was neither particularly prophetic nor especially controversial. It came only after many other religious leaders had already condemned the war, and after years of antiwar activism on the part of the Catholic clergy and laity. *Commonweal* was highly critical of the bishops' equivocation, and said of the *Resolution on Southeast Asia* that "one cannot help but be conscious of how long the statement was in coming."[16] Looking back fifteen years after the fact, William Au dispassionately concluded that "rather than charting a course of leadership, the bishops' resolution seemed to reflect a growing national trend of mainstream disillusionment with the war in Southeast Asia."[17]

Nevertheless, in a number of ways *Resolution on Southeast Asia* was a watershed in the history of the American Catholic hierarchy. It was the first time that the Catholic hierarchy, as a group, publicly dissented from a major American military initiative. And in a sense, it demonstrated that the bishops accepted the reversal of their traditional challenge; they apparently recognized the possibility of a contradiction between patriotic support of U.S. policy and faithfulness to their own Catholic tradition.

In addition, the evolution of their views on the Vietnam War demonstrated to the bishops, and to their successors, that the application of just war principles could lead to dissent from American policy without leading to rejection of American values or intentions.[18] Unlike many others who spoke out against the war, the bishops never questioned the righteousness of America's cause in Vietnam. Rather, they judged that the suffering associated with the war had become disproportionate to an otherwise worthy cause.

Most of the bishops' statements on U.S. defense policy since 1971 have been based on similar judgments. The bishops have not abandoned boosterism and superpatriotism in favor of fundamental disagreement with American interests and values. They merely have begun to point out some of the moral implications of specific methods of advancing those interests. And since the end of the Vietnam War, nuclear weapons has been the issue on which they have done so most pointedly.

NUCLEAR WEAPONS

When in the 1970s the American bishops turned to nuclear weapons, they were able to draw on a long record of Catholic teaching on the subject.[19] That record began with Pope Pius XII, the first pope of the nuclear age, who evaluated nuclear weapons solely in terms of the just war theory. Pius did not believe the atomic bomb was qualitatively different from conventional munitions, and so he argued that its use should be governed by the just war principles of proportionality and discrimination. Pius's successor, Pope John XXIII, however, was not as sure that nuclear weapons did not differ in kind from other forms of destruction. In fact, in his landmark encyclical, *Peace on Earth*, John called for a ban on nuclear weapons, an end to the arms race, and a new age of peace founded on mutual trust rather than a balance of armaments.[20] He even seemed to suggest at one point that the development of the atomic bomb had cast doubt on the contemporary relevance of the whole just war tradition. "In an age such as ours," John wrote, "which prides itself on its atomic energy, it is contrary to reason to hold that war is now a suitable way to restore rights which have been violated."[21]

John's references to the relationship between nuclear weapons and just war theory were taken up directly by the Second Vatican Council in its *Pastoral Constitution on the Church in the Modern World*. Calling for "an evaluation of war with an entirely new attitude," the council solemnly declared that "any act of war aimed indiscriminately at the destruction of entire cities or of extensive areas along with their populations is a crime against God and man himself . . . [that] merits unequivocal and unhesitating condemnation."[22] In addition, while admitting that "many regard [deterrence] as the most effective way by which peace of a sort can be maintained," the council fathers cautioned that "the arms race in which so many countries are engaged is not a safe way to preserve a steady peace."[23]

The pastoral constitution has been called "the controlling text in Catholic moral teaching on war and peace," but it nevertheless left many important questions unanswered.[24] It did not, for example, evaluate the use of smaller, less destructive nuclear weapons; it did not distinguish weapons targeted on military facilities (counterforce) from those targeted on cities (countervalue); and, in truth, it equivocated on deterrence. In short, the Vatican Council did not apply the principles drawn from Catholic teaching to the specific force structures and targeting strategies of the American military. That job was left for the American bishops to carry out, and they began to do so in 1976 through a document called *To Live in Christ Jesus*:

> With respect to nuclear weapons, at least those with massive destructive capability, the first imperative is to prevent their use. As possessors of a vast nuclear arsenal, we must also be aware that not only is it wrong to attack civilian populations, but it is also wrong to threaten to attack them as part of a strategy of deterrence.[25]

In this remarkable statement, the bishops not only disallowed the use of strategic nuclear weaponry, they also condemned the practice of threatening to use them against civilian populations. This rejection of countervalue deterrence was, in the words of one observer, "the most dramatic development in church teaching since Vatican II."[26] It was also, of course, a direct challenge to prevailing American defense policy. Yet it was passed by the bishops' conference without much discussion, and it went virtually unnoticed in the public arena. *To Live in Christ Jesus* dealt primarily with sexual morality, and apparently neither the rank and file bishops nor their readers paid very much attention to the section titled "Peace."

The staff and leadership of the NCCB, however, knew that *To Live in Christ Jesus* represented an important step forward in Catholic teaching. They also realized that, in time, the bishops would have to pass judgment on American defense policies that clearly and specifically violated that teaching. An opportunity to do so presented itself in 1979 when Cardinal John Krol of Philadelphia appeared before a Senate committee to testify in favor of the SALT II arms control treaty. Krol, speaking in the name of the American hierarchy as a whole, restated the position articulated in *To Live in Christ Jesus* that "the primary moral imperative of the nuclear age is to prevent any use of strategic nuclear weapons."[27] He also reiterated the conference's dissatisfaction with deterrence by flatly stating that "the declared intent to use [strategic nuclear weapons] involved in our deterrence policy is wrong."[28] Finally, the cardinal informed the senators that the bishops would "tolerate the possession of nuclear weapons for deterrence as the lesser of two evils" only so long as there was cause for genuine hope of progress toward substantial arms control. But "if that hope were to disappear," he warned, "the moral attitude of the Catholic Church would almost certainly have to shift to one of uncompromising condemnation of both use *and* possession of such weapons."[29]

This, then, was the context within which Bishop Murphy proposed a summary and restatement of the church's position on war and peace. His proposal was, in a sense, the logical next step for bishops who had finally condemned the Vietnam War, and who had tried, for several years, to be forthright in their evaluation of American nuclear policy. However, it is unlikely that Murphy's proposal would have struck such a responsive chord among the bishops had not two other factors convinced a majority of them that a major statement was appropriate at that time.

The first of these factors was the bishops' highly public and frequently stated opposition to abortion. Their mantralike repetition of their commitment to the "right to life" in the 1970s led many people to ask them to extend the same level of commitment to other threats to human life. Surely, peace activists pointed out, the possession of thousands of nuclear warheads and a declared intention to launch those weapons against civilian populations in the event of war, posed a threat to the sanctity of life at least as serious as that posed by abortion. Many bishops apparently came to accept the logic of this argument. Father J. Bryan Hehir, a top aide to the bishops' conference and the primary author of the pastoral letter on war and peace, told me that the bishops' "interest in the abortion issue and the whole way they developed that in terms of right to life had a lot to do with pushing them toward the nuclear question, particularly since people began to argue that the nuclear question was such an enormous threat to life."[30]

The second factor that led the bishops to adopt Murphy's proposal was Ronald Reagan's election to the presidency on a platform that called for a higher defense budget and for a whole series of new nuclear weapons systems. Bishop Thomas Gumbleton, a leader of a Catholic peace organization called Pax Christi America, made the following comments in support of Murphy's proposal:

> We've just elected a president who has stated his conviction that we can have superiority in nuclear weapons, an utter impossibility. We have a Vice-President who has clearly stated that one side could win in a nuclear war, and that we must be prepared to fight one and to win it. When we have this kind of thinking going on, it seems to me that we are getting close to the day when we will wage that nuclear war and it will be the war that will end the world as we know it. We are at a point of urgent crisis. We have to face this question and face it very clearly.[31]

Jim Castelli, a journalist who was granted unparalleled access to the process through which the pastoral letter on nuclear weapons was drafted, wrote that "Reagan's election—with the rhetoric and policies he brought to office— was the single greatest factor influencing the bishops' discussion in November 1980 and all that followed."[32]

THE CHALLENGE OF PEACE

The bishops' main task in writing their pastoral letter was to address directly two important matters that neither they nor Rome had treated fully in the past: (1) How does Catholic teaching on war and peace relate to the specific force structures and targeting doctrines of the American nuclear arsenal? (2) Is deterrence, as actually practiced by the United States in the 1980s, moral? In a lengthy, complex document that took over two years to write, the American bishops provided answers to these questions. They ruled out any militarily significant use of nuclear weapons as instruments of destruction. And they expressed a limited, qualified acceptance of a certain type of deterrence as a device for stabilizing superpower relations while arms control and disarmament proceeded.

The Challenge of Peace redirected the just war theory back to the original presumption against violence and killing. Aware that the theory had often been used as a facile justification for war, the American hierarchy placed the burden of proof on those who wanted to justify war rather than on those who wanted to prevent it. For this reason, the bishops raised the tradition of non-violence, at least for individuals, to a status equal to that of the just war tradi-

100 CHAPTER SEVEN

tion. The two traditions "diverge on some specific conclusions," the bishops acknowledged, "but they share a common presumption against the use of force as a means of settling disputes."[33]

The key question for the bishops, and they argued for American society, was "how it is possible to move from these presumptions to the idea of a justifiable use of lethal force."[34] The bishops' answer to the question, at least in terms of nuclear weapons, was that it is not possible. "To destroy civilization as we know it," they stated, "by waging a 'total war' as today it *could* be waged would be a monstrously disproportionate response to aggression on the part of any nation."[35]

The difference between *The Challenge of Peace* and the church's other documents on modern weapons was that this time the American bishops went beyond general denunciation of mass destruction. They also applied Catholic teaching to a series of potential, real-world uses of nuclear weapons, and they arrived at a number of very specific conclusions. The letter was unambiguous, for example, on the already established matter of counterpopulation warfare:

Under no circumstances may nuclear weapons or other instruments of mass slaughter be used for the purpose of destroying population centers or other predominantly civilian targets . . . this condemnation . . . applies even to the retaliatory use of weapons striking enemy cities after ours have already been struck. No Christian can rightfully carry out orders or policies deliberately aimed at killing non-combatants.[36]

The bishops were almost as categorical in their denunciation of initiation of nuclear war, or what is often referred to as "first use": "We do not perceive any situation in which the deliberate initiation of nuclear warfare, on however a restricted a scale, can be morally justified. Non-nuclear attacks by another state must be resisted by other than nuclear means."[37]

Having thus condemned counterpopulation warfare and rejected first use of nuclear weapons, the bishops turned their attention to so-called limited nuclear warfare. Since tactical and battlefield uses of nuclear weapons had never been dealt with in detail before in official documents of Catholic teaching, the bishops' comments on that subject deserve to be quoted at some length:

The issue at stake is the *real* as opposed to the *theoretical* possibility of a "limited nuclear exchange." . . . The burden of proof remains on those who assert that meaningful limitation is possible. . . . The issue of limited war is not simply the size of weapons contemplated or the strategies projected. The debate should include the psychological and political significance of crossing the boundary from the conventional to the nuclear arena in any form. To cross this divide is to enter a world where we have no experience of control, much testimony against its possibility, and therefore no moral justification for submitting the human community to this risk. We therefore express our view that the first imperative is to prevent any use of nuclear weapons and our hope that leaders will resist the notion that nuclear conflict can be limited, contained, or won in any traditional sense.[38]

Listing these quotes from *The Challenge of Peace* one after the other reveals how unambiguously the bishops wanted "to say 'no' to nuclear war."[39] Through their rejection of the three most likely military uses of nuclear weapons, the bishops virtually ruled out any meaningful use of the American nuclear arsenal. But they went even further than that; the bishops also questioned the use of nuclear weapons as a deterrent to war. As the letter put it, "there are moral limits to deterrence policy as well as to policy regarding use."[40]

In this connection, the bishops restated the position they had taken in *To Live in Christ Jesus* and in Cardinal Krol's testimony on SALT II. "It is not morally acceptable," the bishops declared, "to intend to kill the innocent as part of a strategy of deterring nuclear war."[41] Once again, however, the bishops went beyond their earlier statements to a more detailed treatment of the subject. "'Counterforce targeting,'" they continued, "while preferable from the perspective of protecting civilians, is often joined with a declaratory policy which conveys the notion that nuclear war is subject to precise rational and moral limits. We have already expressed our severe doubts about such a concept."[42]

Despite these deep reservations, however, the American hierarchy could not condemn counterforce deterrence outright in *The Challenge of Peace*. Pope John Paul II, with whom and through whom the bishops exercised their proper teaching authority, limited the bishops' freedom in this regard with his own statement on deterrence in 1982: "In current conditions 'deterrence' based on balance, certainly not as an end in itself but as a step on the way toward a progressive disarmament, may still be judged morally acceptable."[43]

Since the American bishops could not condemn something that the pope found "morally acceptable," their letter, while condemning deterrence that is based on an intention to destroy civilian populations, nevertheless acknowledged that there are two dimensions to the "contemporary dilemma of deterrence." The first is the danger of nuclear war, but the second is the "independence and freedom of nations and entire peoples, including the need to protect smaller nations from threats to their independence and integrity." Given this competing value and "the radical distrust which marks international politics," the bishops allowed that "a balance of forces preventing either side from achieving superiority, can be seen as a means of safeguarding both dimensions."[44] Therefore, the bishops stopped short of a call for unilateral disarmament and expressed their "strictly conditioned moral acceptance of nuclear deterrence." As if to underscore their dissatisfaction with this state of affairs, however, the bishops also concluded that they could not "consider it adequate as a long-term basis for peace."[45]

If *The Challenge of Peace* had stopped there it would still have been a controversial and remarkable document. But the bishops went on to acknowledge and emphasize the very concrete policy implications of the principles they had espoused. The bishops opposed addition of "prompt hard target kill" weapons to the American nuclear arsenal, the development of nuclear war-fighting strategies, and any "proposals which have the effect of lowering the nuclear threshold and blurring the difference between nuclear and conventional weapons." On the other hand, they supported deep, negotiated cuts in the world's nuclear arsenals, a comprehensive nuclear test ban treaty, the strengthening of military command and control capabilities, and the removal of all forward-based tactical nuclear forces that could pose a "use 'em or lose 'em" dilemma to field officers in the early stages of a war in Europe.

Finally, and perhaps most significantly, the bishops called for "immediate, bilateral verifiable agreements to halt the testing, production, and deployment of new nuclear weapons systems."[46] This endorsement of a nuclear freeze, without actually using the word "freeze," indicated the depth of the bishops' dissatisfaction with prevailing American nuclear policy. It also tied the pastoral letter, at least in terms of the public's perception of it, to the large, popular movement that had grown up in support of a nuclear freeze during the early 1980s.

A "MODERN" DOCUMENT

The Challenge of Peace indicated the distance that the bishops had traveled in a relatively short period of time. It was a long way from Cardinal Spellman's reflexive support of U.S. involvement in Vietnam to the judgments and conclusions of the pastoral letter on nuclear weapons. On another level, the letter also indicated the changes that had taken place in the bishops' whole approach to public policy. In chapter 2, I argued that most of the hierarchy's traditional political activities were parochial and defensive in nature. In these terms, the pastoral on war and peace was not a traditional activity. There is nothing parochial about concern over nuclear war, and there was nothing at all defensive about the pastoral letter.

The Challenge of Peace was a forceful, unapologetic analysis and critique of American defense policy that the bishops offered to the whole country in terms that the whole country could understand. Traditionally, the bishops had supported American foreign and defense policy for the purpose of defending the patriotic credentials of an immigrant people. The tone and content of the pastoral letter, however, suggested that the bishops of the 1980s were very confident of their own voice and of their church's place in American society.

Of course, foreign policy by its nature had always been the exception to the local focus of the bishops' traditional political activities. Nevertheless, *The*

Challenge of Peace differed from those earlier activities in that it was a collective effort that was formally voted on by the whole NCCB and was officially promulgated in the name of the entire American hierarchy. In fact, the process through which the letter was written under the direction of committee chairman Bernardin was, at the time, a clear signal of the institutional strength of the national conference and the sense of collegiality among the American bishops.

The final draft of the letter was the product of two and one-half years of debate, discussion, and amendment. Public hearings were held; preliminary drafts were released to the public; comments from Catholics and non-Catholics were solicited and taken seriously; and discussions among the bishops over amendments and final language were extensively covered in the Catholic and secular press. Even leaving aside all other factors, this process alone indicated the changes that had taken place within American Catholicism. It is impossible to imagine the leadership of the old immigrant church conducting its business in this manner.

The pastoral letter was also emblematic of the modern era in the sense that it reflected the seminal influence of the Second Vatican Council on the American bishops and their political activities. It was the council, after all, that called for the expanded scope and national focus that I have been discussing. And the influence of the council, particularly of the *Pastoral Constitution on the Church in the Modern World*, could be seen on virtually every page of the bishops' letter. In its explicit address to Catholics and non-Catholics, its emphasis on principles of Catholic teaching and application of those principles to specific circumstances, and its substantive approach to the problems of modern warfare, the pastoral letter was the direct ecclesiological, theological, and political descendent of the council's constitution. On this point, Father Hehir has called the letter on nuclear weapons "both a product of and a response to the pastoral constitution."[47]

The letter, of course, also significantly affected the bishops' role in the political process. It expanded their policy agenda and fundamentally altered the relationship between that agenda and partisan politics. *The Challenge of Peace* communicated a searching critique of American defense policy to the Catholic laity, it allied the hierarchy with another grass-roots social movement, and it clearly distanced the bishops' conference from the religious new right and its conservative agenda.

CATHOLIC DOVES, THE FREEZE, AND A MORAL AGENDA

There are over 50 million Catholics in the United States, and any document or action with the potential to affect the political attitudes of that many people must be taken seriously. One of the difficulties involved in assessing the effect of *The Challenge of Peace* on Catholic attitudes, however, is that these attitudes themselves are so widely misunderstood. One of the most enduring byproducts of the superpatriotic tradition is that even today, long after the tradition has given way to a more mature, critical approach, Catholics are almost automatically thought to be "hawks" on foreign policy. The facts, as George Gallup and Jim Castelli have amply demonstrated, do not support this perception.[48]

Along with their bishops, American Catholics abandoned their unquestioning support of American foreign policy during the Vietnam War. The only difference between Catholic laypersons and bishops in this regard is that the laypersons changed their minds before the bishops did. In 1969, for example, a majority of Catholics supported "de-Americanization" of the war and a ceasefire; in 1970, a solid plurality of Catholics objected to the invasion of Cambodia; and by January 1971, fully 80 percent of Catholics had come to the position that all American troops should be withdrawn from Vietnam.[49]

As I indicated earlier, the Catholic bishops did not express their own support for a troop withdrawal until November 1971. It is fair to conclude, therefore, that when the bishops advised Catholics "that the speedy ending of the war is a moral imperative," they were not teaching; they were preaching to the already converted. For our purposes, however, the more important point is that Catholics remained relatively dovish even after the Vietnam War ended. By the time the bishops wrote their pastoral letter on nuclear weapons in 1983, many Catholics had already grown quite dissatisfied with American defense policy. In fact, 72 percent of Catholics supported a nuclear freeze in 1982, *before The Challenge of Peace* was published.[50] Catholics of the 1970s and 1980s were simply not the unreconstructed hawks of common perception.

Nevertheless, on the basis of data comparing the attitudes of Catholics and Protestants over time, Andrew Greeley has spoken of the "effective leadership" provided by a pastoral letter that represented "a power and an influence of leadership which does not seem to be matched anywhere in the world."[51] In early 1983, just before the letter was released, 34 percent of both Catholics and Protestants felt that too much was being spent on arms and national defense. In 1984, after the letter was released, the Protestant percentage remained constant while the percentage of Catholics saying they thought too much was being spent on defense jumped a full twenty points to 54 percent. Besides the bishops' letter, Greeley asked, what could have caused this dramatic divergence?[52] "It would appear," he concluded, "that the American bishops provided Catholics [already concerned about the nuclear arms race] with a focus for their concern which was not provided by any parallel agency or institution for American Protestants."[53]

The political significance of the pastoral letter, however, went well beyond its effect on the attitudes of American Catholics. As I argued in the case of abortion, the bishops are able to bring virtually unrivaled resources to any cause or effort they decide to support. They committed those resources to the fight against abortion in the 1970s, and in the process they played a key role in the creation and maintenance of a large social movement. In the case of nuclear weapons, the bishops were not as purposeful, and they did not explicitly lend their institutional resources to a political movement. But the bishops' letter and the campaign for a nuclear freeze were nevertheless related to each other in a number of interesting and significant ways.

The freeze movement and the pastoral letter were both launched in 1980. In the spring, Randall Forsberg of the Institute for Defense and Disarmament Studies wrote "Call to Halt the Nuclear Arms Race," demanding a "mutual freeze on the testing, production, and deployment of nuclear weapons and of missiles and new aircraft designed primarily to deliver nuclear weapons."[54] In the fall, Bishop Murphy proposed a reinvigoration of the church's application of its moral teaching to U.S. defense policy. For the next several years these two efforts, launched separately, developed and advanced together.

Both began as relatively fringe proposals which then gained momentum and urgency in light of Reagan's election to the presidency. Consider the following two quotes, the first from Jim Castelli's account of the pastoral letter, the second from Douglas Waller's book on the freeze:

> Reagan's election—with the rhetoric and policies he brought to office—was the single greatest factor influencing the bishops' discussion in November and all that followed.[55]

> What started out as a relatively minuscule grass-roots [freeze] campaign quickly became a national movement, and Mr. Reagan deserved much of the credit for making it so.[56]

Through 1981 and 1982, as the bishops wrote their letter, the freeze movement grew rapidly. Antinuclear groups sprung up by the hundreds, and town meetings and state legislatures all over the country recorded their official endorsements of a bilateral nuclear freeze. By 1982, a conference of these various groups created the Nuclear Weapons Freeze Campaign to coordinate a nationwide effort, and as Waller observed, "congressmen took notice."[57] As a result of that notice, the Kennedy–Hatfield resolution calling for a freeze was introduced in the Senate, and an identical measure was brought to the House by Representatives Edward Markey and Silvio Conte of Massachusetts. Meanwhile, a number of bishops, particularly those associated with Pax Christi, began to express their own support for the freeze and to encourage their colleagues to do likewise. According to one count, 132 bishops, or nearly one-half of the NCCB, had publicly endorsed the nuclear freeze by the middle of 1982.[58]

The midterm election of 1982 offered the Nuclear Weapons Freeze Campaign its first opportunity to test and flex its political muscles on a national stage. Referenda calling for a freeze were placed on the ballot in nine states, the District of Columbia, and thirty-eight other municipalities and counties. In all, over one-third of the American electorate had the chance to cast a vote on the freeze. And in late October, just days before the election, the NCCB published a draft of the pastoral letter that included language virtually identical to Forsberg's original call for a freeze and to the various referenda pending on ballots across the country.

The NCCB's annual meetings are held every November, of course, and it is unlikely that the release of the draft was timed to influence votes on the freeze. Nor is it possible to accurately calibrate the draft's role in the freeze's impressive showing at the polls. It is clear, however, that the Reagan administration was concerned about the potential impact of the bishops' action. In Waller's words, the bishops' implicit endorsement of the freeze "sent top Reagan administration officials to the bunkers" in the days leading up to the campaign.[59] If nothing else, the events surrounding the election in 1982 drew attention to the close relationship between the letter that the bishops were writing and the nuclear freeze movement.

It became virtually impossible not to notice this relationship once *The Challenge of Peace* and the House freeze resolution had been voted on and passed within twenty-four hours of each other during the first week of May 1983. Reviewing contemporary accounts of the events of that week, one gets the unmistakable impression that the NCCB's letter and the House of Representatives' resolution were two specific manifestations of the public's apprehension concerning the nuclear arms race, and of a growing desire to see it halted. As a matter of fact, the bishops' letter and the congressional resolution actually shared a two-page spread of excerpts and analysis in the 5 May 1983 edition of the *New York Times*.[60]

Simply put, *The Challenge of Peace* was not produced and released in a political vacuum. To the contrary, it was conceived, debated, and resoundingly adopted in a political environment in which the issues of nuclear weapons and arms control had taken an unusually prominent place in the American public policy debate. It would be facile, with the benefit of hindsight, to dismiss the contemporary political significance of the bishops' endorsement of the freeze. We now know, of course, that President Reagan was able to defuse the freeze campaign by toning down his rhetoric and paying greater attention to arms control talks with the Soviet Union. But in 1982 and 1983, when the pastoral was written and released, the freeze campaign was a large, politically potent social movement that was expected to play a powerful role in the upcoming presidential election. The letter and that campaign started out together in 1980, progressed together in 1981 and 1982, and came to a head together in May 1983. In short, the two were closely related, mutually reinforcing developments.

The political significance of the bishops' letter also went beyond its connection to the freeze. As highly visible religious leaders, the American Catholic hierarchy plays a role in setting what might be called the moral agenda of American politics. And *The Challenge of Peace* indicated that, on the basis of their Catholic tradition and their religious faith, the Catholic bishops had come to see American defense policy as a central *moral* issue. Such a declaration would have been controversial no matter when it was made, but it was especially so in 1983. For in 1983 it directly contradicted the beliefs, convictions, and policy proposals of a political coalition that had touted itself as the guardian of moral and religious values in American politics. In other words, it unambiguously alienated the Catholic bishops from the political program and strategy of the religious new right.

In 1976 and 1980, the bishops had been closely identified with a single political cause, the right-to-life movement. But by 1983 the relationship between the bishops' agenda and the partisan political debate and process had become a great deal more complicated, and reactions to that complexity were varied. Republican leaders criticized *The Challenge of Peace* and tried to keep attention focused on abortion and "their" moral issues. Democratic leaders, on the other hand, praised the tone of the bishops' letter and welcomed their moral position on an issue other than abortion, but nimbly sidestepped the rather radical implications of *The Challenge of Peace*.

At the same time, a number of individual bishops also saw fit to respond to this more complex relationship between their moral agenda and the terms and content of American politics. Some of these bishops welcomed the expansion of their collective agenda and celebrated the opportunity it gave them to reformulate their approach to the national political process. Others, to be plain, did not. In fact, a debate ensued within the National Conference of Catholic Bishops over the scope of the bishops' policy agenda and the nature of their participation in national politics. The same debate had also flared within the bishops' conference in 1976, of course, and even to a lesser extent in 1980. But in 1984, the debate spilled out into the open and precipitated the direct participation of several individual bishops in the presidential campaign. This participation was not merely the result of the bishops' new agenda. Rather, it was a result of the new way that that agenda cut across the policy debate and partisan competition between the two major political parties.

CHAPTER EIGHT

The Bishops and Electoral Politics: 1984

HEADING INTO THE 1984 ELECTION, it looked as though the bishops had carved out a new position for themselves on the American political spectrum. Their policy agenda, which included support for a "halt" in the deployment of new nuclear weapons systems and opposition to abortion, was highly unusual and cut rather dramatically across the partisan cleavage of the American electorate. As always, however, the bishops' actual participation in the 1984 election was determined by far more than their own policy views. In this case, the bishops' actions were shaped by the unusually religious tone of the presidential campaign, and by the presence of a prochoice Catholic on the Democratic party's national ticket. The relationship between the bishops' policy positions and these political factors—or, more precisely, the desire of some individual bishops to control and direct this relationship—was the key determining factor in the Catholic hierarchy's involvement in the 1984 national election.

REPUBLICANS AND THE CHALLENGE OF PEACE

For Ronald Reagan and the Republican party, *The Challenge of Peace* was a wholly negative development. The letter condemned American defense policy; it associated the bishops with Reagan's intractable political opponents in the nuclear freeze movement; and it drew attention away from the main issue on which the bishops and Reagan agreed—abortion. In short, the pastoral letter was a potential hindrance to several facets of the Republican electoral strategy in 1984.

As I discussed in previous chapters, the Republican party had been assiduously courting Catholic voters since at least 1964. Republican leaders argued that the traditional cultural ties between the Democratic party and American Catholicism were outdated, and that middle-class suburban Catholics belonged in their party. Reagan had barely won a majority of Catholic votes in 1980, and he and the Republican leadership were anxious to build on that base.[1] They saw 1984 as a crucial opportunity to solidify their hold on the Catholic vote and to draw Catholics more permanently into a new, broader-based Republican coalition. In *The Challenge of Peace*, however, the bishops sharply criticized several of the president's central defense policies. And that criticism was accompanied by a decrease of a full 20 percent in Catholic support for higher defense spending.[2] Even absent any empirical proof of a cause-and-effect relationship between the letter and these attitudes, *The Challenge of Peace* was, by any standard, an unwelcome development for the Republican party.

From the Republican point of view, the bishops' endorsement of the nuclear freeze was equally unwelcome. In 1982 and 1983, as the pastoral letter was being written, the president denounced the freeze as simplistic and counterproductive, and accused leaders of the freeze movement of being dupes of Soviet propaganda and espionage.[3] The bishops' pastoral letter undercut Reagan's efforts to discredit the freeze, however, because it suggested that the concept of a freeze enjoyed significant appeal on its own merits. *The Challenge of Peace* provided the freeze movement with a degree of moral credibility that it would not otherwise have had.

Finally, as I indicated at the end of the last chapter, *The Challenge of Peace* differentiated the bishops from the religious new right in terms of the proper scope of morality's role in American public policy. The Republican party had benefited in 1980 from its identification with an expressly moral agenda. But the bishops' pastoral letter blurred the parameters of that agenda by stressing the public, collective dimension of morality. This more expansive notion of the relationship between moral or religious convictions and public policy could only mean trouble for the Republican party and the political coalition it was trying to build.

For all these reasons, Reagan strenuously lobbied the Catholic hierarchy throughout 1982 and 1983. Officials of his administration wrote letters, both private and public, to Joseph Bernardin and other bishops; some of these same officials met with the drafting committee and its staff to explain and defend American force structures and targeting strategies; diplomatic envoys told the pope of the president's deep displeasure with the letter; and Reagan himself pointedly denounced the campaign for a nuclear freeze in front of Catholic audiences.[4]

As a result of these efforts, a few marginal changes were made in the wording and emphasis of the letter. Later drafts conceded, for example, that the administration was engaged in arms talks with the Soviet Union, and they also included sections of a letter from William Clark to Bernardin in which Clark pointed out the administration's opposition to countercity targeting. None of these changes, however, affected the major conclusions the bishops drew in the letter. In fact, most of the substantial revisions in the document that took place from draft to draft had nothing at all to do with the administration's lobbying. These changes, which for the most part involved interpretation of Scripture and clarifications of the canonical authority associated with the bishops' views, were the results of debate within the bishops' conference and of a "consultation" with leading officials in the Vatican.[5]

That said, a change of a single word between the second and third drafts of the letter did provide an opportunity for the president and other opponents of the bishops' initiative to distort the letter's implications. Bishop John O'Connor, a senior military chaplain and an admiral in the U.S. Navy, was one of the members of the committee that drafted the letter. According to Castelli's account of the drafting process, O'Connor was determined to prevent the letter from being perceived as an endorsement of the increasingly partisan nuclear freeze.[6] He believed that the second draft's call for a "halt [in] the testing, production, and deployment of new strategic weapons" amounted to such an endorsement, and he proposed that the committee change the wording of that section. Acceding to O'Connor's request, the committee replaced the loaded word, "halt," with the much more innocuous "curb."

This change of one single word, as O'Connor surely realized, was highly significant. In terms of semantics alone, "halt" meant a freeze while "curb" did not. But more importantly, "halt" was the word that Randall Forsberg had used in her original call for a nuclear freeze, whereas "curb" had no particular political meaning or resonance. Given this context, the bishops' shift from "halt" to "curb" could not help but be perceived as a pointed retreat from support of the nuclear freeze campaign. As Castelli put it, "the third draft eventually ran 25,000 words, and O'Connor had found the one word that would change the interpretation of the entire document in a politically charged, media heavy climate."[7]

Opponents of the freeze immediately moved to capitalize on the opportunity the bishops had dropped in their laps. A spokesman for Reagan immediately hailed the letter's new "flexibility," and declared that the president was "pleased that the letter explicitly endorsed many of the far-reaching objectives which the administration seeks."[8] Representative Henry Hyde of Illinois, who had sharply criticized earlier drafts of the bishops' letter, wrote to his congressional colleagues that it was "clear that after careful deliberation the Roman Catholic bishops [had] refused to endorse the nuclear arms freeze."[9] Speaking of the upcoming vote in the House of Representatives on the freeze, Hyde added that he hoped "the wisdom of the bishops' second thoughts on the freeze [would] guide the debate and serve as a model for [the House's actions]."[10] In the hands of the freeze's opponents, the difference between "halt" and "curb" became the difference between an endorsement of the freeze and a repudiation of it.

In time, however, these heavy-handed efforts backfired. A number of bishops grew angry at misleading and mischievous interpretations of their letter, and ultimately an overwhelming vote of the full NCCB returned "halt" to the letter. It was not possible, after all, for the bishops' opponents to turn a radical critique of American defense policy into an endorsement of President Reagan's defense agenda. In fact, all the publicity surrounding the controversy only served to underscore the fact that the bishops did indeed support a nuclear freeze.[11]

As it turned out, the bishops' final vote on the halt/curb controversy coincided with the debate on the freeze in the House of Representatives. The bishops' return to "halt," motivated in part by the efforts of Hyde and others, allowed the pastoral letter to be used by Hyde's opponents in the political fight over the freeze. Representative Edward Markey, for example, was able to argue on the floor of the House that "what happened at the bishops' session is a reflection of grass-roots support at the parish level [that is] identical to the grass-roots movement nationwide in support of the freeze."[12]

The two-track strategy for countering *The Challenge of Peace*, then, was a failure. The lobbying effort was unsuccessful, and the attempt to distort the letter's meaning proved counterproductive. But by the time the final version of the letter was released in the name of the entire hierarchy, the president had shifted to a third, more subtle approach. He simply praised the bishops for their effort, and then dismissed the fruits that effort had borne. "I think [the bishops'] purpose is the same as ours," the president offered in an interview. "[The letter] really is a legitimate effort to do exactly what we're doing and that is to try to find ways toward world peace."[13]

This final reaction to *The Challenge of Peace* did not mean, however, that Reagan was going to ignore the bishops or their policy agenda entirely. To the contrary, he continued to associate himself whenever possible with the bishops' commitment to the right to life; he just refused to be drawn into the bishops' expansion of that commitment to include issues other than abortion. The president dealt with the bishops' agenda selectively, in other words. He emphasized the moral issues on which he and the bishops agreed, and tried to obscure those on which they disagreed. When all was said and done, his Democratic opponents adopted pretty much the same approach.

DEMOCRATS AND THE CHALLENGE OF PEACE

In chapters 4 and 5 I was able to report in some detail on Republican attempts to hasten and benefit from the decline of the Democratic New Deal coalition. I discussed the draft of Goldwater, Nixon's new majority, and the rise of the new right, and I argued that all of these developments were aggressive, carefully coordinated political strategies. In contrast, Democratic responses to the decay of their own majority have been much less clearly defined. Political scientists Benjamin Ginsberg and Martin Shefter have identified several Democratic attempts to reassert dominance over the American electorate. None of these attempts have been particularly impressive.[14] The Democratic strategies have included efforts to reconstitute the old New Deal coalition; forge a new majority around a New Politics movement of peace activists, civil rights advocates, and environmentalists; and build an alliance between organized labor and remnants of the New Politics movement. All in all, with the possible exception of McGovern's original appeal to New Politics activists in 1972, these Democratic responses to the demise of their electoral majority have been remarkably ad hoc and fundamentally defensive.

The year 1984 was no exception. Walter Mondale, faced with the unenviable task of building an electoral majority for a party that had lost two of the last three presidential elections by overwhelming margins, adopted a blend of past Democratic approaches. He tried to salvage what was left of the old New Deal party and combine it with segments of the electorate that were most solidly opposed to Reagan's program. In more specific terms, Mondale appealed to organized labor, blacks, and senior citizens, all of whom had been adversely affected by Reaganomics; young professionals and holdovers from the New Politics movement, both of whom opposed the Republican social agenda; and women, who it was hoped could be energized by the selection of a female vice-presidential candidate.

In one sense, Mondale's strategy in 1984 was very similar to Ford's in 1976. Resigned to losing the South, Mondale knew that to have a chance at beating Reagan he would have to carry the heavily Catholic states of the Northeast and Midwest. Mondale was never as explicit as Ford had been about a Catholic strategy for winning in these states, but Robert Beckel, his campaign manager, indicated in an interview with me that the Democrats fully appreciated how important Catholics were to their electoral fortunes in 1984. "We always assumed that electorally it was going to be very difficult for us to win in the South," Beckel said. "So it was absolutely essential that we swept the Northeast and Midwest. And when you talk about the Northeast and the upper tier Midwest you talk ethnic, and when you talk ethnic you talk Catholic."[15]

The Challenge of Peace, in a number of ways, could have been of help to Mondale. First of all, the letter was very well received within the Catholic community where it reinforced attitudes that were much closer to the Democratic approach to defense issues than to the Republican. Second, the letter offered the possibility at least that the conflict between the Catholic bishops and the national Democratic party, a conflict that had flared in 1976 over the abortion issue, could be ameliorated in 1984 by agreement on issues like the nuclear freeze.

The bishops' implied endorsement of the freeze (how else could one read the return to "halt"?) was advantageous for Mondale in another sense as well. Originally a product of the professional peace community, the freeze had become by 1984 a sprawling middle-class movement and the leading symbol of widespread unease with Reagan's defense program. Mondale hoped his own support for a freeze would facilitate the delicate task of holding remnants of the New Deal coalition and the New Politics movement together in one Democratic party. He figured he could placate New Politics activists by backing the freeze without simultaneously alienating more traditional Democratic voters. To the extent that their pastoral letter both increased support for the freeze among middle-class Catholics, and debunked notions that the freeze was a radical, irresponsible proposal, the Catholic bishops made Mondale's tenuous balancing act that much easier.

Finally, Reagan's rhetoric and the support he enjoyed among very vocal evangelical Christians made it seem in the early 1980s that religious and moral values were the sole preserves of the Republican party. *The Challenge of Peace* established, however, that not all of America's religious leaders supported Reagan's version of morality and values. In fact, the Catholic bishops declared that *their* religious tradition, the tradition of 50 million Americans, had led them to reject many of Reagan's defense policies. Religious and moral values, it appeared, could serve as the basis for criticism of the Republican platform as well.

In sum, for all the reasons that *The Challenge of Peace* was a political disadvantage for the Republicans, it was a political advantage for the Democrats. For that reason, while Republican leaders tried to derail the bishops' letter, Democratic leaders cautiously welcomed it. Charles Manatt, the Democratic National Committee chairman, chose Georgetown University, a Catholic institution, as the setting for a speech outlining what he called a "Democratic consensus" on arms control. The speech, which received front-page coverage in both the Catholic and secular press, listed all the policy areas on which the pastoral letter and the Democratic platform agreed.[16] Manatt did not embrace all of the bishops' fundamental critiques of American defense doctrine, of course, but he did express the Democratic party's "general support" for the contents of the pastoral letter.[17]

As I said, however, the Democrats' response to the bishops and the pastoral letter was rather cautious. Abortion was still a major stumbling block to agreement between the Catholic hierarchy and the Democratic national leadership. Mondale had apparently learned from Carter's naive mistakes in 1976, and he had no intention of inviting a dialogue with the bishops that might degenerate into a debate on abortion. He decided it was probably wise to keep his distance from the Catholic hierarchy during the presidential campaign. "We weren't going to be able to repair ourselves on abortion," Beckel told me. "Mondale was in favor of abortion, it was as simple as that. So we never spent resources nor time trying to convince the Catholic bishops that they ought to be for Walter Mondale."[18]

In an important sense, then, the Democrats' response to the bishops' expanded policy agenda in 1984 was very similar to the Republicans'; both parties approached the bishops' agenda selectively. They acknowledged and welcomed areas of agreement with the hierarchy when possible, while seeking to avoid any direct engagement with the Catholic leadership when it came to issues on which they disagreed.

At the beginning of this chapter, I noted that the Catholic bishops had staked out a new political position for themselves by developing an agenda that sharply diverged from the platforms of both political parties. By 1983, in other words, the bishops had associated themselves with a set of policy positions that, *if taken together*, could not be perceived as favoring one party or candidate over the other. The parties' reactions to *The Challenge of Peace*, however, suggested to the bishops that their positions would probably not be taken together during the 1984 campaign. Rather, the bishops could expect that bits and pieces of their agenda would be used by various candidates in various ways, but that no candidate would engage them on all of the positions they had adopted. These expectations regenerated the debate within the Catholic hierarchy between those bishops who wanted to emphasize abortion and those who preferred to identify themselves with a broader range of issues. These two groups of bishops disagreed over the relationship that the hierarchy's various policy positions should have to each other, and how that relationship should be presented publicly. But in so doing, they also disagreed over the way that their agenda as a whole should relate to the political process, to the partisan competition between the two major parties.

THE CONSISTENT ETHIC OF LIFE

Cardinal Bernardin opened the public version of the bishops' debate in late 1983. He argued, in a speech at Fordham University in New York, that the bishops' views on the various issues should be conceived of, not as separate and distinct positions, but rather as a coherent and seamless whole. Bernardin, of course, played a very important role in creating the common perception that the Catholic hierarchy was primarily an antiabortion lobby. In 1976 he had rejected arguments within the church that his emphasis on abortion was too narrow. As president of the NCCB, he had held meetings with the presidential candidates that year and had characterized the candidates' views on abortion as "disappointing" and "encouraging," respectively. But Bernardin also played a very important role in the expansion of the bishops' agenda and in the shift in the bishops' approach to politics after 1976. He was chairman of the ad hoc committee that drafted *The Challenge of Peace*, and he was chairman of the bishops' standing committee on pro-life activities. He was, in other words, the American hierarchy's leading spokesman on both nuclear weapons and abortion. And by 1983 he was also, thanks to appointments by the pope, the archbishop of Chicago and a cardinal.

Bernardin was, in short, uniquely qualified to articulate the Catholic hierarchy's priorities and to shape the bishops' participation in the 1984 election. That is just what he attempted to do through his now famous speech at Fordham:

> I am convinced that the pro-life position of the church must be developed in terms of a comprehensive and consistent ethic of life. . . . The principle which structures both cases, war and abortion, needs to be upheld in both places. It cannot be successfully sustained on one count and simultaneously eroded in a similar situation. . . . I contend the viability of the principle depends upon the consistency of its application.[19]

At one level, this linking together of the church's prolife positions into a consistent ethic of life was a theological approach that grew out of Bernardin's interpretation of Catholic principles and teachings. At another level, however, the consistent ethic was also a political strategy designed to prevent a recurrence of either the bishops' divisive and partisan role of 1976 or their distorted, indirect role of 1980. Bernardin wanted to prevent the bishops' varied and cross-cutting agenda from being misrepresented by opportunistic candidates and from being overrun by the dynamics of single-issue politics. Reflecting on this political aspect of his consistent ethic, Bernardin later said:

> It was urgent, I felt, that a well developed theological and ethical framework be provided that could link the various life issues while at the same time pointing out that the issues are not all the same. It was my fear that without such a framework or vision the bishops of this country would be severely pressured by those who wanted to push a particular issue with little or no concern for the rest. With such a theological basis we would be able to argue convincingly on all the issues on which we had taken a position in recent years.[20]

Bernardin is a very influential member of the National Conference of Catholic Bishops, and the consistent ethic of life, or as some called it, the seamless garment, quickly received the support of many American bishops. In fact, his approach was incorporated into the political responsibility statement of 1984 wherein the bishops collectively expressed their hope "that voters will examine the positions of candidates on the full range of issues as well as their integrity, philosophy, and performance."[21]

This is not to say, however, that Bernardin spoke for all of the American bishops when he gave his speech at Fordham University, because he most certainly did not. Between 1976 and 1984 Bernardin personally, and with him the NCCB institutionally, moved away from a singular preoccupation with abortion toward a greater public emphasis on a broad range of issues. But over that same period of time, a number of bishops who remained deeply committed to a primary emphasis on abortion had also risen to visible and influential positions in the American hierarchy. Two of these bishops—John O'Connor of New York and Bernard Law of Boston—forcefully and publicly advocated the old abortion-centered approach during the presidential campaign of 1984.

THE BISHOPS AND ELECTORAL POLITICS, 1984

In early September 1984, the bishops of New England, under Law's leadership, declared that abortion was still the single most important issue in American national politics. "While nuclear holocaust is a future possibility," they said, "the holocaust of abortion is a present reality. . . . Indeed, we believe that the enormity of the evil makes abortion the critical issue of the moment."[22] In a similar vein, O'Connor would later say that he was "totally repelled by the possibility of nuclear war [but] even more repelled by the actuality of the war against the unborn. . . . If the unborn in a mother's womb is unsafe," O'Connor contended, "it becomes ludicrous for the bishops to address the threat of nuclear war or the great problems of the homeless or the suffering of the aged."[23]

In both of these statements, the subordination of the nuclear question to the issue of abortion and the direct conclusion that abortion was the most important issue in the election were direct refutations of Bernardin's assertion that "the pro-life position of the church must be developed in terms of a comprehensive and consistent ethic of life." These statements were attempts, in other words, to counter Bernardin's consistent ethic and to draw attention to the church's teaching on abortion and to the candidates' positions on that single issue.

These efforts to redirect the church's priorities and energies back to abortion did not go unchallenged by other members of the American hierarchy. Twenty-three bishops, all members of Pax Christi, released an unusually direct response to Law and the other bishops of New England just days before the election. Rejecting the depiction of abortion as "the critical issue of the moment," these bishops declared that "one cannot examine abortion as though that were the only moral issue facing our people. . . . Without imposing our moral convictions on anyone," they continued, "it does seem the place of religious leaders to ask that moral evaluation be brought to the entire spectrum of life issues and to encourage our people to be wary of any narrowing of moral vision to focus on only one issue."[24]

Bernardin also explicitly rejected the notion that abortion was a more urgent issue and a more pressing reality than the danger of nuclear war. The two issues, he argued, are "linked at the level of moral principle [and] are also comparable questions in terms of national policy. . . . The possibility of a nuclear war," he warned, "is a clear and present danger."[25]

All of these statements reveal the depth of conviction that characterized the bishops' debate in 1984. It was the same basic debate, of course, that had been going on for a decade or more, the same debate that had swirled around the *Pastoral Plan for Pro-Life Activities* and the meetings with the candidates in 1976. But this time the debate was more clearly drawn, and a few prominent bishops were widely recognized as the primary participants. In addition, the debate moved out from behind the private walls of the National Conference of Catholic Bishops and became public. One of the reasons for this was the aggressive and forthright styles of these primary participants. O'Connor, for one, said what he thought and said it in public. But the major reason the bishops' disagreement was so public in 1984 was that it closely paralleled the partisan political discussion of that year. In 1984, the bishops argued over the policy priorities of the largest church in America in the middle of a presidential campaign in which, according to *Time* magazine, "the prominence and complexity of religious issues may [have been] greater than in any previous election."[26]

In part, the religious issue of the campaign concerned the propriety of using religious rhetoric and imagery for partisan gain. Mondale, for example, accused Reagan of blurring the lines of separation between church and state and of trying to "transform policy debates into theological disputes."[27] And Reagan, while assuring the voters that he was a faithful defender of the First Amendment, reminded his opponent that "faith and religion play a central role in the political life of our nation and always have."[28]

This aspect of the religious issue was the subject of a good deal of attention in 1984, but it was not really the heart of the matter. In truth, Reagan was right. Faith and religion *have* always played a critical role in American politics, and beyond the American Civil Liberties Union, Mondale was not going to get very far arguing that they should be kept out of the campaign altogether. What he could argue, however, and what he did argue in fact, was that Reagan was *mis*using religion by inappropriately identifying the shared religious sentiments of the American people with a partisan program. "Most Americans would be surprised to learn," Mondale remarked sarcastically, "that God is a Republican."[29]

The central facet of the religious issue in 1984, in other words, was not *whether* religion and Christian morality should influence public policy and politics, but rather *where* that influence should begin and end. For Reagan, morality was a matter of individual behavior. He stressed issues like abortion and prayer in public schools, and he accused those who disagreed with him on those matters, especially on the latter, of being intolerant of religion. For Walter Mondale, on the other hand, morality was a far more collective or societal matter. He emphasized the moral dimensions of issues like poverty and the nuclear arms race, and he argued that his personal religious convictions had broad policy implications. "I believe the reason I am in politics," Mondale said at one point, "is because of my faith, what I believe it teaches me about what Christianity should involve: nondiscrimination, freedom, reaching out to lighten the burden on the vulnerable."[30]

Mondale and Reagan were really offering contradictory answers to a series of crucial questions concerning the relationship between religion and politics in the United States. Is abortion the major moral issue facing the American people? Or are the nuclear arms race and the plight of the poor equally important moral considerations? What is, after all, the proper scope of Christian morality's influence on the formulation and implementation of American public policy? When the religious issue of 1984 is framed in this way, it is easy to see why the media and the candidates were so interested in the bishops and their policy agenda. The questions that occupied the presidential candidates were exactly the same ones that occupied the National Conference of Catholic Bishops. And the different answers that, for example, Bernardin and O'Connor gave to these questions suggested entirely different relationships between Catholic teaching and American politics. In fact, those answers can be said to have had contradictory partisan implications.

Bernardin envisioned his consistent ethic of life as a politically neutral, issue-oriented approach. He wanted to prevent the kind of partisan haggling with candidates that had occurred in 1976, and he spoke proudly of the "unique position" that the bishops could hold in 1984 because of the cross-cutting nature of their most prominently articulated policy positions.[31] Given the terms of the debate I have outlined above, however, the consistent ethic was not really neutral. Yes, it retained the opposition to abortion that kept Bernardin and his supporters at odds with the Democratic platform. But the codification of the bishops' policy stances into a consistent ethic of life, and the deemphasis of abortion as a political litmus test that this development inevitably implied, meshed much more closely with the Democratic approach to religion's role in American public life than it did with the Republican.

Like the Democrats, supporters of the consistent ethic or seamless garment stressed the societal, collective dimension of morality. Like Mondale and Ferraro, they argued that issues beyond abortion and individual behavior had to be assessed in light of moral values. Father Bryan Hehir, a strong proponent of Bernardin's approach, framed the American moral/political agenda in a way that was virtually identical to the Democratic response to Reagan's religious rhetoric. "We should remember," Hehir admonished in 1984, "that fairness in economics and restraint on nuclear arms control are moral and religious issues too."[32]

At the very least, a major attraction of the broader agenda for Bernardin, Hehir, and many others was that it would prevent the Republican party from claiming the bishops' tacit support on the basis of a shared opposition to abortion. But for the other group of bishops, still committed to the notion that abortion was the most important issue in American politics, this was not a positive development. Apparently, bishops like O'Connor, Law, and their supporters were willing to have their opposition to abortion identified with the moral agenda being advanced in 1984 by Ronald Reagan and the Republican party.

These bishops contend that they were merely speaking out on the issues, and they did not seek out such an identification. But their claims of nonpartisanship rang as hollow in 1984 as Bernardin's similar claims had in 1976. To say in the heat of a campaign that you are "disappointed" in the views of one candidate and "encouraged" by the views of another is at least to imply support for the latter candidate. In the same way, to call abortion the "critical" issue of a campaign in which the Republican candidate pointedly opposes abortion and the Democratic candidate just as pointedly supports it, is to suggest, albeit indirectly, a preference for that Republican candidate. In fact, an off-hand remark made by John O'Connor during the campaign indicated how difficult it is in such cases to distinguish positions on issues from preferences for candidates. Taking the podium at a right-to-life rally immediately after a taped message of support from the president had been played, O'Connor asked the crowd, "I didn't tell you to vote for Reagan did I?"[33] Well, no, not exactly.

The dispute within the Catholic hierarchy in 1984 concerned the position that abortion should hold on the bishops' policy agenda, and the way that agenda as a whole would relate to the candidates' discussion of religion and morality. But the actions of Law and O'Connor also concerned the matter of Catholic officeholders and the degree to which those officeholders should enact Catholic teaching on abortion into law. In 1984, Mario Cuomo, the Catholic governor of New York and the keynote speaker at the Democratic national convention, presented a platform that supported legal abortion as a political program dedicated to compassion and traditional family values. And Geraldine Ferraro, also a Catholic, and the Democratic candidate for the vice-presidency, forthrightly and passionately defended the right of all American women to have an abortion. Cuomo and Ferraro both claimed that they *personally* accepted the church's moral teaching on abortion, but implicit in their *political* position was an argument that abortion was only one among many important moral issues that Catholic politicians have to face.

This position, to put it plainly, was utterly unacceptable to the bishops who saw abortion as the preeminent evil in modern American society. In June 1984, Archbishop O'Connor had said that he personally could not see "how a Catholic in conscience could vote for an individual explicitly expressing himself or herself as favoring abortion."[34] Unwilling to allow such a statement to stand unchallenged, Cuomo charged that O'Connor had stepped over the line of acceptable behavior by presuming to tell Catholics how to vote. "Now you have the Archbishop of New York," the governor pointed out, "saying that no Catholic can vote for Ed Koch, no Catholic can vote for . . . Pat Moynihan, or Mario Cuomo—anybody who disagrees with him on abortion."[35]

On the face of it, O'Connor's statement had seemed to contradict the NCCB's collective policy of not "instruct[ing] persons how they should vote by endorsing candidates."[36] And in his response to Cuomo, O'Connor appeared to retreat to at least the tone of that policy. "It is neither my responsibility nor my desire," he countered, "to evaluate the qualifications of any individual of any party for any public office or of any individual holding public office. My sole responsibility is to present as clearly as I can the formal official teaching of the Catholic Church. I leave to those interested in such teachings whether or not the public statements of officeholders and candidates accord with this teaching."[37] In one sense, O'Connor's statement imposed a self-limitation, and Cuomo declared himself "delighted to have the clarification."[38] But in a more fundamental sense, O'Connor's statement neatly sidestepped the crucial issue. The question in 1984 was not the Catholic Church's teaching on abortion; nothing could have been clearer. The question was how that teaching would be related to other politically charged teachings within a context in which neither of the major parties agreed with all of the church's positions. One answer to this question had already been offered by Bernardin. Another, conflicting answer, was offered in the heat of the presidential campaign by O'Connor, and by Law and his colleagues in New England.

Soon after Archbishop Law declared that abortion was the critical issue of the campaign, O'Connor once again focused on Catholic politicians who supported legal abortion. He did not tell Catholics how to vote this time; instead, he accused one particular Catholic politician of misrepresenting her church's teaching:

> Geraldine Ferraro has said some things relevant to Catholic teaching which are not true. . . . The only thing I know about her is that she has given the world to understand that Catholic teaching is divided on the subject of abortion. . . . As an officially approved teacher of the Catholic Church all I can judge is that what has been said about Catholic teaching is wrong. It's wrong.[39]

Although O'Connor did not say so in his original statement, "giving the world to understand that Catholic teaching is divided on the subject of abortion" referred to a letter that Ferraro had signed two years earlier. The letter, from a group called Catholics for a Free Choice, was sent to members of Congress inviting them to attend a briefing on abortion and the special problems associated with that issue for Catholic politicians. The offending section of the letter said that the "briefing will show us that the Catholic position on abortion is not monolithic and that there can be a range of personal and political responses to it."[40] Once it became clear that O'Connor had based his criticism on this letter, Ferraro pointed out that she had taken the term "monolithic" to refer to the views of individual Catholics rather than to Catholic doctrine. O'Connor was not mollified. "The teaching of the Catholic Church is monolithic on abortion," he declared, "and it is stated in a letter signed by Ferraro that it is not monolithic. Now that, to me, is a pretty basic disagreement."[41]

After several days of troublesome controversy, Ferraro finally answered the archbishop directly. "I believe the Catholic Church's position on abortion is monolithic," she conceded. "But I do believe that there are a lot of Catholics who do not share the view of the Catholic Church."[42] While she was on the subject, Ferraro also suggested that her dispute with O'Connor was part of a broader imposition of religion on the political process. "To me, my religion is a very personal and private matter," Ferraro said. "But when some people try to use religion for their partisan political advantage, then the freedom of all of us is at risk, and I feel compelled to respond."[43]

If Ferraro thought this speech would ease the pressure on her, she was mistaken. As it happened, she gave this speech in Scranton, Pennsylvania, where O'Connor had been bishop for a brief period between his tenure at the Military Ordinariate and his appointment to New York City. James Timlin, O'Connor's successor, chose to hold his first press conference as bishop of Scranton immediately following Ferraro's speech. Referring to the vice-presidential candidate throughout his remarks as "Geraldine," Timlin summarily rejected Ferraro's views on abortion. He termed her position that she would not "impose" her own moral opposition to abortion on others "absurd" and "not a rational position." To be acceptable to the Catholic Church, Bishop Timlin declared, Ferraro "would have to say that she is personally against abortion and would do all she can within the law to stop the slaughter of innocent human beings."[44]

The point of these actions by O'Connor and Timlin was to make clear that as Catholic bishops they would not accept Catholic politicians who acquiesced in legal abortion. The challenges to Cuomo and Ferraro were ways of asserting that, *The Challenge of Peace* and Bernardin's consistent ethic notwithstanding, abortion was still the first priority of a major segment of the American Catholic hierarchy. They were also, of course, ways of damaging the campaign of the Democratic candidate for vice-president of the United States. The bishops involved in these matters denied that they intended to harm Ferraro's candidacy. Archbishop Law, for example, argued that his statement on the primacy of abortion was neither a partisan declaration nor a particular slap at Ferraro. His words were "directed at all candidates and all voters," he said. Even when trying to assert his even-handedness, however, Law could not help but reveal the immediate target of his statement. "I think," he added, "Geraldine Ferraro is a candidate."[45]

O'Connor also claimed that he harbored "no ill will whatsoever towards Ferraro or Ferraro's candidacy."[46] In fact, throughout his entire interaction with Ferraro, he sought to leave the impression that he was merely clarifying misleading statements she had made about Catholic teaching. This interpretation obscured the aggressiveness of his initiative, however. The archbishop did not respond spontaneously to statements Ferraro had made during the campaign. Instead, he actively sought out a dispute with her over an ambiguous phrase in a two-year-old document, and then directed as much attention as possible to that dispute.

All of these bishops—Bernardin, Law, O'Connor, Timlin, and others— were responsible for their own actions, of course. They took those actions independently, and to a degree, they did so for reasons having to do with the internal politics of American Catholicism rather than the external politics of the presidential campaign. Nevertheless, each of these bishops was also responding to the specific political context in which he found himself. Bernardin's original formulation of the consistent ethic of life, for example, was an attempt to prevent politicians from using selected segments of the bishops' policy agenda for partisan purposes. It was, in part, a reaction to a particular set of political conditions and to a particular relationship between those conditions and the bishops' teachings. Law's characterization of abortion as the critical issue of the day and O'Connor's attacks on Ferraro were also reactions to political conditions and to the relationship between those conditions and the NCCB's agenda. They were attempts to counterbalance Bernardin's consistent ethic, to reinforce the identification of the Catholic hierarchy with the antiabortion cause, and to prevent prochoice Catholics from taking solace from their agreement with the bishops on issues other than abortion. In every case, individual bishops who participated in the 1984 campaign did so in reaction to the actual or anticipated use of Catholic teaching for partisan political purposes.

In terms of any effect that these bishops had on the election, we must begin with the realization that Reagan's victory in 1984 was extraordinarily sweeping. He won among men and women, among the old, young, and middle aged, and among the well educated and the poorly educated. He carried the East, West, North, and South. He swept all income groups except those making less than $12,500 per year, and all occupation groups except those without occupations. Only minorities and Jews rejected the Reagan juggernaut.[47] It would be silly, in light of this landslide, to claim that John O'Connor, or a group of Catholic bishops, or anyone really other than Reagan himself, had a very significant impact on that outcome.

It does not even seem fruitful to try to isolate the bishops' influence on the Catholic vote in 1984. Reagan received 55 percent of that vote, but I would not want to attribute that result to support he received from individual Catholic bishops.[48] One could just as easily argue from this 55 percent figure that a relatively high percentage of American Catholics stubbornly held onto their affiliation with the Democratic party in 1984. Regardless of how one interprets the result, however, it seems entirely safe to assume that Reagan would have been reelected in 1984 no matter what the bishops did or did not do.

This is not to argue, however, that the bishops had no effect on the campaign in 1984. In fact, their impact on less tangible aspects of the campaign was rather substantial, and that impact is likely to have several long-term implications. First of all, O'Connor and a few of his colleagues played an important role in the deflation of Ferraro's candidacy in the late summer of 1984. Ferraro's nomination for the vice-presidency was supposed to be the shot in the arm that Mondale needed to mount a serious challenge to Reagan. Coming out of the Democratic national convention, Ferraro was a fresh face, a historic figure, and a major source of positive news coverage for the Democratic ticket. In very short order, however, that image was tarnished by controversy concerning her husband's business dealings and her family's finances. And just as Ferraro was emerging from the crisis over her financial affairs, she became embroiled in a public argument with a major leader of her church over one of the most emotional and trying issues in American politics. The challenge from Archbishop O'Connor meant more controversy for Ferraro, more distractions, and more negative publicity at the time when she was most anxious to get out to begin campaigning against Reagan and Bush.

News reports at the time suggested that this succession of controversies in August and September was more than a coincidence. Jamie Gangel of NBC News reported, for example, that "high Republican sources" had told her that the Republican campaign was out to "get Ferraro without creating a backlash."[49] These sources told Gangel that Reagan's campaign director Ed Rollins and Reagan's political aide Lyn Nofziger had coordinated a strategy to make sure that "any advantage Ferraro brought to the ticket [was] destroyed" without dirtying the hands of the Republican ticket. As part of this strategy, "Reagan/Bush intermediaries contacted high church officials . . . to encourage their public criticism of Ferraro."[50]

If Gangel's story is accurate, then the pressure that several bishops put on Ferraro was even more partisan in origin and motivation than I have suggested. I have argued that this pressure was inescapably partisan in its implications. But Gangel claims, in so many words, that at least some of these bishops were involved in a secret plot with Republican officials to discredit a Democratic nominee for national office. Gangel's story, however, has never been verified elsewhere. Rollins explicitly denied at the time that he was involved in any such strategy, and Nofziger refused to comment on the story. Unfortunately, Gangel, though she stuck to her story, would not reveal her "high Republican sources" to me. We do not need evidence of a conspiracy or coordinated strategy, however, to conclude that Ferraro's dealings with O'Connor, Timlin, and other bishops damaged her candidacy. Whether instigated by Reagan's men or not, the controversy with the bishops, coming as it did on the heels of the financial inquiries, distracted Ferraro and kept her off balance in the critical early days of the campaign.

Rollins concluded at the time that, following the financial flap and the public dispute with O'Connor, Ferraro was "not the factor that she was a week after San Francisco."[51] Not surprisingly, Robert Beckel, Mondale's campaign manager, put the matter a bit more sharply. Responding to my question of whether O'Connor's criticism of Ferraro had any significant impact on the campaign, Beckel said, "Did it disrupt our campaign? Absolutely. Did it disrupt Ferraro's campaign specifically? Unquestionably. Did it cost us resources and time? Absolutely. Did it help the Republicans? No question."[52]

Beckel, with his understandably short-term perspective, did not mention another significant political effect of the bishops' actions. Ferraro was not only thrown off balance as the Democratic candidate for vice-president, she was also put on the defensive as the *Catholic* candidate for vice-president. In the summer of 1984 most political analysts considered Ferraro's Catholicism to be an asset to the Democratic ticket. A Catholic running mate would presumably help Mondale compete in the heavily Catholic Northeast and Midwest, areas of the country that were crucial to his slim electoral chances. And Ferraro's Catholicism and evident devotion to her religion would provide a powerful counterpoint to Reagan's public piety. As one op-ed writer in the *New York Times* put it, Ferraro and her faith could "neutralize Mr. Reagan's attempts to convince the American people that St. Peter was a registered Republican."[53]

This asset, of course, never paid a dividend. Instead, Ferraro ended up defending her Catholicism, not from the nativists who had hounded Al Smith, nor from the Protestant ministers who had challenged John Kennedy, but rather from her own archbishop. In the short term, the public row with O'Connor, and the great publicity that surrounded it, created an impression that Ferraro was out of step with her church. In the longer term, it conveyed the powerful message that Catholic politicians would pay a high price of controversy and rancor for taking a prochoice position on abortion. Given the current make-up of the party, it is a fact of political life that any Catholic hoping to be on a Democratic national ticket in the foreseeable future would have to be prochoice. And all other things being equal, the Democrats may not wish to court the extra controversy and negative publicity now associated with prochoice Catholic politicians. After the experience of 1984, everyone knows that for at least some Catholic bishops abortion is still the most important litmus test for judging a given candidate's fitness for political office.

Everyone also knows that the struggle within the American hierarchy is still very much alive. During the 1984 campaign a number of Catholic bishops debated the relative merits of a broad multiissue agenda and a more narrow abortion-centered approach. The debate was over the church's policy agenda and political priorities, but it was also over the right to determine what Catholics and the general American public would perceive that agenda and those priorities to be. And at this level of perception, those bishops in favor of sustaining a greater emphasis on abortion and of resisting the extension of the church's prolife political commitment to other issues, won a clear and portentous victory.

Recall the hierarchy's new position heading into the 1984 campaign. *The Challenge of Peace* had unmistakably communicated the bishops' pointed interest in politically charged issues other than abortion. It looked like the bishops' radical critique of American defense policy would prevent them from being associated with the Republican party and the rest of the conservative social agenda. That is why Charles Manatt had welcomed the pastoral letter, and why President Reagan had done everything he could to derail it. Both sides thought that the bishops might highlight the moral dimension of issues other than abortion, thereby implying that the Republican party did not hold a monopoly on religious values or Christian morality. During the actual campaign, however, a few articulate, committed bishops with access to the national media played a very different role. Rather than encouraging attention to issues on which the NCCB and Reagan disagreed, these bishops successfully focused the media's and the public's attention back onto abortion.

The *New York Times* of 6 September 1984, for example, contained a story about Mondale's plan to call the Soviet leadership on his "very first day as President" in order to energize the then moribund arms control process.[54] Given *The Challenge of Peace* and its ringing endorsement of more aggressive arms control, one would have thought that this was just the kind of proposal the American Catholic hierarchy would support. To be sure, many bishops undoubtedly did support Mondale's proposal. But the same edition of the *Times* that reported Mondale's resolve also quoted Bernard Law: "We are not saying you must vote for a particular candidate. But we are saying that when you make up your mind [abortion] is the critical issue."[55]

A few days later, Mondale said he planned to draw as much attention as possible to the issues on which the differences between himself and Reagan were most stark. "Mondale Plans to Focus on Issues Where He Says Reagan Is Weak" was the *New York Times* headline of a story that quoted Mondale's pollster saying that "war and peace stands out as an absolutely fundamental issue where the voters see Reagan as off in the wrong direction and Mondale headed in the right one."[56] Again, one would think that the bishops who had published *The Challenge of Peace* a year earlier would welcome attention to the issue of war and peace, and surely many of them did. However, the headline over the very next column on the *Times'* front page read: "O'Connor Critical of Ferraro's Views."[57]

In short, while the Democrats tried to emphasize and exploit the issue of war and peace, an issue with which the NCCB as a conference had closely associated itself, a few individual bishops courted and received publicity for their position that abortion should be the central issue of the campaign, at least for Catholics. The image that all this publicity created was precisely what Cardinal Bernardin had sought to avoid with his consistent ethic of life. Bernardin had constructed a theological and political framework in which other moral issues would be linked to abortion, but as it turned out his "fear that without such a framework or vision the bishops of this country would be severely pressured by those who wanted to push a particular issue with little or no concern for the rest" proved to be very well founded.

It was not, however, simply that the bishops were pressured by political forces. It was also that several influential and highly visible bishops simply did not accept the consistent ethic of life, or at least they did not accept its political implications. These bishops preferred to push abortion over all the other issues, and in 1984 they effectively counterbalanced, if they did not eclipse, those bishops who did not. As a matter of fact, some observers mistakenly took these relatively few bishops to be speaking and acting on behalf of the entire American Catholic hierarchy. Mary McGrory of the *Washington Post*, for example, indiscriminately charged that "*the hierarchy of the church is acting like an arm of the Reagan reelection committee.*"[58]

We have seen in this chapter just how inappropriate McGrory's inclusive and sweeping judgment was. By 1984 it was no longer appropriate to speak of "the bishops" as a collectivity in terms of the political process. The bishops did not act as a conference in 1984, nor did they speak through their conference's leadership. To the contrary, individual bishops and small groups of bishops acted on their own, often in direct conflict with each other, in order to press their own notions of how Catholic teaching should affect the American political process.

By 1984 a split had also developed among the bishops concerning the fundamental matter of the NCCB's proper role and authority. O'Connor, for example, believes that while national episcopal conferences serve very useful collegial and organizational purposes, their very limited authority should not be confused with the primary teaching authority that an individual bishop wields in his own diocese. Other bishops, while recognizing the centrality of individual episcopal authority, give greater credence to the need for national, collective initiatives on social and political matters. This dispute over the NCCB's proper role in the modern American church has far-reaching and absolutely fundamental implications for the future of the bishops' participation in the political process. For that reason, I will turn to this dispute in greater detail in the following chapter.

CHAPTER NINE

Economics, 1988, and the Future

THROUGHOUT THE PREVIOUS CHAPTERS I have argued that the relationship between religion and politics in the United States is a complex and double-edged one. Yes, religion has an effect on American politics. But the Catholic bishops' activities over the last two decades illustrate that the role of American churches and religious leaders is also a function of the structures and processes of the American political system. A substantial shift in governmental authority and policy initiative to Washington, D.C., for example, led the bishops to adopt a more collective, national approach to public policy matters. And the bishops' participation in several recent national election campaigns has been shaped, in part, by the platforms and electoral strategies of the political parties and their national candidates.

The bishops' positions on central political issues such as abortion and nuclear weaponry have occupied polar opposites of the American ideological spectrum and cut across the partisan cleavage of the American party system. As a result, politicians have sought to associate themselves with limited aspects of the bishops' agenda, and the bishops have engaged in a protracted debate among themselves over the way their political priorities should be developed and articulated. As I have indicated in earlier chapters, the relationship between the bishops' policy agenda and the emerging electoral strategies of the major political parties was the key determinant of the bishops' participation in the 1976, 1980, and 1984 campaigns.

In this chapter, I will look at how this relationship can also separate the bishops from the electoral process. I will apply the expressly political framework I have used throughout to the bishops' pastoral letter on the American economy and to their involvement in the national election of 1988. I will offer a brief textual analysis of the bishops' economic pastoral, assess the letter in terms of the Catholic hierarchy's "modern" political style, and evaluate the relationship between the bishops' economic views and the platforms of the Democratic and Republican parties in 1988. I will argue that in this case that relationship distanced the bishops from the political process and, to a significant degree, determined that the bishops would play a marginal role in the contest between George Bush and Michael Dukakis. The chapter will end with a series of comments concerning the role that the Catholic bishops are likely to play in the American political process in the years to come.

ECONOMIC JUSTICE FOR ALL

In *Economic Justice for All: Catholic Social Teaching and the U.S. Economy*, released in 1986, the American bishops applied the Catholic Church's general teachings on economic matters to the particular social and political circumstances of the contemporary United States.[1] "Economic life raises important social and moral questions for each of us and for society as a whole," the bishops wrote. "We are trying to look at economic life through the eyes of faith, applying traditional church teaching to the U.S. economy."[2] All of the moral precepts included in the letter, and all of the policy implications drawn from them, were based on a single fundamental principle: the dignity of all human persons as expressed by full participation in the life of the community. "We judge any economic system by what it does *for* and *to* people, and by how it permits all to *participate* in it," the bishops declared. "The economy should serve people, not the other way around."[3] In light of this principle, the bishops argued in favor of what they called a fundamental option for the poor: "As Christians we are called to respond to the needs of *all* our brothers and sisters, but those with the greatest needs require the greatest response."[4]

The bishops also held that a proper commitment to full participation for all Americans required the development of a set of inalienable economic rights to complement the political rights guaranteed by the U.S. Constitution:

> The economic challenge of today has many parallels with the political challenge that confronted the founders of our nation. . . . Their efforts were arduous and their goals imperfectly realized, but they launched an experiment in the protection of civil and political rights that has prospered through the efforts of those who came after them. *We believe the time has come for a similar experiment in securing economic rights: the creation of an order that guarantees the minimum conditions of human dignity in the economic sphere for every person.*[5]

The bishops were no more content to articulate moral principles in *Economic Justice for All* than they had been in *The Challenge of Peace*, their pastoral letter on nuclear weapons. To the contrary, the bishops applied those principles to the conditions of modern American life as they saw them, and they arrived at a lengthy series of very specific policy proposals. They called for a renewed commitment to full employment as the "foundation of a just economy"; they stressed the need for an "urgent" confrontation with the problem of poverty in America, particularly in light of the discriminatory and disenfranchising effects of poverty on American women and minorities; and they called for an evaluation and reform of the nation's food production system, as well as of America's commercial relations with the dependent economies of the developing world.[6] The bishops suggested that the government take a more active role in each of these main policy areas in order to protect the economic rights of all citizens and to foster "distributive justice."

The bishops' pastoral letter on the U.S. economy closely conformed to the model of their modern political activities that I developed in chapter 3. It was a collective statement released in the name of the entire National Conference of Catholic Bishops, and its subjects—unemployment, poverty, agriculture, and international economic relations—could not be reduced to the status of "Catholic issues." In *Economic Justice for All* the bishops said "the tragedy [of unemployment] is compounded by the unequal and unfair way it is distributed."[7] They also said the fact that "so many people are poor in a nation as rich as ours is a social and moral scandal that we cannot ignore."[8] In an earlier era, statements like these would have had a defensive and parochial tone, in that a substantial segment of the American poor were Catholic. By 1986, however, Catholics were, for the most part, middle-class, well-educated citizens. *Economic Justice for All* was not a defense of the economic interests of these Catholics; it was simply the Catholic hierarchy's contribution to a national debate on the future of American economic policy.

As such, *Economic Justice for All*, like many of the bishops' modern political activities, was decidedly national in focus. In passage after passage, the bishops directly addressed the responsibilities of the federal government:

· We recommend increased support for direct job creation programs targeted on the long term unemployed and those with special needs.[9]
· We believe Congress should raise the minimum wage.[10]
· National eligibility standards and a national minimum benefit level for public assistance programs should be established.[11]
· The current [farm] crisis calls for special measures to assist otherwise viable family farms that are threatened by bankruptcy or foreclosure.[12]

Economic statements made by the Catholic hierarchy in earlier eras, such as the *Program of Social Reconstruction* in 1919, had addressed the national aspects of the economy as well, of course. But in the modern era, given the New Deal of the 1930s and the Great Society of the 1960s, the economic responsibilities of the national government had grown enormously. *Economic Justice for All* was more national in focus than earlier efforts had been because the policy issues in question had become more national.

This national approach, of course, was facilitated by the strong episcopal conference the American bishops had established and by the powerful sense of collegiality they had adopted. The collective nature of the bishops' earlier economic pronouncements did not come close to that of *Economic Justice for All*. The *Program of Social Reconstruction*, for example, was a recapitulation of one of Monsignor John Ryan's personal speeches. It was written by Ryan alone, and it was adopted and released by the administrative board of the

National Catholic Welfare Council before many of the other American bishops had even read it, much less approved it.[13] In contrast, *Economic Justice for All* was the product of six years of highly public work by an ad hoc committee expressly acting in the name of the National Conference of Catholic Bishops as a whole. That committee, like the committee that produced *The Challenge of Peace*, held extensive hearings, circulated preliminary drafts, and invited comments and suggestions from a wide audience. Only after this process had run its course was the final document passed and released by a plenary session of the full NCCB.

Economic Justice for All and *The Challenge of Peace*, then, were direct results of the less parochial scope and more national focus that the bishops gradually adopted after the Second Vatican Council. The two letters also significantly expanded the American hierarchy's public policy agenda and put the bishops at odds with many of their allies on the question of abortion. However, the extent to which a given policy position or pastoral letter actually affects the bishops' involvement in the political process is not determined solely by the content of the position itself or even by how that position relates to others the bishops have taken in the past. It is also determined by the relationship the particular position or letter has to the central political debates and major partisan cleavages of its day. And on this point, the most significant in terms of the bishops' involvement in the political process, the two major pastoral letters of the mid-1980s differed markedly.

The Challenge of Peace was released at a time when the issues of arms control and nuclear weapons occupied an unusually prominent place on the national political agenda. It may be a dim memory now, but in 1983 and 1984 nuclear weapons and arms control were heated partisan issues that deeply divided the parties and their national candidates. The freeze movement was a potent political force, and the Democratic party emphasized arms control as a moral issue on which *they* spoke for the traditional values and aspirations of the American people. In fact, President Reagan's concern over the support the bishops' letter would give to the nuclear freeze and to the Democratic moral agenda led to his strenuous and public efforts to influence the final content of the letter.

As a result of its relationship to the political discussion of the time, *The Challenge of Peace* substantially altered the bishops' approach to the national political campaign in 1984. Faced with the fact that their agenda cut across the moral debate between the parties, the bishops split among themselves over how their agenda should be articulated and advanced. That split, which grew out of various bishops' responses to a series of political developments, rather than out of any internal inconsistency in the bishops' agenda itself, led to the active participation of several of those bishops in the presidential campaign.

In contrast, the pastoral letter on the U.S. economy has had, to this point at least, a marginal effect on the bishops' role in American politics. *Economic*

Justice for All, like *The Challenge of Peace*, was highly publicized at the time of its release and was the subject of a great deal of comment, both positive and negative. But compared with *The Challenge of Peace*, *Economic Justice for All* was much less directly related to the central political debates and cleavages of its time. Unlike their support for a "halt" in the deployment of nuclear weapons, for example, the bishops' calls for distributive justice and economic rights were not tied to a grass-roots political movement. In fact, the bishops' economic program of increased governmental intervention in the economy, a greater commitment of resources to social programs, and the development of a bill of economic rights rang decidedly hollow in the mid-1980s.

Economic issues sharply divided the parties, of course, but Democrats and Republicans argued over *how sharply* social programs should be cut, not *whether* they should be cut at all. In that context, the bishops' pastoral letter conjured up images that were very much out of political favor. Their economic principles were too "liberal," their approach to the economy too activist, and their proposed policies too likely to result in higher personal income taxes. These views may have been prophetic, or they may have just been out of step. But either way, they allowed Reagan to take a much more passive attitude to *Economic Justice for All* than he had taken to the bishops' letter on war and peace. This time the president said nothing publicly on the matter, and left the job of opposing the bishops' initiative to conservative Catholics like William Simon and Michael Novak.[14] More significantly, both George Bush and Michael Dukakis were also able to completely ignore the bishops' letter on the economy during their presidential campaign in 1988.

THE BISHOPS AND ELECTORAL POLITICS: 1988

The issues the bishops discussed in *Economic Justice for All*, like the distribution of national income or the demographics of American poverty, were on the margins of the political discussion in 1988. The major issues were competence, crime, experience, and patriotism, and the only real economic discussion, if you could call it that, concerned reading the candidates' lips on the subject of income taxes. As a result, the split within the NCCB over the hierarchy's political priorities that once again could have led various individual bishops to engage in overt political action, was far less pointed and far less politically significant than it had been four years earlier.

It did not have to be thus, of course. A more activist Democratic platform, and a more class-based Democratic electoral strategy would have breathed considerable political life into the bishops' letter. Less talk of competence, duty, and fiscal responsibility, and more of economic justice and redistribution of income would have drawn more attention to the bishops' pronouncements on these issues. Consider, for example, how easily the Democrats could have tied a class-based strategy to the following sections of the bishops' economic pastoral:

• Unemployment is a tragedy no matter whom it strikes, but the tragedy is compounded by the unequal way it is distributed in our society.[15]

• That so many people are poor in a nation as rich as ours is a social and moral scandal that we cannot ignore.[16]

• Defense Department expenditures in the United States are almost $300 billion per year. The rivalry and mutual fear between the superpowers diverts into projects that threaten death, minds and money that could better human life.[17]

Agreement between these sections of the letter and the Democratic platform would have once again sparked the central disagreement within the National Conference of Catholic Bishops. Those bishops who were particularly committed to the church's call for economic justice would have emphasized economic issues, and may have even responded favorably to the Democrats' approach to them. However, those bishops who were particularly committed to a more abortion-centered approach to public policy would have protested an explicit association of a prochoice political platform with Catholic social teaching. An association of the Democratic party with the bishops' economic policy proposals, in other words, would have led various bishops once again to articulate contradictory notions of how Catholic teaching should affect the American political discussion. Such an association might have also led some of these bishops to active participation in the national political campaign. The important point is that such a scenario would have been only partially the result of decisions made by Catholic bishops themselves. It also would have been the result of strategic political decisions made by the national Democratic party.

As it was, most American bishops approached 1988 with a certain degree of wariness, anxious to prove that they were not given to partisan political maneuvering. In fact, these anxieties, along with related fears that the partisan activities of church-affiliated prolife groups were jeopardizing the church's tax exemption, led the legal staff at the United States Catholic Conference to warn the bishops about the possible consequences of direct involvement in the 1988 election.[18]

"During an election campaign," read a message from the conference's lawyers to the bishops, "[tax] exempt organizations remain free to address issues of concern to them and their membership, even when such issues are relevant to the campaign. However, such discourse must focus on issues and not personalities."[19] Therefore, the message continued, individual bishops should refrain from participating in political rallies and from placing themselves in circumstances that might suggest they were officially identifying themselves with a particular candidate or party.

As for the hierarchy's collective policy agenda in 1988, the National Conference of Catholic Bishops once again put itself on record in support of "political responsibility" and a varied multiissue agenda. Revealing the strength of Bernardin's seamless garment within the NCCB, the bishops' administrative board declared that "we are convinced that a consistent ethic of life should be the moral framework from which we address all issues in the political arena."[20] During the presidential campaign, the leaders of the bishops' conference tried to avoid a repeat of the controversies of 1984. A few bishops did appear publicly with Bush during the campaign, and one, Archbishop Whealon of Hartford, publicly renounced his membership in the Democratic party to protest its position on abortion.[21] But on the whole, the Catholic bishops resolved to be less active politically in 1988 than they had been in 1984 or, for that matter, in 1976.

That said, however, the extent of the bishops' political activities was no more a simple matter of choice on the bishops' part in 1988 than it had been in those other years. Even had the bishops, collectively or individually, wanted to take a more active role in the 1988 campaign, they would have found political circumstances decidedly inhospitable to such a role. One of these circumstances, as I have already pointed out, was the Democratic decision not to pursue a political program and strategy based upon the class divisions in American society. Whatever its effect would have been on Democratic electoral fortunes in 1988, such an approach would have placed the bishops in a much more prominent political position. It would have drawn attention to the bishops' letter on the economy, reenergized the split over political priorities within the American hierarchy, and raised the possibility of direct political action by various individual bishops.

Another factor mitigating against an active role for the bishops in 1988 was the Democratic candidate's apparent appreciation for the tenuous and limited relationship between the positions taken by the Catholic hierarchy and the votes cast by Catholic citizens. In 1976, Jimmy Carter sought a cordial relationship with the bishops because he believed that a rift with them would deny him the Catholic votes he needed to rebuild the New Deal coalition. That belief led Carter to a series of public exchanges with Bernardin, and to an ill-advised insistence on a face-to-face meeting with the NCCB's executive committee.

Dukakis did not repeat Carter's mistake of creating a public forum in which a policy disagreement between the Democratic party and the Catholic Church could be transformed into a personal dispute between the Democratic candidate and the Catholic hierarchy. Dukakis knew that it was impossible to finesse the matter of abortion with the bishops. Just as importantly, he also knew, from Carter's experience in 1976, that his disagreement with the bishops on that issue was not a barrier to success with Catholic voters. Like Carter, Dukakis needed Catholic votes if he was going to rebuild the New Deal coalition. But unlike Carter, Dukakis did not seek those Catholic votes through a relationship with the Catholic hierarchy, and so he did not hand the bishops a public role in his presidential campaign.

The general tone of the campaign in 1988 also did not encourage the participation of the Catholic bishops, nor of other religious leaders for that matter.
In 1984 the bishops were looked upon as important moral and religious
spokesmen in a political campaign that was drenched in religious rhetoric.
That year, a debate between several bishops who favored a consistent ethic of
life and others who favored a more abortion-centered approach roughly paralleled a partisan dispute over the proper scope and character of religion's role
in the American political process. In 1988, religion played a relatively limited
role in the presidential campaign, despite the presence of the Reverend Jesse
Jackson and televangelist Pat Robertson in the nomination struggles of their
respective parties. Perhaps religious rhetoric suited George Bush less well
than it did Ronald Reagan. But whatever the reason, the more secular tone of
the campaign meant that the bishops' debate over their policy priorities was
less closely tied to the candidates' strategies and rhetoric. The bishops' internal disagreement was far from settled, but everyone from the presidential
candidates, to the national press, to the bishops themselves paid far less attention to it in 1988.

Moreover, abortion was less prominently featured in 1988 than it had been
in other recent elections. Bush and Dukakis disagreed over abortion, and each
sought to reap political benefits from his position on the issue. But in 1988
other symbolic social issues took centerstage. Bush and Republican strategists
used crime and patriotism to divide the Democratic coalition against itself,
and their strategy was remarkably successful. However, Willie Horton and the
pledge of allegiance were not symbols that invited responses from members of
the Catholic hierarchy.

The Democratic national ticket in 1988 also did not elicit direct responses
or challenges from Catholic bishops. Most American bishops prefer not to
address particular political candidates directly, especially since the controversy of 1976. John O'Connor, Bernard Law, and several others were able to
finesse this point in 1984, however, because the candidate they personally
challenged was a Catholic. O'Connor, for one, claimed that he was challenging only Geraldine Ferraro's characterization of Catholic teaching on abortion
rather than her own personal position on the issue, or her candidacy in general. Regardless of the merits of such an argument, nothing like it could have
been made in 1988. As non-Catholics, Michael Dukakis and Lloyd Bentsen
never characterized Catholic "teachings" or Catholic "positions." Therefore,
unlike Ferraro, they were never personally and directly challenged on the
matter by members of the Catholic hierarchy.

It is difficult to explain a nonevent, of course, and the National Conference
of Catholic Bishops and several of its most prominent members did decide to
back off a bit from the political fray in 1988. Nevertheless, the bishops' relatively limited involvement in the Bush–Dukakis contest must also be attrib-
uted to the fact that the most pointed policy debates between the candidates

and the most significant electoral strategies adopted by the parties involved neither the Catholic bishops nor the most prominent items on the bishops' policy agenda.

Imagine if Jesse Jackson had succeeded in having the Democratic platform emphasize distributive justice and economic rights; or if the Republican party had run a more straightforwardly religious campaign, thereby sparking another debate over the role of religion in American politics; or if Mario Cuomo or another prochoice Catholic had gained a place on the Democratic national ticket; or if Bush had placed abortion, rather than crime and patriotism, at the center of his social issues agenda. Any one or more of these conditions would have substantially altered both the tenor of the 1988 campaign and the Catholic hierarchy's role in it. However, not a single one of them would have been the result of actions or decisions taken by the bishops themselves. Rather, they would have been the result of political decisions associated with the efforts of one or both parties to construct an enduring electoral majority.

LOOKING TO THE FUTURE

The bishops were active participants in the national campaigns of 1976 and 1984, but not of 1988, because of the nature of the competition between the political parties. In the same way, the bishops' political role in the future will be shaped to a large extent by developments in the agenda of American politics and in the alignment of the American party system. I argued in chapter 3, for example, that a shift in the locus of American public policy to Washington D.C., along with a change in the social status of American Catholicism, devalued the bishops' traditional political role of defending the interests of Catholics in local politics. I also argued that a new, more outward-looking mission, and a new, more cohesive national conference, allowed the bishops to focus on a wider range of issues and to channel their political energies into national, collective activities. This more national, less parochial style is not necessarily a permanent feature of the bishops' approach to politics, however. As they did in the past, changing political circumstances and evolving ecclesiastical structures could once again substantially alter the bishops' participation in the political process.

A change in the locus of initiative and jurisdiction on a few crucial policy issues, for example, could deeply influence the bishops' political activities. Neofederalism and reassertion of local prerogatives in areas such as education, social welfare, and sexual morality would require more local intervention by individual bishops and less collective coordination by the National Conference of Catholic Bishops. We are already seeing such a shift on the issue of abortion. As a result of the Supreme Court's decision in 1989 to uphold the restrictive provisions of Missouri's abortion law, abortion has once again become a highly divisive issue at the state level of politics.[22] To be sure, the bishops' national conference continues to oppose abortion and support local efforts to ban it. But a good deal of attention has already shifted to individual bishops and state conferences of bishops and their relationships with local state legislators. Just as Roe v. Wade and the nationalization of abortion law in 1973 drew the bishops more deeply into national politics in the 1970s and 1980s, the court's retreat from Roe v. Wade will draw more of the bishops' energy and resources back to local political struggles in the 1990s.[23]

The nature of the American Catholic population, and of its relationship to the hierarchy, may also be entering an era of substantial change. In what I termed the traditional era, individual bishops participated in local politics in order to defend the political, social, and economic interests of a persecuted immigrant people. In the modern era, this defense was no longer needed as Catholics became one of the most prosperous and well-educated segments of the American population. Today, however, many American Catholics are once again recent immigrants, this time from the nations of Latin America.[24] These newcomers, faced with many of the same economic, social, and educational barriers that European Catholics faced upon their arrival in the United States years ago, may turn to their bishops and priests for leadership, representation, and protection. A promising subject for future research, in fact, is the relationships between individual bishops and the local political leaders of these new Catholic immigrants. It will be especially interesting to see to what extent these relationships, and the political activities that grow from them, eclipse the National Conference of Catholic Bishops and its national agenda and activities.

As I indicated at the end of chapter 8, a debate has already erupted within the American hierarchy on the question of the proper role and authority of the National Conference of Catholic Bishops. Some American bishops continue to emphasize the importance of collective activities, but others have begun to question the conference's right to articulate the church's agenda and to formulate the hierarchy's collective approach to the political process. As a result of this very fundamental dispute, the collective identity of the American Catholic hierarchy is today quite a bit stronger when it comes to articulating individual policy positions than it is when it comes to ordering the priority of those positions at politically sensitive times.

This is so because the national conference, either through its elected leadership or through a vote of a majority of its members, is simply not in a position to control the statements and actions of individual bishops. The NCCB may set guidelines or articulate a collective agenda, but the local bishops retain primary authority over the teaching of Catholic doctrine and practice in their own dioceses. Individual bishops are entirely free, in other words, to articulate for themselves how they think Catholic teaching should be applied to particular political circumstances. They do not have to square their own interpretations or actions with those of other individual bishops or with those of their national episcopal conference. Church officials, by the way, harbor no illusions on this point. Monsignor Daniel Hoye, general secretary of the United States Catholic Conference, remarked in an interview with me that "the national conference cannot put a muzzle on individual bishops. It is," he said, "just not part of the nature of the beast."[25]

More importantly, it has become apparent over the last several years that a powerful segment of the American hierarchy is anxious to limit the role of that beast, to reassert the preeminent authority of individual local bishops.[26] And it has also become apparent that this goal is shared by powerful forces in the Vatican as well. The American hierarchy established the National Conference of Catholic Bishops in response to provisions of the Second Vatican Council's *Decree on the Bishops' Pastoral Office in the Church*. The council, as I pointed out in chapter 3, judged that many of the functions of the modern hierarchy could be carried out more efficiently and effectively if performed through the auspices of national and regional bodies. Recently, however, the Vatican has suggested that these episcopal conferences have overstepped their bounds and exaggerated their own teaching authority at the expense of the local bishops' prerogatives.

Theological and Juridical Status of Episcopal Conferences, a treatise on this important matter, was sent by the Vatican to all episcopal conferences for their consideration and comment in 1987.[27] Decidedly ambivalent, if not negative, in tone, this document questioned the authentic collegiality of episcopal conferences, cast doubt on the theological foundations of their development, and challenged the notion that they can exercise legitimate teaching authority. A series of questions that appeared at the end of the statement revealed the Vatican's intention to lower the profile of episcopal conferences like the NCCB, particularly in the eyes of the Catholic laity:

> As episcopal conferences are not organs of magisterium [teaching authority] in the strict sense, how can it be made clearer to the faithful that the positions taken by them in doctrinal matters must be interpreted in the light of doctrine already set forth by the Roman pontiff and the episcopal college united with him?
>
> Do the faithful see the distinction between the documents which come from the pope, from the episcopal college, and from their bishops and those which come from the episcopal conference and from its organs?[28]

The officers of the National Conference of Catholic Bishops took this document to be a serious challenge and threat to the vitality and viability of their episcopal conference. As a result, they authorized a prestigious committee of the NCCB's past presidents to frame a response to the Vatican's initiative. The committee's response, released in late 1988, was sharply critical. "While we recognize the work that has gone into it," the committee said of the Vatican's statement, "we do not believe that the working document is suitable as a basis for discussion, and we believe that it should be replaced with another draft."[29] Given the steadfastly formal and respectful lexicon of communications between bishops and the Vatican, the American response was a remarkably dismissive rejection.

It is too early to tell what the outcome will be of this discussion concerning national and regional episcopal conferences. However, it is not too early to say that the outcome of this discussion will have far-reaching effects on the political activities of the American Catholic hierarchy. Changes in the content of the national political agenda may result in shifts in the scope and focus of the bishops' political energies. But if the bishops hope to retain a role in national debates on a range of issues from Central America and nuclear weaponry, to poverty, unemployment, and for now at least abortion, they are going to have to do so, in large part, at the national level through their national conference. The bishops' ability to act collectively and nationally could be hindered substantially by efforts based here and in Rome to limit the NCCB's role and discredit its authority.

Throughout this book, I have argued that the bishops' political activities, particularly in terms of their participation in the national electoral process, have been shaped by the renewed political competition that followed the breakdown of the Democratic New Deal coalition in the 1960s. Paying particular attention to a number of recent presidential campaigns, I maintained that political strategies designed to appeal to Catholic voters or to enhance the salience of moral and religious issues have placed the bishops at the center of an evolving American party system. The bishops' future political role, of course, will be determined in part by the collective statements of the National Conference of Bishops and by the specific activities of individual bishops. However, as in the past, it will also be determined by the terms of the debate between the parties, and by the particular electoral strategies pursued by Republican and Democratic candidates for national office.

The post–New Deal party system remains in flux. The Republican party has established itself as the majority party in presidential politics, but it has been unable to effect a true partisan realignment of the national electorate as a whole. The Democratic party retains a formidable edge in terms of partisan affiliation, and a virtually unassailable majority in the House of Representatives. For the foreseeable future, therefore, both parties will continue to search for programs and strategies that can attract and hold a broad-based electoral majority. Those programs and strategies, in turn, will continue to shape the nature and the significance of the American Catholic hierarchy's participation in the electoral process.

Since 1968 the "social issue" has been the Republican party's key tool in an effort to divide the Democratic coalition against itself. The specific character of the issue has changed from campaign to campaign, but Republicans have argued consistently that the national leadership of the Democratic party is out of step with "the silent majority," or with "mainstream America," or with "traditional values." At the presidential level, at least, these efforts have been quite successful. Thanks in part to the support of social conservatives, Republican presidential candidates have dominated the South and made significant advances with Northern ethnic voters. It is safe to assume not only that the Republicans will continue to push and exploit the social issues at the presidential level, but also that they will apply that strategy to other political levels as well. Republicans will try to convince socially conservative Democrats to do more than vote for Republican presidential candidates; they will try to convince them actually to become Republicans.

In terms of the Catholic bishops' political activities, the important thing to watch in this regard will be the position that abortion holds on the national social agenda. As I argued in chapter 4, the Republican party's adoption of the antiabortion cause in the 1970s had far-reaching effects on the bishops' involvement in American politics. The Republican decision, and the partisan dispute over abortion it spawned, bestowed partisan implications on the bishops' antiabortion activities, drew the bishops into the national political process, and in time led several individual members of the hierarchy to call for renewed emphasis on other "prolife" issues. At the moment, there are few matters in American politics less certain than the role abortion will play in partisan politics over the next several years. Latent prochoice energies have been released by the Supreme Court's retreat from Roe v. Wade, and those energies may prove troublesome for prolife political candidates. The Republicans used abortion to split the Democratic party in the 1970s, but they are now learning that the issue can cut across their own coalition as well.

The bishops have responded in two ways to these changes in the political status of abortion. In April 1990, the bishops' committee for prolife activities announced that it intended to engage a polling firm and a public relations firm for the purpose of devising more effective means of publicizing and popularizing opposition to abortion.[30] The Catholic hierarchy, in other words, has rededicated itself to applying the church's institutional resources to the task of outlawing abortion. These resources, as always, are substantial, and the bishops may yet be able to revitalize the prolife movement that they played such an important role in launching in the first place.

The bishops have also increased their attention to, and pressure on, Catholic candidates and officeholders who take a prochoice position on abortion. At its annual meeting in November 1989, the National Conference of Catholic Bishops declared that "no Catholic can responsibly take a 'pro-choice' stand when the 'choice' in question involves abortion."[31] Some members of the conference have applied this dictum with considerable vigor. Bishop Leo T. Maher of San Diego, for example, barred prochoice Assemblywoman Lucy Kilea from communion because, in his words, Kilea had placed herself in "complete contradiction to the moral teachings of the Catholic Church."[32] In another case, Bishop Austin Vaughan of Orange County, New York, warned Governor Mario Cuomo that he was in "serious risk of going to hell" because of his views on abortion.[33]

A number of individual bishops have apparently decided to fight a kind of rearguard action to make it more difficult for Catholic candidates to either deemphasize abortion or rationalize support of it. But these actions by individual bishops are politically significant, in partisan terms, only if the parties or the given set of candidates disagree on abortion. If the Republican party, in the face of internal pressure, moves away from its straightforwardly antichoice position, however, then the bishops' pressures on prochoice Catholic candidates will be much less noteworthy. It so happens, for example, that Kilea is a Democrat and her political opponent in 1989 was a prolife Republican. But what if a prochoice Catholic were to run against another prochoice candidate? It is hard to see what political meaning the bishops' pressure would have in such a case, unless it was to discourage the nomination of Catholic candidates in the first place.

Over the last several years, of course, many bishops have sought to blunt the partisan edge of the bishops' stand on abortion by including it in a broader agenda, a consistent ethic of life that cuts across the partisan divisions of American politics. But this effort, particularly as it relates to the bishops' positions on nuclear weapons and deterrence, has been losing its own political edge over the last few years. Democrats and Republicans have moved toward a rough bipartisan agreement on the direction that arms control and superpower relations should take in the near future. To be sure, very real disagreements over specific weapons systems and particular provisions of one treaty or another do persist, both between the parties and between various factions within the parties. But these disagreements cannot compare with the deep partisan split over the very desirability of arms control that existed during Reagan's first administration.

It was that split, and the closely related notion that nuclear weapons and arms control could serve as the centerpiece of an alternative moral policy agenda for the Democratic party, that made *The Challenge of Peace* a politically significant document in the first place. The bishops' fundamental doubts regarding the morality of nuclear deterrence, after all, were never relevant to the American political debate; no serious candidate for national political office could express only "strictly conditioned moral acceptance" of nuclear deterrence, the centerpiece of American defense policy for the last forty years. What was relevant, however, was the bishops' strongly phrased insistence on more aggressive arms control, an insistence that placed the bishops in opposition to their political allies on abortion and in support of a morally based policy position of the Democratic party. If there is less partisan conflict concerning arms control in the future, then *The Challenge of Peace*, or any restatement of the principles and policy prescriptions it contained, will receive less attention, have less political impact, and result in a less urgent debate among the bishops over their public policy priorities. This will not be because the bishops will have changed their position on nuclear weapons, but rather because the particular political conditions in which that position was originally articulated will no longer pertain.

Political developments and conditions will determine the future status and impact of the bishops' pastoral letter on the economy as well. In this case, the key factor will be the electoral strategy adopted by the Democratic party. The Democrats are clearly the minority party in presidential politics, having lost every presidential election since 1964, save the post-Watergate Republican debacle in 1976. As a result, the Democrats have constantly debated and struggled among themselves over the question of which political strategies will be most likely to reestablish lasting control of the White House.

In 1972, George McGovern set out to build a so-called New Politics coalition of peace activists, minorities, women, and liberal professionals; he lost forty-nine states. In 1976, Jimmy Carter faced a scandal-ridden Republican party headed by a presidential candidate who had recently pardoned Richard Nixon. Given the weakness of the opposition, Carter was able to regain traditional Democratic constituencies such as the South and organized labor, bring them together with the new constituencies of McGovern's campaign, and resurrect a reasonable facsimile of the old New Deal coalition. That success was short-lived, however, and Carter's coalition flew apart in 1980, and remained apart in 1984 and 1988.

Nevertheless, Carter in 1980, Mondale in 1984 (insofar as that doomed candidacy had a strategy), and Dukakis in 1988 all tried to recreate the success of 1976 under far less advantageous conditions. They all appealed, that is, to a hybrid coalition made up of traditional constituencies of the New Deal party and enduring elements of the New Politics movement. They pined after the South, or at least parts of it; they actively courted organized labor and urban ethnics of the Midwest and Northeast; and they tied themselves to the women's movement, the environmental movement, the gay rights movement, and a variety of other so-called special interest groups. In the process, of course, they failed to repair the racial and class-based fissures that destroyed the New Deal coalition in the first place, and they suffered three decisive and devastating defeats at the polls.

In 1984 and 1988, Jesse Jackson and his supporters proposed an alternative electoral strategy. They argued that the way to elect Democratic presidents was to expand the base of the Democratic party for the purpose of constructing a new political coalition of the poor, minorities, working-class whites, and liberal activists. This strategy, they maintained, would allow the Democrats to compete with the Republicans in both the North and the South without having to accommodate social conservatives who had abandoned the party in 1972 and 1980. Such an electoral appeal, of course, would require a revamped platform committing the Democratic party to unequivocal support for minority rights and affirmative action, to unhesitating endorsement of the activist liberal agenda, and to a relatively radical reordering of American economic priorities.

This strategic debate within the Democratic party will dominate the nomination process again in 1992, and perhaps for years to come. It grows out of fundamental tensions within the fractious Democratic coalition, and it cannot be willed away. More importantly for our purposes, this debate will also have a powerful impact on the Catholic bishops and their political activities. The outcome of this debate will decide the future of the Democratic party's economic platform, and that platform, in turn, will decide the political status of the bishops' pastoral letter on the economy.

I expect that the Democrats will continue for a time with the failed political strategies of the past. A switch to Jackson's approach would involve too much change, too many racial overtones, in short too many social and political threats to the forces that have dominated the Democratic party for decades. Besides, it is far from clear that the alternative strategy would be any more successful than Carter's, Mondale's, or Dukakis's have been. I also expect, therefore, that *Economic Justice for All* will remain in the political background. Neither a Democratic party unwilling to emphasize the political consequences of class divisions, nor a Republican party unwilling to admit that such divisions even exist, is likely to associate itself with the bishops' egalitarian principles and redistributive policy prescriptions. Absent such an explicit political association, the letter will attract relatively little attention and result in relatively little political action by either the NCCB's leadership or other individual bishops.

Of course, out of either political necessity or plain exasperation, the Democrats might adopt a substantially different political strategy and a significantly more activist economic platform. In that case, the Democratic party would derive valuable moral support and even religious sanction from the Catholic hierarchy's ringing call for distributive justice and economic rights. An association between the bishops' pastoral letter and the Democratic economic platform would also substantially reorient the relationship between the bishops' agenda and the American political process. That new relationship would almost certainly reenergize the dispute within the bishops' conference and set the stage for direct political action by various individual bishops.

I readily acknowledge the speculative nature of these observations. My intention is not to predict confidently either the future course of American party politics or the future participation of the Catholic hierarchy in the American political process. It is rather to indicate that party politics and the evolution of the national partisan alignment will continue to have a substantial influence on the Catholic bishops. It is to argue once again that the bishops' political activities will continue to be shaped by political factors and developments over which the bishops have no control. The content of the bishops' pastoral letters on nuclear weapons and the economy will not change, nor will their commitment to the antiabortion cause. What may well change, however, and what will determine the extent to which these policy positions involve the bishops in the electoral process, are the platforms and strategies of two political parties that are seeking to establish control of a shifting and uncertain American party system.

In the coming years, the American bishops and the Vatican will determine the status and authority of the National Conference of Catholic Bishops. But national and local political developments will determine whether the NCCB will be a central element of the bishops' political activities. Similarly, the American bishops will continue to develop their policy positions on the basis of the Second Vatican Council's mandate to apply the general principles of Catholic teaching to their particular national context. But the electoral strategies pursued by the major political parties and their candidates will determine the extent to which, and the ways in which, those positions will involve the bishops in the political process. The electoral importance of Catholic voters, the political salience of moral/religious issues, and the relative stability of the national partisan alignment will all affect the future activities of the American Catholic hierarchy. That is the way that religion and politics have mixed in the past, and that is the way that they will continue to do so in the future.

Before I end, I want to address one final matter, namely the unique position that abortion occupies on the Catholic hierarchy's public policy agenda. Abortion is not simply one issue among many for the bishops. It is rather the bedrock, non-negotiable starting point from which the rest of their agenda has developed. The bishops' positions on other issues have led to political action and political controversy but abortion, throughout the period I have examined, has been a consistently central feature of the Catholic hierarchy's participation in American politics.

There are several reasons for the special status of abortion. The first of these has to do with the personal styles of the individual bishops involved. Those bishops committed to the abortion-centered approach to public policy, whether they be Bernardin in 1976, Medeiros in 1980, O'Connor in 1984, or Whealon in 1988, have simply been more willing to relate their agenda directly to the political process than have the advocates of the consistent ethic of life. One reason for this, I suspect, is that Bernardin, the consistent ethic's leading spokesman, was burned in his one direct contact with partisan politics in 1976. Bernardin is now firmly committed to avoiding direct participation in the political debate, even if that commitment leaves the road clear for other bishops to emphasize the political implications of the bishops' opposition to abortion.

Another reason that the abortion-centered approach has been related more directly to politics than has the consistent ethic of life is that there is an absolute consensus among the American bishops that abortion is evil and must be morally and politically resisted. Bishops can be found who do not agree with all of the conclusions and implications of *The Challenge of Peace* or *Economic Justice for All*. But you will not find, either now or in the foreseeable future, a bishop who is not strongly opposed to abortion. Cardinal Bernardin, for example, may be the leading spokesman for the broad, *nonabortion-centered* approach to the bishops' policy agenda, but he was also the chairman of the bishops' committee for prolife activities for many years. Consider how Bernardin phrased his views on abortion in an interview with me: "In no way have I ever backed off from a very aggressive stance regarding abortion, or to put it more positively the need for legal protection of the unborn. I've always stood up and been counted on that. . . . I've always taken a very prolife stance in regard to that."[34]

Bernardin not only opposes abortion, he also seems anxious to stress that his formulation of the consistent ethic of life has not diminished his fervent devotion to his church's antiabortion cause. In light of the desire of some bishops to stress abortion above all other issues, and the equally strong desire of those who favor a broader agenda to defend their antiabortion credentials, it is little wonder that abortion receives the greatest amount of the bishops' collective attention.[35]

The American hierarchy's consensus on abortion, of course, is a function of the strong antiabortion position held by the popes and the universal Catholic Church. Abortion, unlike many other public policy issues, is not a matter on which individual episcopal conferences are free to apply church doctrine to their own political and social circumstances. The official Catholic Church is opposed to all direct abortions, plain and simple, and it is up to all Catholic bishops to teach, advocate, and further that position. In fact, the Vatican has even made clear the political implications of this position. A document titled *Vatican Declaration on Abortion* decreed in 1974:

> A Christian can never conform to a law which is in itself immoral, and such is the case of a law which would admit in principle the licitness of abortion. *Nor can a Christian take part in a propaganda campaign in favor of such a law, or vote for it*. Moreover, he may not collaborate in its application.[36]

Taken on face value, this statement rather clearly prohibits Catholic office-holders from supporting legal abortion. Moreover, it does not stretch its implications too far to suggest that it comes very close to prohibiting Catholic voters from voting for prochoice political candidates as well. The document can be interpreted, in other words, as support from the Vatican for an effort on the part of Catholic bishops to challenge prochoice Catholic politicians and to encourage Catholic voters to support antiabortion candidates. On the other hand, there is not, nor is there likely to be in the future, a comparably specific and demanding Vatican policy on the *political* implications of nuclear weaponry, social welfare, capital punishment, or any other issue of dispute between American political parties and candidates. As a result, American bishops who are especially concerned about abortion are freer to relate that concern directly to the political process and to votes than are bishops who are especially concerned about nuclear war, capital punishment, or a consistent prolife agenda.

But here again, as always, it is not enough simply to look at the bishops and the level of their commitments. Abortion has often been the centerpiece of the bishops' political activities not only because of the reasons just cited, but also because of the particular way their position on that issue has intersected with the political process. The bishops' position on abortion is clearer and more politically accessible than their positions on other issues. "Right-to-life" has been a political rallying cry and a powerful tool of partisan mobilization. And since 1976, the national Republican party has officially and formally agreed with the bishops that Roe v. Wade was decided wrongly and should be either overturned by constitutional amendment or reversed by subsequent judicial action. Some faction or other of the party may disagree with the bishops on this or that specific application of the antiabortion principle. But the principle itself is crystal clear and the agreement based on it, at least through 1990, has been direct and substantial.

On the other hand, the bishops' political alliances on issues like nuclear weapons and the economy have been far less direct. Mondale, for example, agreed with the bishops in 1984 on the matter of a bilateral nuclear freeze. But he did not—and given the political realities of the day could not—run for president from a platform that offered only "strictly conditioned moral acceptance" of the American nuclear deterrent. Similarly, Dukakis agreed with the bishops in 1988 that the economic priorities established under President Reagan had exacerbated the divisions and injustices of the American economic system. But Dukakis did not advocate, as the bishops did, a radical redistribution of national income or a sweeping reintroduction of the federal government into the economic process. This is not to suggest that the general moral and political *direction* of the bishops' policy positions have not paralleled those of the Democratic party. In some cases they have. However, it is to suggest that these agreements between the Catholic hierarchy and the Democratic party have been agreements of moral tone and inference rather than of specific policy or law.

The same cannot be said of the bishops' agreement with politicians or political interest groups who oppose abortion, of course. The bishops have been deeply committed to restricting legal abortion in the United States, and that commitment has been directly related to a clear, durable, and highly partisan dispute. As a result of both that commitment and that relationship, political strategies that have called attention to abortion and to the Catholic Church's opposition to it have involved the bishops more directly in the political process than have strategies that emphasized other issues on the bishops' collective agenda. As with all aspects of the bishops' political activities, in other words, the terms of the partisan debate and the nature of the parties' electoral strategies have played an important role in establishing abortion as the central element of the Catholic hierarchy's participation in contemporary American politics.

Notes

Chapter One

1. V. O. Key, "A Theory of Critical Elections," *Journal of Politics* 17 (1955): 4.

2. For a discussion of the Catholic vote at the national level, see George Gallup, Jr., and Jim Castelli, *The American Catholic People: Their Beliefs, Practices, and Values* (New York: Doubleday, 1987), pp. 126–27.

3. This lack of understanding is not limited to politicians. See Andrew M. Greeley, *The Catholic Myth: The Behavior and Beliefs of American Catholics* (New York: Charles Scribner's Sons, 1990).

4. Robert Beckel, interview with author, 14 Dec. 1987.

5. For these figures, as well as a wealth of other data concerning religion in the United States, see *The Gallup Report*, May 1985 and July 1985.

6. See, in particular, Robert Booth Fowler, *Religion and Politics in America* (Metuchen, N.J.: Theological Library Association and Scarecrow, 1985); A. James Reichley, *Religion in American Public Life* (Washington, D.C.: Brookings Institution, 1985); and Kenneth D. Wald, *Religion and Politics in the United States* (New York: St. Martin's, 1987). Eric Hanson restricted himself to Catholicism, but from a global rather than American perspective. See Eric O. Hanson, *The Catholic Church in World Politics* (Princeton: Princeton University Press, 1987).

7. Mary T. Hanna, *Catholics and American Politics* (Cambridge: Harvard University Press, 1979). More recently, Hanna has narrowed her focus to the Catholic hierarchy itself. See, for example, Mary T. Hanna, "Bishops as Political Leaders," in Charles Dunn, ed., *Religion in American Politics* (Washington, D.C.: Congressional Quarterly, 1988), pp. 75–86; and Mary T. Hanna, "From Civil Religion to Prophetic Church: The Bishops and the Bomb," in Charles Dunn, ed. *American Political Theology* (New York: Praeger, 1984), pp. 144–54.

8. J. Brian Benestad, *The Pursuit of a Just Social Order: Policy Statements of the U.S. Catholic Bishops, 1966–1980* (Washington, D.C.: Ethics and Public Policy Center, 1982).

9. Walter Dean Burnham, *Critical Elections and the Mainsprings of American Politics* (New York: W. W. Norton, 1970), p. 10.

10. James L. Sundquist, *Dynamics of the Party System: Alignment and Realignment of Political Parties in the United States* (Washington, D.C.: Brookings Institution, 1983).

11. John E. Chubb and Paul E. Peterson, "Realignment and Institutionalization," in John E. Chubb and Paul E. Peterson, eds., *The New Direction in American Politics* (Washington, D.C.: Brookings Institution, 1985), p. 3.

12. A similar argument was made in terms of racial issues in Edward G. Carmines and James A. Stimson, *Issue Evolution: Race and the Transformation of American Politics* (Princeton: Princeton University Press, 1989).

Chapter Two

1. Henry J. Browne, "Catholicism in the United States," in James Ward Smith and A. Leland Jamison, eds., *The Shaping of American Religion* (Princeton: Princeton University Press, 1961), p. 78.

2. James Hennesey, S.J., *American Catholics: A History of the Roman Catholic Community in the United States* (New York: Oxford University Press, 1981), p. 65.

3. See Annabelle M. Melville, *John Carroll of Baltimore: Founder of the American Catholic Hierarchy* (New York: Charles Scribner's Sons, 1955), pp. 203–13.

4. Ibid., pp. 199–200.

5. Browne, "Catholicism in the United States," p. 78.

6. Melville, *John Carroll of Baltimore*, p. 286.

7. For Carroll's views before the war, see ibid., p. 273. For his actions after the war began, see Thomas O'Brien Hanley, S.J., ed., *The John Carroll Papers, 1807–1815* (Notre Dame: University of Notre Dame Press, 1976), 3: 192–95.

8. Ray Allen Billington, *The Protestant Crusade 1800–1860: A Study of the Origins of American Nativism* (New York: Rinehart, 1938), p. 39.

9. Peter Guilday, *The Life and Times of John England, First Bishop of Charleston*, 2 vols. (New York: America, 1927), 1: vii–viii.

10. Ibid., 1: 455.

11. Ibid., 2: 117.

12. *Pastoral Letter to the Laity*, in Hugh J. Nolan, ed., *Pastoral Letters of the United States Catholic Bishops*, 4 vols. (Washington, D.C.: United States Catholic Conference, 1984), 1: 41.

13. Quoted in Guilday, *Life and Times of John England*, 2: 221.

14. *Pastoral Letter of 1837*, in Nolan, *Pastoral Letters*, 1: 82.

15. Ibid., 1: 90.

16. Ibid., 1: 133.

17. See Billington, *Protestant Crusade*, pp. 143–55.

18. Hugh J. Nolan, *The Most Reverend Francis Patrick Kenrick, Third Bishop of Philadelphia 1830–1851* (Washington, D.C.: Catholic University of America Press, 1948), p. 320.

19. Richard Shaw, *Dagger John: The Unquiet Life and Times of Archbishop John Hughes of New York* (New York: Paulist, 1977), p. 197.

20. John Tracy Ellis, *American Catholicism* (Chicago: University of Chicago Press, 1969), p. 66.

21. Ibid., p. 90.

22. Dorothy Dohen, *Nationalism and American Catholicism* (New York: Sheed and Ward, 1967), p. 140.

23. See Hennesey, *American Catholics*, pp. 151–52.

24. Browne, "Catholicism in the United States," p. 78.

25. For a book-length treatment of the Knights of Labor, see Henry J. Browne, *The Catholic Church and the Knights of Labor* (Washington, D.C.: Catholic University of America Press, 1949).

26. John Tracy Ellis, *The Life of James Cardinal Gibbons, Archbishop of Baltimore 1834–1921*, 2 vols. (Milwaukee: Bruce, 1952), 4: 519.

and the Bishops' Program of 1919 (Washington, D.C.: Catholic University of America Press, 1986), p. 53.

57. Ibid., p. 88.

58. See James M. O'Toole, "Prelates and Politicos: Catholics and Politics in Massachusetts, 1900–1970," in James M. O'Toole and Robert E. Sullivan, eds., *Catholic Boston: Studies in Religion and Community, 1870–1970* (Boston: Archdiocese of Boston, 1985), pp. 27–31.

59. McAvoy, *History of the Catholic Church*, p. 403.

60. McKeown, "War and Welfare," p. 111.

61. McAvoy, *History of the Catholic Church*, p. 388.

62. Hennesey, *American Catholics*, p. 235.

63. *Statement on Unemployment* and *Statement on Economic Rights*, in Nolan, *Pastoral Letters*, 1: 366–70.

64. *Present Crisis*, in ibid., 1: 375–403.

65. Hennesey, *American Catholics*, p. 260.

66. See David J. O'Brien, *American Catholics and Social Reform: The New Deal Years* (New York: Oxford University Press, 1968), especially p. 55.

67. Ibid., p. 214.

68. George Q. Flynn, *Roosevelt and Romanism: Catholics and American Diplomacy, 1937–1945* (Westport, Conn.: Greenwood, 1976), p. 89.

69. Hennesey, *American Catholics*, p. 280.

70. Quoted in Flynn, *Roosevelt and Romanism*, p. 193.

71. Dohen, *Nationalism and American Catholicism*, p. 150.

72. Ibid., p. 151.

73. Flynn, *Roosevelt and Romanism*, p. 223.

74. Nolan, *Pastoral Letters*, 2: 29.

75. Ibid., 2: 63.

76. Flynn, *Roosevelt and Romanism*, p. 224.

77. O'Brien, *American Catholics and Social Reform*, pp. 95–96.

78. Garry Wills, *Bare Ruined Choirs* (Garden City: Doubleday, 1972), pp. 15–37.

79. See, in particular, Paul Blanshard, *American Freedom and Catholic Power* (Boston: Beacon, 1949).

80. See William M. Halsey, *The Survival of American Innocence: Catholicism in an Era of Disillusionment, 1920–1940* (Notre Dame: University of Notre Dame Press, 1980).

81. See *Statement on Secularism* and *The Christian in Action*, in Nolan, *Pastoral Letters*, 2: 74–81, 82–89.

82. Jay P. Dolan, *The American Catholic Experience: A History from Colonial Times to the Present* (Garden City: Doubleday, 1985), p. 356.

83. O'Toole, "Prelates and Politicos," pp. 57–58.

84. John Cooney, *The American Pope: The Life and Times of Francis Cardinal Spellman* (New York: Dell, 1984), pp. 229–30.

Chapter Three

1. Eugene Kennedy, *Re-Imagining American Catholicism: The American Bishops and Their Pastoral Letters* (New York: Vintage, 1985), p. 14.

27. Quoted in Browne, *Catholic Church and the Knights of Labor*, p. 374.

28. See James Edmund Roohan, *American Catholics and the Social Ques 1865–1900* (New York: Arno, 1976), p. 398.

29. Donald L. Kinzer, *An Episode in Anti-Catholicism: The American Prote Association* (Seattle: University of Washington Press, 1964), p. 45.

30. James H. Moynihan, *The Life of Archbishop John Ireland* (New York: Ha 1953), pp. 33–34.

31. Gerald P. Fogarty, *The Vatican and the American Hierarchy from 1870 to .* (Stuttgart: Anton Hiessemann, 1982), p. 45.

32. Irish-Americans made up more than one-half of the American hierarchy in 1 See Hennesey, *American Catholics*, p. 194.

33. Fogarty, *Vatican and the American Hierarchy*, p. 72.

34. Ibid., p. 65.

35. Thomas T. McAvoy, *A History of the Catholic Church in the United S* (Notre Dame: University of Notre Dame Press, 1969), p. 277.

36. See Aaron I. Abell, *American Catholic Thought on the Social Question* (In apolis: Bobbs-Merrill, 1968), p. 66.

37. Robert D. Cross, *The Emergence of Liberal Catholicism in America* (C bridge: Harvard University Press, 1958), p. 183.

38. Text in Thomas T. McAvoy, *The Great Crisis in American Catholic His 1895–1900* (Chicago: Henry Regnery, 1957), pp. 379–91.

39. Ellis, *American Catholicism*, p. 121.

40. Robert Emmet Curran, S.J., *Michael Augustine Corrigan and the Shapir Conservative Catholicism in America 1878–1902* (New York: Arno, 1978), p. iv.

41. Thomas T. McAvoy, "The Catholic Minority after the Americanist Cor versy, 1899–1917: A Survey," *Review of Politics* 21 (1959): 57.

42. Moynihan, *Life of Archbishop John Ireland*, p. 169.

43. For Corrigan's and McQuaid's public support of the war, see Curran, *Mic Augustine Corrigan*, p. 489.

44. See Robert Emmett Curran, S.J., "The McGlynn Affair and the Shaping o New Conservatism in American Catholicism," *Catholic Historical Review* 66 (19 184–204.

45. McAvoy, "Catholic Minority," p. 61.

46. Ibid., p. 64.

47. McAvoy, *History of the Catholic Church*, p. 243.

48. James W. Sanders, *The Education of an Urban Minority: Catholics in Chica 1833–1965* (New York: Oxford University Press, 1977), p. 34.

49. Ibid.

50. McAvoy, *History of the Catholic Church*, p. 338.

51. Nolan, *Pastoral Letters*, 1: 244.

52. Charles Shanabruch, *Chicago's Catholics: The Evolution of an American Id tity* (Notre Dame: University of Notre Dame Press, 1981), p. 193.

53. Elizabeth McKeown, "War and Welfare: A Study of American Catholic Lead ship" (Ph.D. diss., University of Chicago, 1972).

54. Hennesey, *American Catholics*, p. 227.

55. See *Program of Social Reconstruction*, in Nolan, *Pastoral Letters*, 1: 255–

56. Joseph McShane, S.J., *"Sufficiently Radical": Catholicism, Progressivi*

2. David O'Brien, *Renewal of American Catholicism* (New York: Oxford University Press, 1972), p. 138.

3. See Andrew M. Greeley and Peter H. Rossi, *The Education of Catholic Americans* (Chicago: Aldine, 1966); Andrew M. Greeley, William McCready, and Kathleen McCourt, *Catholic Schools in a Declining Church* (Kansas City: Sheed and Ward, 1976); Andrew M. Greeley, *The American Catholic: A Social Portrait* (New York: Basic, 1977); Andrew M. Greeley, *American Catholics since the Council: An Unauthorized Report* (Chicago: Thomas More, 1985); and Andrew M. Greeley, *The Catholic Myth: The Behavior and Beliefs of American Catholics* (New York: Charles Scribner's Sons, 1990).

4. The results of this study are presented in Greeley, et al., *Catholic Schools in a Declining Church*, p. 43.

5. Ibid.

6. Ibid.

7. Ibid., p. 74.

8. Greeley, *American Catholic*, p. 47.

9. O'Brien, *Renewal of American Catholicism*, p. 7.

10. Eugene Kennedy, *The Now and Future Church: The Psychology of Being an American Catholic* (Garden City: Doubleday, 1984), p. 17.

11. Ibid., p. 11.

12. See, in particular, Lawrence H. Fuchs, *John F. Kennedy and American Catholicism* (New York: Meredith, 1967); and Albert J. Menendez, *John F. Kennedy: Catholic and Humanist* (Buffalo: Prometheus, 1979).

13. John Cogley and Rodger Van Allen, *Catholic America* (Kansas City: Sheed and Ward, 1986 [expanded and updated edition]), p. 96.

14. Ibid., p. 96.

15. For a discussion of Ryan's views on the church-state question, see Francis L. Broderick, *Right Reverend New Dealer: John A. Ryan* (New York: Macmillan, 1963), pp. 118–20.

16. For Smith, see Charles C. Marshall, "An Open Letter to the Honorable Alfred E. Smith," *Atlantic Monthly* (Apr. 1927): pp. 540–49; and Alfred E. Smith, "Catholic and Patriot: Governor Smith Replies," *Atlantic Monthly* (May 1927): 721–28. For Kennedy, see Menendez, *John F. Kennedy*, pp. 120–25.

17. See *Declaration on Religious Liberty*, in Walter M. Abbott, ed., *The Documents of Vatican II* (New York: Guild, 1966), pp. 675–96.

18. Ibid., p. 678.

19. Ibid., p. 679.

20. John Courtney Murray, "Commentary on Declaration on Religious Freedom," in Vincent A. Yzermans, ed., *American Participation in the Second Vatican Council* (New York: Sheed and Ward, 1967), p. 668.

21. Ibid., p. 627.

22. See William A. Scott and Frances M. Scott, *The Church Then and Now: Cultivating a Sense of Tradition* (Kansas City: Leaven, 1984), p. 58.

23. See *Pastoral Constitution on the Church in the Modern World* in Abbott, *Documents of Vatican II*, pp. 199–308.

24. George C. Higgins, "Commentary on Pastoral Constitution on the Church in the Modern World," in Yzermans, *American Participation*, p. 263.

25. *Pastoral Constitution*, in Abbott, *Documents of Vatican II*, pp. 199–200.

26. Ibid., pp. 200, 201.

27. Ibid., p. 245.

28. Ibid., pp. 201–2.

29. Ibid., pp. 255–56.

30. Ibid., p. 245.

31. See, in particular, Leo XIII's *Rerum Novarum*, Pius XI's *Quadragesimo Anno*, and John XXIII's *Mater et Magistra*, in David M. Byers, ed., *Justice in the Marketplace: Collected Statements of the Vatican and the U.S. Catholic Bishops on Economic Policy* (Washington, D.C.: National Conference of Catholic Bishops, 1985).

32. *Pastoral Constitution*, in Abbott, *Documents of Vatican II*, pp. 273–74.

33. Ibid., p. 293.

34. Ibid., p. 294.

35. Ibid., p. 295.

36. Monsignor George Higgins, interview with author, 17 Sept. 1986.

37. *Pastoral Constitution*, in Abbott, *Documents of Vatican II*, p. 291.

38. Yzermans, *American Participation*, p. 254.

39. Ibid., p. 220.

40. Ibid., p. 221.

41. Theodore J. Lowi, "Europeanization of America? From United States to United State," in Theodore J. Lowi and Alan Stone, eds., *Nationalizing Government: Public Policies in America* (Beverly Hills: Sage, 1978), p. 15.

42. Ibid., p. 16.

43. Titles and descriptions of statutes are based on review of *Congressional Quarterly* for the relevant years.

44. Alfred H. Kelly, Winfred A. Harbison, and Herman Belz, *The American Constitution: Its Origins and Development* (New York: W. W. Norton, 1983), p. 635.

45. Ibid.

46. Ibid., p. 655.

47. Ibid., p. 645.

48. Ibid., p. 651.

49. Ibid., p. 647.

50. Lowi, "Europeanization of America?" p. 25.

51. Luke Eugene Ebersole, *Church Lobbying in the Nation's Capital* (New York: Macmillan, 1951), p. 52.

52. Monsignor George Higgins, interview with author, 17 Sept. 1986.

53. George A. Kelly, *The Battle for the American Church* (Garden City: Doubleday, 1979), p. 370.

54. See *Decree on the Bishops' Pastoral Office in the Church*, in Abbott, *Documents of Vatican II*, pp. 396–429.

55. Ibid., pp. 424–25.

56. Ibid., pp. 425–26.

57. "NCWC: New Life and Vigor," *America* (19 Nov. 1966): 643.

58. "The Bishops Meet," *Commonweal* (2 Dec. 1966): 245.

59. Ibid., p. 245.

60. "NCWC," p. 643.

61. Herbert Vorgrimler, ed., *Commentary on the Documents of Vatican II*, 5 vols. (New York: Herder and Herder, 1967), 2: 285n.

62. Ibid.

63. Monsignor George Higgins, interview with author, 17 Sept. 1986.

64. See *Dogmatic Constitution on the Church*, in Abbott, *Documents of Vatican II*, pp. 14–101.

65. Kennedy, *Re-Imagining American Catholicism*, p. 12.

66. *Dogmatic Constitution*, in Abbott, *Documents of Vatican II*, p. 40.

67. Ibid., p. 42.

68. See Vorgrimler, *Commentary on the Documents of Vatican II*, 1: 195.

69. Ibid., p. 198.

70. Ibid., p. 43.

71. *Dogmatic Constitution*, in Abbott, *Documents of Vatican II*, p. 46.

72. For a discussion of Jadot's influence and of the intricate process by which Catholic bishops are appointed, see Thomas J. Reese, "The Selection of Bishops," *America* (25 Aug. 1984): 65–72. Reese also pointed out that Jadot's criteria of appointment apparently fell out of favor in the Vatican once John Paul II had ascended to the papacy. "John Paul II," Reese said, ". . . stress[ed] unity and fidelity to the magisterium" (ibid., p. 71).

73. Kennedy, *Now and Future Church*, p. 20.

74. Ibid., p. 22.

75. Robert Olmstead, "Bishops Chart New Course with Dearden at the Helm," *National Catholic Reporter* (23 Nov. 1966): 1.

76. Tom Blackburn, "Archbishop John F. Dearden," *National Catholic Reporter* (7 Dec. 1966): 1–2.

Chapter Four

1. For the history of the church's teaching on abortion, see John Connery, S.J., *Abortion: The Development of the Roman Catholic Perspective* (Chicago: Loyola University Press, 1977).

2. *Pastoral Constitution*, in Abbott, *Documents of Vatican II*, pp. 255–56.

3. *Human Life in Our Day*, in Nolan, *Pastoral Letters*, 3: 181.

4. Ibid., 3: 181.

5. *Statement on Abortion (1969), Statement on Abortion (1970), Declaration on Abortion*, and *Population and the American Future: A Response*, in Nolan, *Pastoral Letters*, 3: 198–99, 254–55, 271, 298–300.

6. *Statement on Abortion (1970)*, in ibid., 3: 254.

7. Ibid.

8. Ibid.

9. *Declaration on Abortion*, in Nolan, *Pastoral Letters*, 3: 271.

10. *Statement on Abortion (1970)*, in Nolan, *Pastoral Letters*, 3: 254.

11. *Statement on Abortion (1969)*, in Nolan, *Pastoral Letters*, 3: 199.

12. Bishop James McHugh, interview with author, 4 Mar. 1987.

13. *Statement on Abortion (1973)*, in Nolan, *Pastoral Letters*, 3: 366.

14. *Statement of the Committee for Pro-Life Affairs*, in uscc, *Documentation on the*

Right-to-Life and Abortion (Washington, D.C.: United States Catholic Conference, 1974), p. 59.

15. Ibid., p. 60.

16. Bishop James McHugh, interview with author, 4 Mar. 1987.

17. *Resolution of the Pro-Life Committee*, in Nolan, *Pastoral Letters*, 3: 384–85.

18. Minutes of NCCB's Mar. 1975 meeting, p. 36.

19. "Testimony of United States Catholic Conference on Constitutional Amendment Protecting Unborn Human Life before the Sub-Committee on Constitutional Amendments of the Senate Committee on the Judiciary," in USCC, *Documentation on the Right-to-Life*, pp. 1–44.

20. Ibid., p. 28.

21. Raymond Tatalovich and Byron W. Daynes, *The Politics of Abortion: A Study of Community Conflict in Public Policy Making* (New York: Praeger, 1981), p. 157. See *Pastoral Plan for Pro-Life Activities*, in Nolan, *Pastoral Letters*, 4: 81–91.

22. *Pastoral Plan for Pro-Life Activities*, in Nolan, *Pastoral Letters*, 4: 87.

23. Ibid., p. 89.

24. Bishop James McHugh, interview with author, 4 Mar. 1987.

25. *Pastoral Plan for Pro-Life Activities*, in Nolan, *Pastoral Letters*, 4: 89.

26. See Richard Rashke, "Little Dissent When Bishops Meet," *National Catholic Reporter* (5 Dec. 1975): 6.

27. Minutes of the NCCB's Nov. 1975 meeting, p. 13; Bishop Thomas Gumbleton, interview with author, 27 Mar. 1987.

28. Paul J. Weber, "Bishops in Politics: The Big Plunge," *America* (20 Mar. 1976): 220.

29. See Gallup and Castelli, *American Catholic People*, pp. 93–98.

30. Burnham, *Critical Elections*, p. 8.

31. For an insider's account, see William A. Rusher, *The Rise of the Right* (New York: Morrow, 1984).

32. E. E. Schattschneider, *The Semi-Sovereign People: A Realist's View of Democracy in America* (New York: Holt, Rinehart and Winston, 1960), pp. 81, 88.

33. Sundquist, *Dynamics of the Party System*, p. 13.

34. Ibid., p. 312.

35. Ibid., p. 300.

36. Kevin B. Phillips, *The Emerging Republican Majority* (Garden City: Anchor, 1969), p. 25.

37. Ibid., p. 26.

38. Rusher, *Rise of the Right*, p. 221.

39. Ibid., p. 257.

40. Richard M. Scammon and Ben J. Wattenberg, *The Real Majority* (New York: Coward-McCann, 1970), pp. 40–43.

41. Ibid., p. 40.

42. See Sundquist, *Dynamics of the Party System*, p. 300; and Schattschneider, *Semi-Sovereign People*, pp. 81, 88.

43. Phillips, *Emerging Republican Majority*, p. 69.

44. Ibid., p. 72.

45. "Abortion Makes Strange Bedfellows: GOP and God," *Commonweal* (19 Oct. 1970): 37.

46. Bishop James McHugh, interview with author, 4 Mar. 1987.

47. Patrick J. Buchanan, *The New Majority: President Nixon at Mid-Passage* (Philadelphia: Girard Bank, 1973), p. 62.

48. Patrick J. Buchanan, *Conservative Votes, Liberal Victories: Why the Right Has Failed* (New York: Quadrangle, 1975), p. 172.

49. Ibid., p. 175.

Chapter Five

1. *Pastoral Plan for Pro-Life Activities*, in Nolan, *Pastoral Letters*, 4: 87.

2. Monsignor George Higgins, interview with author, 11 Mar. 1987.

3. Bishop James McHugh, interview with author, 4 Mar. 1987.

4. See Nolan, *Pastoral Letters*, 4: 92–98, 99–119, 126, 128.

5. *Political Responsibility: Reflections on an Election Year*, in Nolan, *Pastoral Letters*, 4: 129–47.

6. Ibid., 4: 131.

7. Ibid., 4: 133.

8. Ibid., 4: 134–36.

9. Catholics preferred Nixon to McGovern by 52 percent to 48 percent. For a recent discussion of the history of the Catholic vote, see Gallup and Castelli, *American Catholic People*, pp. 126–38.

10. Stuart Eizenstat, telephone interview with author, 12 Mar. 1987.

11. The quote is from David M. Alpern, "Courting the Catholics," *Newsweek* (20 Sept. 1976): 16.

12. See "Democratic Platform 1976," in Donald Bruce Johnson, ed., *National Party Platforms: Volume 2, 1960–1976*, 2 vols. (Urbana: University of Illinois Press, 1978), 2: 926.

13. United States Catholic Conference (USCC) news release, 22 June 1976. These news releases were provided to me by the USCC Office of Public Affairs.

14. USCC news release, 23 June 1976.

15. Castelli's interview with Carter was reproduced in *Origins* (2 Sept. 1976): 170–72.

16. *Origins* (2 Sept. 1976): 172.

17. The platform endorsed the "efforts of those who seek enactment of a constitutional amendment to restore protection of the right-to-life for unborn children." See "Republican Platform 1976," in Johnson, *National Party Platforms*, 2: 976. For Bernardin's statement, see *Origins* (2 Sept. 1976): 173.

18. Bishop James Rausch is deceased. I discussed his activities in 1976 with several of his former staff members and colleagues at the United States Catholic Conference.

19. The quote is from John Carr, former Rausch aide and now a leading official of the USCC, interview with author, 10 Mar. 1987.

20. Thomas Farmer, interview with author, 24 Apr. 1987. Many of the details concerning Rausch's contacts with the Carter campaign were relayed to me in this interview.

21. Mondale recalled that he had worked "very closely" with Rausch in 1976. Personal correspondence with author, 3 Sept. 1987.

22. See Martin Schram, *Running for President 1976: The Carter Campaign* (New

York: Stein and Day, 1977), p. 224. Several of Carter's aides told me that it would be impossible to overestimate Carter's self-confidence at the end of the summer of 1976.

23. I discussed this meeting with Bernardin on 23 Mar. 1988, and with Carter's aide Greg Schneiders on 17 Mar. 1987. Bernardin was the presiding bishop at the meeting and Schneiders was the only aide to accompany Carter to it.

24. Greg Schneiders, telephone interview with author, 17 Mar. 1987.

25. See *Origins* (2 Sept. 1976): 170.

26. *Origins* (16 Sept. 1976): 207.

27. See Charles Mohr, "Abortion Stand by Carter Vexes Catholic Bishops," *New York Times*, 1 Sept. 1976, p. A1.

28. Ibid.

29. Alpern, "Courting the Catholics," p. 16.

30. "Flare-up over Abortion," *Time* (13 Sept. 1976): 21.

31. Quoted in Alpern, "Courting the Catholics," *Newsweek*, 20 Sept. 1976, p. 16.

32. See James W. Naughton, "Ford Hopes Linked to Catholic Vote," *New York Times*, 5 Sept. 1976, p. A1.

33. Ibid.

34. Janis Johnson, "President Hints at Abortion 'Concern,'" *Washington Post*, 9 Aug. 1976, p. A10.

35. *Origins* (23 Sept. 1976): 216.

36. Ibid., p. 218.

37. "On Abortion, the Bishops v. the Deacon," *Time* (20 Sept. 1976): 11.

38. Edward Walsh, "Bishops Like Ford's Stand on Abortion," *Washington Post*, 11 Sept. 1976, p. A1.

39. The letter was reproduced in a USCC news release, 13 Sept. 1976.

40. Based on the statement reproduced in a USCC news release, 1 Sept. 1976.

41. Ibid.

42. Based on the statement reproduced in a USCC news release, 13 Sept. 1976.

43. Ibid.

44. Quoted in Rick Casey, "Bishops 'Encouraged' by Ford's Abortion Stand," *National Catholic Reporter* (17 Sept. 1976): 1.

45. Cardinal Joseph Bernardin, interview with author, 23 Mar. 1976.

46. Ibid.

Chapter Six

1. *Origins* (23 Sept. 1976): 216.

2. John Carr, interview with author, 10 Mar. 1987.

3. USCC news release, 17 Sept. 1976.

4. Marjorie Hyer, "Some Catholics Lament Bishops' Abortion Stress," *Washington Post*, 11 Sept. 1976, p. A4.

5. USCC news release, 17 Sept. 1976.

6. USCC news release, 21 Sept. 1976.

7. Monsignor George Higgins, interview with author, 11 Mar. 1987.

8. *Resolution of the Administrative Committee*, in Nolan, *Pastoral Letters*, 4: 157.

9. Ibid., p. 158.

10. Ibid., p. 157.

11. Jim Castelli, "How Catholics Voted," *Commonweal* (3 Dec. 1976): 780.

12. Ibid.

13. Maris A. Vinovskis, "Abortion and the Presidential Election of 1976: A Multivariate Analysis of Voting Behavior," in Carl E. Schneider and Maris A. Vinovskis, eds., *The Law and Politics of Abortion* (Lexington: Lexington Books, 1980), pp. 184–205.

14. Ibid., p. 200.

15. *Political Responsibility: Choices for the 80s*, in Nolan, *Pastoral Letters*, 4: 317–29.

16. Cited in Andrew H. Merton, *Enemies of Choice: The Right to Life Movement and Its Threat to Abortion* (Boston: Beacon, 1981), p. 115.

17. Activist Richard Viguerie said of Rockefeller's appointment: "As a conservative Republican, I could hardly have been more upset if Ford had selected Teddy Kennedy." See Richard A. Viguerie, *The New Right: We're Ready to Lead* (Falls Church: Viguerie Company, 1980), p. 51.

18. See William A. Rusher, *The Making of a New Majority Party* (New York: Sheed and Ward, 1975).

19. "New Right Plans Move to Change Congress," *Congressional Quarterly* (23 Oct. 1976): 3027.

20. Richard John Neuhaus, "The Right to Fight," *Commonweal* (9 Oct. 1981): 558.

21. Jepsen's campaign was reported in Alan Crawford, *Thunder on the Right: The New Right and the Politics of Resentment* (New York: Pantheon, 1980), pp. 272–75.

22. Ibid., p. 273.

23. Connie Paige, *The Right to Lifers: Who They Are, How They Operate, Where They Get Their Money* (New York: Summit, 1983), p. 135.

24. Ibid., p. 136.

25. For a discussion of the Browns' relationship with the new right, see Merton, *Enemies of Choice*, pp. 160–65.

26. Viguerie, *New Right*, pp. 66, 69–70.

27. Merton, *Enemies of Choice*, p. 164.

28. Albert Menendez, *Religion at the Polls* (Philadelphia: Westminster, 1977), p. 104.

29. "God and Politics: Mixing More Than Ever," *Congressional Quarterly* (23 Sept. 1978): 2565.

30. The creation of the religious new right and its relations with secular political leaders were the subject of a series of articles in the *New York Times* in Aug. 1980. See John Herbers, "Ultraconservative Evangelicals: A Surging New Force in Politics," *New York Times*, 17 Aug. 1980, p. A1; Dudley Clendinen, "Christian New Right's Rush to Power," *New York Times*, 18 Aug. 1980, p. B7; Kenneth A. Briggs, "Evangelicals Turning to Politics Fear Moral Slide Imperils Nation," *New York Times*, 19 Aug. 1980, p. D17; and Dudley Clendinen, "Reverend Falwell Inspires Evangelical Vote," *New York Times*, 20 Aug. 1980, p. B22.

31. See Dinesh D'Souza, *Falwell before the Millennium: A Critical Biography* (Chicago: Regnery Gateway, 1984); and Peggy L. Shriver, *The Bible Vote: Religion and the New Right* (New York: Pilgrim, 1981).

32. Neuhaus, "Right to Fight," p. 558.

33. Weyrich in particular felt that abortion could prove to be the Achilles' heel of the Democratic coalition (ibid.).

34. D'Souza, *Falwell before the Millennium*, p. 95.

35. For a discussion of this impact, see Seymour Martin Lipset and Earl Rabb, "The Election and the Evangelicals," *Commentary* (Mar. 1981): 25–31.

36. A. James Reichley, "The Reagan Coalition," *Brookings Review* 1/2 (1986): 6.

Chapter Seven

1. The most complete account of the drafting of the letter is Jim Castelli, *The Bishops and the Bomb: Waging Peace in a Nuclear Age* (Garden City: Image, 1983).

2. George Weigel, *Tranquillitus Ordinis: The Present Failure and Future Promise of American Catholic Thought on War and Peace* (Oxford: Oxford University Press, 1987), p. 257.

3. Dohen, *Nationalism and American Catholicism*, p. 175.

4. Ibid., p. 1.

5. Ibid., pp. 124, 165.

6. For a book-length treatment of the Catholic antiwar movement, see Charles A. Meconis, *With Clumsy Grace: The American Catholic Left, 1961–1975* (New York: Seabury, 1979).

7. *Peace on Earth*, in David J. O'Brien and Thomas A. Shannon, eds., *Renewing the Earth: Catholic Documents on Peace, Justice and Liberation* (Garden City: Image, 1977), p. 154.

8. Robert Hyer, *Nuclear Disarmament: Key Statements of Popes, Bishops, Councils, and Churches* (New York: Paulist, 1982), pp. 19, 23.

9. "The Bishops and Vietnam," *Commonweal* (5 Apr. 1966): 94.

10. For clear explications of the just war theory, see J. Bryan Hehir, "The Just-War Ethic and Catholic Theology: Dynamics of Change and Continuity," and James F. Childress, "Just War Criteria," in Thomas A. Shannon, ed., *War or Peace? The Search for New Answers* (Maryknoll, N.Y.: Orbis, 1980), pp. 15–39, 40–58.

11. Paul Ramsey, *The Just War: Force and Political Responsibility* (New York: Scribner's, 1968), p. 195.

12. *Peace and Vietnam*, in Nolan, *Pastoral Letters*, 3: 74.

13. Ibid., 3: 76.

14. *Human Life in Our Day*, in Nolan, *Pastoral Letters*, 3: 191.

15. *Resolution on Southeast Asia*, in Nolan, *Pastoral Letters*, 3: 289.

16. "On Selecting Bishops," *Commonweal* (10 Dec. 1971): 243.

17. William A. Au, *The Cross, the Flag, and the Bomb: American Catholics Debate War and Peace, 1960–1983* (Westport, Conn.: Greenwood, 1985), p. 180.

18. A similar argument was made in William A. Au, "Papal and Episcopal Teaching on War and Peace: The Historical Background to 'The Challenge of Peace: God's Promise and Our Response,'" in Charles J. Reid, Jr., ed., *Peace in a Nuclear Age: The Bishops' Pastoral Letter in Perspective* (Washington, D.C.: Catholic University of America Press, 1986), pp. 98–119.

19. Two fine reviews of this record are J. Bryan Hehir, "Reflections on Recent Teaching," in Hyer, *Nuclear Disarmament*, pp. 1–11; and David Hollenbach, "The

Challenge of Peace in the Context of Recent Church Teachings," in Phillip J. Murnion, ed., *Catholics and Nuclear War: A Commentary on "The Challenge of Peace"—The U.S. Catholic Bishops' Pastoral Letter on War and Peace* (New York: Crossroad, 1983), pp. 3–15.

20. *Peace on Earth*, in O'Brien and Shannon, *Renewing the Earth*, p. 151.
21. Ibid., p. 154.
22. *Pastoral Constitution*, in Abbott, *Documents of Vatican II*, pp. 293–94.
23. Ibid., pp. 294–95.
24. Hehir, "Reflections on Recent Teaching," p. 5.
25. *To Live in Christ Jesus*, in Nolan, *Pastoral Letters*, 4: 192.
26. Au, *Cross, the Flag, and the Bomb*, p. 194.
27. Hyer, *Nuclear Disarmament*, p. 103.
28. Ibid., p. 104.
29. Ibid.
30. Reverend J. Bryan Hehir, interview with author, 28 July 1987.
31. Castelli, *Bishops and the Bomb*, p. 18.
32. Ibid., p. 15.
33. *The Challenge of Peace: God's Promise and Our Response*, in John Tracy Ellis, ed., *Documents of American Catholic History*, 3 vols. (Wilmington: Michael Glazer, 1987), 3: 823.
34. Ibid., p. 812.
35. Ibid., pp. 817–18.
36. Ibid., pp. 831–32.
37. Ibid., p. 832.
38. Ibid., pp. 834–35.
39. Ibid., p. 827.
40. Ibid., p. 841.
41. Ibid.
42. Ibid., p. 843.
43. Ibid., p. 839.
44. Ibid., p. 840.
45. Ibid., p. 843.
46. Ibid., p. 845.
47. J. Bryan Hehir, "From the Pastoral Constitution of Vatican II to The Challenge of Peace," in Murnion, *Catholics and Nuclear War*, p. 71.
48. See Gallup and Castelli, *American Catholic People*, pp. 77–90.
49. Ibid., pp. 78–79.
50. Greeley, *American Catholics since the Council*, p. 47.
51. Ibid., p. 94.
52. Ibid., pp. 93–94
53. Ibid., p. 96.
54. Douglas Waller, *Congress and the Nuclear Freeze: An Inside Look at the Politics of a Mass Movement* (Amherst: University of Massachusetts Press, 1987), pp. 305–7.
55. Castelli, *Bishops and the Bomb*, p. 15.
56. Waller, *Congress and the Nuclear Freeze*, p. 37.
57. Ibid., p. 161.

58. Castelli, *Bishops and the Bomb*, p. 60.
59. Waller, *Congress and the Nuclear Freeze*, p. 161.
60. See "Excerpts from U.S. Bishops' Pastoral Letter on War and Peace"; "Excerpts from House Arms Freeze Measure"; Kenneth A. Briggs, "Bishops, Gratified, Prepare to Teach Letter on Peace"; and David Shribman, "House Passes Modified Nuclear Freeze Resolution," *New York Times*, 5 May 1983, pp. B16–17.

Chapter Eight

1. For the 1980 voting data, see Paul Lopatto, *Religion and the Presidential Election* (New York: Praeger, 1985), p. 55.
2. See Greeley, *American Catholics since the Council*, p. 93.
3. In an Oct. 1982 speech Reagan claimed that the freeze movement was "inspired not by the sincere, honest people who want peace, but by some who want the weakening of America." See George Lardner, Jr., "Soviets' Role in Nuclear Freeze Limited, FBI Says," *Washington Post*, 26 Mar. 1983, p. A7.
4. See, for example, Caspar Weinberger's letter to Joseph Bernardin in *Origins* (21 Oct. 1982): 292–94; William Clark's letter to Bernardin in *Origins* (2 Dec. 1982): 398–401; and Reagan's address to the Knights of Columbus in *Origins* (26 Aug. 1982): 171–75.
5. For documentation of the Vatican consultation and an examination of its effect on the pastoral letter, see *Origins* (7 Apr. 1983): 690–96.
6. See especially Castelli, *Bishops and the Bomb*, pp. 137–40.
7. Ibid., p. 140.
8. Bernard Gwertzman, "Administration Hails New Draft of Arms Letter," *New York Times*, 7 Apr. 1983, p. A1.
9. Castelli, *Bishops and the Bomb*, p. 150.
10. Ibid.
11. One indicator of the attention the controversy received was that William Safire devoted one of his "On Language" columns to the difference between "halt" and "curb." See William Safire, "Curb the Halting," *New York Times Magazine*, 22 May 1983, pp. 12–15.
12. David Maraniss, "House Passes Nuclear Freeze Resolution," *Washington Post*, 5 May 1983, p. A8.
13. "Transcript of the President's News Conference on Foreign and Domestic Matters," *New York Times*, 5 May 1983, p. D22.
14. See Benjamin Ginsberg and Martin Shefter, "A Critical Realignment? The New Politics, the Reconstituted Right, and the Election of 1984," in Michael Nelson, ed., *The Elections of 1984* (Washington, D.C.: Congressional Quarterly, 1985), pp. 10–18.
15. Robert Beckel, interview with author, 14 Dec. 1987.
16. Phil Gailey, "Democrats Urge Steps to Prevent Nuclear Warfare: Party Chief, Backing Bishops' Letter, Asks for Freeze and Reductions in Arsenals," *New York Times*, 21 Sept. 1983, p. A1.
17. Ibid.
18. Robert Beckel, interview with author, 14 Dec. 1987.
19. For a text of the speech, see *Origins* (29 Dec. 1983): 491–49.

20. Bernardin in a speech at the University of Portland. I am grateful to the office of Senator Mark Hatfield (R-Oreg.) for making a videotape of this speech available to me.

21. See *Political Responsibility: Choices for the 80s*, in *Origins* (12 Apr. 1984): 733.

22. For the text of the statement, see *Origins* (20 Sept. 1984): 217.

23. See Wayne Barrett, "Holier Than Thou" *Village Voice* (25 Dec. 1984): 16.

24. For the text of the statement, see *Origins* (1 Nov. 1984): 311.

25. See *Origins* (8 Nov. 1984): 326.

26. Kurt Anderson, "For God and Country," *Time* (10 Sept. 1984): 8.

27. Walter Shapiro, "Politics and the Pulpit," *Newsweek* (17 Sept. 1984): 24.

28. Anderson, "For God and Country," p. 9.

29. Kenneth M. Pierce, "God and the Ballot Box," *Time* (17 Sept. 1984): 26.

30. Fay S. Joyce, "Mondale Explains Role of Religion," *New York Times*, 8 Sept. 1984, p. A8.

31. See Bernardin's Fordham speech in *Origins* (29 Dec. 1983): 491.

32. Kenneth L. Woodward, "Faith, Hope, and Votes," *Newsweek* (17 Sept. 1984): 35.

33. "O'Connor Critical of Ferraro's Views," *New York Times*, 9 Sept. 1984, p. 34.

34. "Archbishop Contends Abortion Is Key Issue," *New York Times*, 25 June 1984, p. D13.

35. Sam Roberts, "Cuomo to Challenge Archbishop over Criticism of Abortion Stand," *New York Times*, 3 Aug. 1984, p. B2.

36. *Political Responsibility: Choices for the 80s*, in *Origins* (12 Apr. 1984): 733.

37. Robert D. McFadden, "Archbishop Asserts That Cuomo Misinterpreted Stand on Abortion," *New York Times*, 4 Aug. 1984, p. A1.

38. Ibid.

39. "O'Connor Critical of Ferraro's Views," p. A1.

40. The text of the letter was reprinted in the *New York Times*, 11 Sept. 1984, p. A26.

41. Robert D. McFadden, "O'Connor–Ferraro Dispute on Abortion Unresolved," *New York Times*, 11 Sept. 1984, p. A1.

42. Jane Perlez, "Ferraro Acts to Still Abortion Dispute," *New York Times*, 12 Sept. 1984, p. B9.

43. Jane Perlez, "Ferraro Says Religion Won't Influence Policy," *New York Times*, 13 Sept. 1984, p. B16.

44. Ibid.

45. Fox Butterfield, "Archbishop of Boston Cites Abortion as 'Critical' Issue," *New York Times*, 6 Sept. 1984, p. B13.

46. McFadden, "O'Connor–Ferraro Dispute on Abortion Unresolved," p. A26.

47. For a detailed "Portrait of the Electorate" in 1984, see *New York Times*, 8 Nov. 1984, p. A19.

48. Ibid.

49. "NBC Nightly News," 21 Sept. 1984. I am grateful to Jamie Gangel of NBC for providing me with a transcript and a videotape of this broadcast.

50. Ibid.

51. Ibid.

52. Robert Beckel, interview with author, 14 Dec. 1987.

53. Robert S. McElvaine, "Liberals Go Back to the Flag," *New York Times*, 2 Sept. 1984, p. E15.

54. Bernard Weinraub, "Mondale Pledges Immediate Effort for Arms Freeze," *New York Times*, 6 Sept. 1984, p. A1.

55. Butterfield, "Archbishop of Boston Cites Abortion as 'Critical' Issue," p. B13.

56. Bernard Weinraub, "Mondale Plans to Focus on Issues Where He Says Reagan Is Weak," *New York Times*, 9 Sept. 1984, p. A1.

57. "O'Connor Critical of Ferraro's Views," p. A1.

58. Mary McGrory, "Ferraro's Performance Shows the Wit, Grit of a Born Politician," *Washington Post*, 25 Sept. 1984, p. A2, emphasis added.

Chapter Nine

1. The history of this teaching is charted in David M. Byers, ed., *Justice in the Marketplace: Collected Statements of the Vatican and the U.S. Catholic Bishops on Economic Policy, 1891–1984* (Washington, D.C.: United States Catholic Conference, 1985).

2. *Economic Justice for All,* in Ellis, *Documents of American Catholic History,* 3: 981.

3. Ibid., 3: 983.

4. Ibid., 3: 985.

5. Ibid., 3: 985.

6. Ibid., 3: 1039, 1072, 1095, 1111.

7. Ibid., 3: 998.

8. Ibid.

9. Ibid., 3: 1069.

10. Ibid., 3: 1087.

11. Ibid., 3: 1093.

12. Ibid., 3: 1106.

13. For the story of Ryan's speech being transformed into an NCWC statement, see McShane, *"Sufficiently Radical,"* pp. 155–56.

14. See *Toward the Future: Catholic Social Teaching and the U.S. Economy* (New York: American Catholic Committee, 1984).

15. *Economic Justice for All*, in Ellis, *Documents of American Catholic History*, 3: 998.

16. Ibid.

17. Ibid., p. 999.

18. The United States Catholic Conference was sued by a group called Abortion Rights Mobilization, which claimed that church officials had forfeited their tax exemption by "participat[ing] in or interven[ing] in political campaigns in all parts of the country." The suit died in May 1990, when the Supreme Court let stand a lower court ruling that the prochoice group had no standing to bring the case. For an account of Abortion Rights Mobilization v. U.S. Catholic Conference, see Linda Greenhouse, "Suit on Church Tax Status and Abortion Fails," *New York Times*, 1 May 1990 p. A18.

19. "USCC General Counsel's Memorandum on Tax-Exempt Entities and Political Campaign Activities," in *Origins* (1 Sept., 1988): 185.

20. *Political Responsibility: Choices for the Future*, in *Origins* (5 Nov. 1987): 372.

21. On Bush's meetings with individual bishops, the *New York Times* reported that "quietly but persistently Vice-President Bush has gone out of his way in recent weeks to court leading Roman Catholic clergymen in the Northeast and Midwest." See Bernard Weinraub, "Campaign Courtesy: Bush Calls on Bishop," *New York Times*, 3 Oct. 1988, p. A22. For a discussion of Whealon's activities in particular, see *National Catholic Reporter* (14 Oct. 1988): 2.

22. The case was Webster v. Reproductive Health Services. For excerpts from opinions, see *New York Times*, 4 July 1989, pp. 12–13.

23. Bishop Francis Mugavero of Brooklyn, for example, responded immediately to the Supreme Court decision by calling for legislative action "by our elected officials" to "protect unborn life to the maximum degree possible." See ibid., p. 31.

24. Gallup and Castelli reported in 1987 that 16 percent of American Catholics were Hispanic. See Gallup and Castelli, *American Catholic People*, p. 3. These authors also discuss the special circumstances of Hispanic Catholics (pp. 139–48).

25. Monsignor Daniel Hoye, interview with author, 9 Feb. 1988.

26. Cardinal John O'Connor of New York is often cited as a leader of this segment of the American hierarchy. An interview I conducted with O'Connor on 27 Aug. 1987 was dominated by his arguments concerning the proper relationship between the national conference and individual local bishops.

27. *Theological and Juridical Status of Episcopal Conferences*, in *Origins* (7 Apr. 1988): pp. 731–37.

28. Ibid., p. 737.

29. See *Origins* (1 Dec. 1988): 402.

30. Ari L. Goldman, "Catholic Bishops Hire Firms to Market Fight on Abortion," *New York Times*, 6 Apr. 1990, p. A1.

31. Peter Steinfels, "Bishops Warn Politicians on Abortion," *New York Times*, 8 Nov. 1989, p. A18.

32. Ari L. Goldman, "Legislator Barred from Catholic Rite," *New York Times*, 17 Nov. 1989, p. A18.

33. Sam Howe Verhovek, "Cleric Assails Cuomo Stand on Abortion," *New York Times*, 24 Jan. 1989, p. B1.

34. Cardinal Joseph L. Bernardin, interview with author, 23 Mar. 1988.

35. When NCCB's administrative board voted in early 1990 to contract a polling firm and a public relations concern to help them further the cause of restricting abortion, the vote of the fifty-member board was unanimous. See Peter Steinfels, "Knights Aiding Anti-Abortion Effort," *New York Times*, 13 May 1990, p. A18.

36. *Vatican Declaration on Abortion*, in *Origins* (12 Dec. 1974): 390, emphasis added.

Bibliography

Documents

Congressional Quarterly
The Gallup Report
National Catholic News Service
Origins

Interviews

Robert Beckel (14 Dec. 1987)
Cardinal Joseph Bernardin (23 Mar. 1988)
Reverend Edward Bryce (29 Jan. 1987)
John Carr (10 Mar. 1987)
Stuart Eisenstat (12 Mar. 1987)
Thomas Farmer (24 Apr. 1987)
Bishop Thomas Gumbleton (27 Mar. 1987)
Reverend J. Bryan Hehir (29 June 1987; 28 July 1988)
Monsignor George Higgins (17 Sept. 1986; 11 Mar. 1987)
Monsignor Daniel Hoye (9 Feb. 1988)
James Jennings (24 Mar. 1987)
Bishop James McHugh (4 Mar. 1987)
Cardinal John O'Connor (27 Aug. 1987)
Larry O'Rourke (9 Mar. 1987)
Greg Schneiders (17 Mar. 1987)

Works Cited

Abbott, Walter M., ed. *The Documents of Vatican II*. New York: Guild, 1966.
Abell, Aaron I. *American Catholic Thought on the Social Question*. Indianapolis: Bobbs-Merrill, 1968.
"Abortion Makes Strange Bedfellows: GOP and God." *Commonweal* (19 Oct. 1970): 37.
Alpern, David M. "Courting the Catholics." *Newsweek* (20 Sept. 1976): 16–18.
Anderson, Kurt. "For God and Country." *Time* (10 Sept. 1984): 8–10.
"Archbishop Contends Abortion Is Key Issue." *New York Times*, 25 June 1984, p. D13.
Au, William A. *The Cross, the Flag, and the Bomb: American Catholics Debate War and Peace, 1960–1983*. Westport, Conn.: Greenwood, 1985.
———. "Papal and Episcopal Teaching on War and Peace: The Historical Background to 'The Challenge of Peace: God's Promise and Our Response.'" *Peace in a Nuclear Age: The Bishops' Pastoral Letter in Perspective*. Ed. Charles J. Reid, Jr. Washington, D.C.: Catholic University Press of America, 1986, 98–119.
Barrett, Wayne. "Holier Than Thou." *Village Voice* (25 Dec. 1984): 10–24.
Benestad, J. Brian. *The Pursuit of a Just Social Order: Policy Statements of the U.S.*

Catholic Bishops, 1966–1980. Washington, D.C.: Ethics and Public Policy Center, 1982.

Billington, Ray Allen. *The Protestant Crusade 1800–1860: A Study of the Origins of American Nativism*. New York: Rinehart, 1938.

Blackburn, Tom. "Archbishop John F. Dearden." *National Catholic Reporter* (7 Dec. 1966): 1–2.

Blanshard, Paul. *American Freedom and Catholic Power*. Boston: Beacon, 1949.

Briggs, Kenneth A. "Evangelicals Turning to Politics Fear Moral Slide Imperils Nation." *New York Times*, 19 Aug. 1980, p. D17.

———. "Bishops, Gratified, Prepare to Teach Letter on Peace." *New York Times*, 5 May 1983, p. B17.

Broderick, Francis L. *Right Reverend New Dealer: John A. Ryan*. New York: Macmillan, 1963.

Browne, Henry J. *The Catholic Church and the Knights of Labor*. Washington, D.C.: Catholic University of America Press, 1949.

———. "Catholicism in the United States." *The Shaping of American Religion*. Eds. James Ward Smith and A. Leland Jamison. Princeton: Princeton University Press, 1961, 72–121.

Buchanan, Patrick J. *The New Majority: President Nixon at Mid-Passage*. Philadelphia: Girard Bank, 1973.

———. *Conservative Votes, Liberal Victories: Why the Right Has Failed*. New York: Quadrangle, 1975.

Burnham, Walter Dean. *Critical Elections and the Mainsprings of American Politics*. New York: W. W. Norton, 1970.

Butterfield, Fox. "Archbishop of Boston Cites Abortion as 'Critical' Issue." *New York Times*, 6 Sept. 1984, p. B13.

Byers, David M., ed. *Justice in the Marketplace: Collected Statements of the Vatican and the U.S. Catholic Bishops on Economic Policy, 1891–1984*. Washington, D.C.: United States Catholic Conference, 1985.

Carmines, Edward G., and James A. Stimson. *Issue Evolution: Race and the Transformation of American Politics*. Princeton: Princeton University Press, 1989.

Casey, Rick. "Bishops 'Encouraged' by Ford's Abortion Stand." *National Catholic Reporter* (17 Sept. 1976): 1.

Castelli, Jim. "How Catholics Voted." *Commonweal* (3 Dec. 1976): 780–82.

———. *The Bishops and the Bomb: Waging Peace in a Nuclear Age*. Garden City: Image, 1983.

Childress, James F. "Just War Criteria." *War or Peace? The Search for New Answers*. Ed. Thomas A. Shannon. Maryknoll, N.Y.: Orbis, 1980, 40–58.

Chubb, John E., and Paul E. Peterson. "Realignment and Institutionalization." *The New Direction in American Politics*. Eds. John E. Chubb and Paul E. Peterson. Washington, D.C.: Brookings Institution, 1985, 1–30.

Clendinen, Dudley. "Christian New Right's Rush to Power." *New York Times*, 18 Aug. 1980, p. B7.

———. "Reverend Falwell Inspires Evangelical Vote." *New York Times*, 20 Aug. 1980, p. B22.

Cogley, John, and Rodger Van Allen. *Catholic America*. Kansas City: Sheed and Ward, 1986.

Connery, John, S.J. *Abortion: The Development of the Roman Catholic Perspective.* Chicago: Loyola University Press, 1977.

Cooney, John. *The American Pope: The Life and Times of Francis Cardinal Spellman.* New York: Dell, 1984.

Crawford, Alan. *Thunder on the Right: The New Right and the Politics of Resentment.* New York: Pantheon, 1980.

Cross, Robert D. *The Emergence of Liberal Catholicism in America.* Cambridge: Harvard University Press, 1958.

Curran, Robert Emmett, S.J. *Michael Augustine Corrigan and the Shaping of Conservative Catholicism in America, 1878–1902.* New York: Arno, 1978.

———. "The McGlynn Affair and the Shaping of the New Conservatism in American Catholicism." *Catholic Historical Review* 66 (1980): 184–204.

Dohen, Dorothy. *Nationalism and American Catholicism.* New York: Sheed and Ward, 1967.

Dolan, Jay P. *The American Catholic Experience: A History from Colonial Times to the Present.* Garden City: Doubleday, 1985.

D'Souza, Dinesh. *Falwell before the Millennium: A Critical Biography.* Chicago: Regnery Gateway, 1984.

Ebersole, Luke Eugene. *Church Lobbying in the Nation's Capital.* New York: Macmillan, 1951.

Ellis, John Tracy. *The Life of James Cardinal Gibbons: Archbishop of Baltimore, 1834–1921.* 2 vols. Milwaukee: Bruce, 1952.

———. *American Catholicism.* Chicago: University of Chicago Press, 1969.

———, ed. *Documents of American Catholic History.* 3 vols. Wilmington: Michael Glazer, 1987.

"Flare-Up over Abortion." *Time* (13 Sept. 1976): 21.

Flynn, George Q. *Roosevelt and Romanism: Catholics and American Diplomacy, 1937–1945.* Westport, Conn.: Greenwood, 1976.

Fogarty, Gerald P. *The Vatican and the American Hierarchy from 1870 to 1965.* Stuttgart: Anson Hiessemann, 1982.

Fowler, Robert Booth. *Religion and Politics in America.* Metuchen, N.J.: Theological Library Association and Scarecrow, 1985.

Fuchs, Lawrence H. *John F. Kennedy and American Catholicism.* New York: Meredith, 1967.

Gailey, Phil. "Democrats Urge Steps to Prevent Nuclear Warfare: Party Chief, Backing Bishops' Letter, Asks for Freeze and Reductions in Arsenals." *New York Times,* 21 Sept. 1983, p. A1.

Gallup, George, Jr., and Jim Castelli. *The American Catholic People: Their Beliefs, Practices, and Values.* New York: Doubleday, 1987.

Ginsberg, Benjamin, and Martin Shefter. "A Critical Realignment? The New Politics, the Reconstituted Right, and the Election of 1984." *The Elections of 1984.* Ed. Michael Nelson. Washington, D.C.: Congressional Quarterly, 1985, 1–25.

"God and Politics: Mixing More Than Ever." *Congressional Quarterly* (23 Sept. 1978): 2565.

Goldman, Ari L. "Catholic Bishops Hire Firms to Market Fight on Abortion." *New York Times,* 6 Apr. 1990, p. A1.

———. "Legislator Barred from Catholic Rite." *New York Times,* 17 Nov. 1989, p. A18.

Greeley, Andrew M. *The American Catholic: A Social Portrait*. New York: Basic, 1977.

———. *American Catholics since the Council: An Unauthorized Report*. Chicago: Thomas More, 1985.

———. *The Catholic Myth: The Behavior and Beliefs of American Catholics*. New York: Charles Scribner's Sons, 1990.

Greeley, Andrew M. and Peter H. Rossi. *The Education of Catholic Americans*. Chicago: Aldine, 1966.

Greeley, Andrew M., William McCready, and Kathleen McCourt. *Catholic Schools in a Declining Church*. Kansas City: Sheed and Ward, 1976.

Greenhouse, Linda. "Suit on Church Tax Status and Abortion Fails." *New York Times*, 1 May 1990, p. A18.

Guilday, Peter. *The Life and Times of John England, First Bishop of Charleston*. 2 vols. New York: America, 1927.

Gwertzman, Bernard. "Administration Hails New Draft of Arms Letter." *New York Times*, 7 Apr. 1983, p. A1.

Halsey, William M. *The Survival of American Innocence: Catholicism in an Era of Disillusionment, 1920–1940*. Notre Dame: University of Notre Dame Press, 1980.

Hanley, Thomas O'Brien, S.J., ed. *The John Carroll Papers*. 3 vols. Notre Dame: University of Notre Dame Press, 1976.

Hanna, Mary T. *Catholics and American Politics*. Cambridge: Harvard University Press, 1979.

———. "From Civil Religion to Prophetic Church: The Bishops and the Bomb." *American Political Theology*. Ed. Charles Dunn. New York: Praeger, 1984, 144–54.

———. "Bishops as Political Leaders." *Religion in American Politics*. Ed. Charles Dunn. Washington, D.C.: Congressional Quarterly, 1988, 75–86.

Hanson, Eric O. *The Catholic Church in World Politics*. Princeton: Princeton University Press, 1987.

Hennesey, James, S.J. *American Catholics: A History of the Roman Catholic Community in the United States*. New York: Oxford University Press, 1981.

Hehir, J. Bryan. "The Just War Ethic and Catholic Theology: Dynamics of Change and Continuity." *War or Peace? The Search for New Answers*. Ed. Thomas A. Shannon. Maryknoll, N.Y.: Orbis, 1980, 15–39.

———. "Reflections on Recent Teaching." *Nuclear Disarmament: Key Statements of Popes, Bishops, Councils, and Churches*. Ed. Robert Hyer. New York: Paulist, 1982, 1–11.

———. "From the Pastoral Constitution of Vatican II to the Challenge of Peace." *Catholics and Nuclear War: A Commentary on "The Challenge of Peace"—The U.S. Catholic Bishops' Pastoral Letter on War and Peace*. Ed. Phillip J. Murnion. New York: Crossroad, 1983, 71–87.

Herbers, John. "Ultraconservative Evangelicals: A Surging New Force in Politics." *New York Times*, 17 Aug. 1980, p. A1.

Higgins, George C. "Commentary on Pastoral Constitution on the Church in the Modern World." *American Participation in the Second Vatican Council*. Ed. Vincent A. Yzermans. New York: Sheed and Ward, 1967, 262–69.

Hollenbach, David. "The Challenge of Peace in the Context of Recent Church Teachings." *Catholics and Nuclear War: A Commentary on "The Challenge of Peace"—*

The U.S. Catholic Bishops' Pastoral Letter on War and Peace. Ed. Phillip J. Murnion. New York: Crossroad, 1983, 3–15.

Hyer, Marjorie. "Some Catholics Lament Bishops' Abortion Stress." *Washington Post*, 11 Sept. 1976, p. A4.

Hyer, Robert. *Nuclear Disarmament: Key Statements of Popes, Bishops, Councils, and Churches*. New York: Paulist, 1982.

Johnson, Donald Bruce, ed. *National Party Platforms: Volume 2, 1960–1987*. 2 vols. Urbana: University of Illinois Press, 1978.

Johnson, Janis. "President Hints at Abortion 'Concern.'" *Washington Post*, 9 Aug. 1976, p. A10.

Joyce, Fay S. "Mondale Explains Role of Religion." *New York Times*, 8 Sept. 1984, p. A8.

Kelly, Alfred H., Winfred A. Harbison, and Herman Belz. *The American Constitution: Its Origins and Development*. New York: W. W. Norton, 1983.

Kelly, George A. *The Battle for the American Church*. Garden City: Doubleday, 1979.

Kennedy, Eugene. *The Now and Future Church: The Psychology of Being an American Catholic*. Garden City: Doubleday, 1984.

———. *Re-Imagining American Catholicism: The American Bishops and Their Pastoral Letters*. New York: Vintage, 1985.

Key, V. O. "A Theory of Critical Elections." *Journal of Politics* 17 (1955): 3–18.

Kinzer, Donald L. *An Episode in Anti-Catholicism: The American Protective Association*. Seattle: University of Washington Press, 1964.

Lardner, George, Jr. "Soviets' Role in Nuclear Freeze Limited, FBI Says." *Washington Post*, 26 Mar. 1983, p. A7.

Lay Commission. *Toward the Future: Catholic Social Teaching and the U.S. Economy*. New York: American Catholic Committee, 1984.

Lipset, Seymour Martin, and Earl Rabb. "The Election and the Evangelicals." *Commentary* (Mar. 1981): 25–31.

Lopatto, Paul. *Religion and the Presidential Election*. New York: Praeger, 1985.

Lowi, Theodore J. "Europeanization of America? From United States to United State." *Nationalizing Government: Public Policies in America*. Eds. Theodore J. Lowi and Alan Stone. Beverly Hills: Sage, 1978, 15–29.

McAvoy, Thomas T. *The Great Crisis in American Catholic History, 1895–1900*. Chicago: Henry Regnery, 1957.

———. "The Catholic Minority after the Americanist Controversy, 1899–1917: A Survey." *Review of Politics* 21 (1959): 53–82.

———. *A History of the Catholic Church in the United States*. Notre Dame: University of Notre Dame Press, 1969.

McElvaine, Robert D. "Liberals Go Back to the Flag." *New York Times*, 2 Sept. 1984, p. E15.

McFadden, Robert D. "Archbishop Asserts That Cuomo Misinterpreted Stand on Abortion." *New York Times*, 4 Aug. 1984, p. A1.

———. "O'Connor–Ferraro Dispute on Abortion Unresolved." *New York Times*, 11 Sept. 1984, p. A1.

McGrory, Mary. "Ferraro's Performance Shows the Wit, Grit of a Born Politician." *Washington Post*, 25 Sept. 1984, p. A2.

McKeown, Elizabeth. "War and Welfare: A Study of American Catholic Leadership." Ph.D. diss., University of Chicago, 1972.

McShane, Joseph, S.J. *"Sufficiently Radical": Catholicism, Progressivism, and the Bishops' Program of 1919*. Washington, D.C.: Catholic University of America Press, 1986.

Maraniss, David. "House Passes Nuclear Freeze Resolution." *Washington Post*, 5 May 1983, p. A8.

Marshall, Charles C. "An Open Letter to the Honorable Alfred E. Smith." *Atlantic Monthly* (Apr. 1927): 540–49.

Meconis, Charles A. *With Clumsy Grace: The American Catholic Left, 1961–1975*. New York: Seabury, 1979.

Melville, Annabelle M. *John Carroll of Baltimore: Founder of the American Catholic Hierarchy*. New York: Charles Scribner's Sons, 1955.

Menendez, Albert J. *Religion at the Polls*. Philadelphia: Westminster, 1977.

———. *John F. Kennedy: Catholic and Humanist*. Buffalo: Prometheus, 1979.

Merton, Andrew H. *Enemies of Choice: The Right to Life Movement and Its Threat to Abortion*. Boston: Beacon, 1981.

Mohr, Charles. "Abortion Stand by Carter Vexes Catholic Bishops." *New York Times*, 1 Sept. 1976, p. A1.

Moynihan, James H. *The Life of Archbishop John Ireland*. New York: Harper, 1953.

Murray, John Courtney. "Commentary on Declaration on Religious Freedom." *American Participation in the Second Vatican Council*. Ed. Vincent A. Yzermans. New York: Sheed and Ward, 1967, 668–76.

Naughton, James W. "Ford Hopes Linked to Catholic Vote." *New York Times*, 5 Sept. 1976, p. A1.

"NCWC: New Life and Vigor." *America* (19 Nov. 1966): 643.

Neuhaus, Richard John. "The Right to Fight." *Commonweal* (9 Oct. 1981): 555–59.

———. *The Naked Public Square: Religion and Democracy in America*. Grand Rapids: Eerdmans, 1984.

"New Right Plans Move to Change Congress." *Congressional Quarterly* (23 Oct. 1976): 3027.

Nolan, Hugh J. *The Most Reverend Francis Patrick Kenrick, Third Bishop of Philadelphia, 1830–1851*. Washington, D.C.: Catholic University of America Press, 1948.

———, ed. *Pastoral Letters of the United States Catholic Bishops*. 4 vols. Washington, D.C.: United States Catholic Conference, 1984.

O'Brien, David J. *American Catholics and Social Reform: The New Deal Years*. New York: Oxford University Press, 1968.

———. *Renewal of American Catholicism*. New York: Oxford University Press, 1972.

O'Brien, David J., and Thomas A. Shannon, eds. *Renewing the Earth: Catholic Documents on Peace, Justice and Liberation*. Garden City: Image, 1977.

"O'Connor Critical of Ferraro's Views." *New York Times*, 9 Sept. 1984, p. 34.

Olmstead, Robert. "Bishops Chart New Course with Dearden at the Helm." *National Catholic Reporter* (23 Nov. 1966): 1.

"On Abortion, the Bishops v. the Deacon." *Time* (20 Sept. 1976): 11.

"On Selling the Bishops." *Commonweal* (10 Dec. 1971): 243.

O'Toole, James M. "Prelates and Politicos: Catholics and Politics in Massachusetts, 1900–1970." *Catholic Boston: Studies in Religion and Community, 1870–1970*. Eds. James M. O'Toole and Robert E. Sullivan. Boston: Archdiocese of Boston, 1985, 15–66.

Paige, Connie. *The Right to Lifers: Who They Are, How They Operate, Where They Get Their Money*. New York: Summit, 1983.

Perlez, Jane. "Ferraro Acts to Still Abortion Dispute." *New York Times*, 12 Sept. 1984, p. B9.

———. "Ferraro Says Religion Won't Influence Policy." *New York Times*, 13 Sept. 1984, p. B16.

Phillips, Kevin B. *The Emerging Republican Majority*. Garden City: Anchor, 1969.

Pierce, Kenneth M. "God and the Ballot Box." *Time* (17 Sept. 1984): 26–27.

"Portrait of the Electorate." *New York Times*, 8 Nov. 1984, p. A19.

Ramsey, Paul. *The Just War: Force and Political Responsibility*. New York: Scribner's, 1968.

Rashke, Richard. "Little Dissent When Bishops Meet." *National Catholic Reporter* (5 Dec. 1975): 6.

Reese, Thomas J. "The Selection of Bishops." *America* (25 Aug. 1984): 65–72.

Reichley, A. James. "The Reagan Coalition." *Brookings Review*, 1/2 (1986): 6–9.

———. *Religion in American Public Life*. Washington, D.C.: Brookings Institution, 1985.

Roberts, Sam. "Cuomo to Challenge Archbishop over Criticism of Abortion Stand." *New York Times*, 3 Aug. 1984, p. B2.

Roohan, James Edmund. *American Catholics and the Social Question, 1865–1900*. New York: Arno, 1976.

Rusher, William A. *The Making of a New Majority Party*. New York: Sheed and Ward, 1975.

———. *The Rise of the Right*. New York: Morrow, 1984.

Safire, William. "Curb the Halting." *New York Times Magazine*, 22 May 1983, pp. 12–15.

Sanders, James W. *The Education of an Urban Minority: Catholics in Chicago, 1833–1965*. New York: Oxford University Press, 1977.

Scammon, Richard M., and Ben J. Wattenberg. *The Real Majority*. New York: Coward-McCann, 1970.

Schattschneider, E. E. *The Semi-Sovereign People: A Realist's View of Democracy in America*. New York: Holt, Rinehart and Winston, 1960.

Schram, Martin. *Running for President 1976: The Carter Campaign*. New York: Stein and Day, 1977.

Scott, William A., and Frances M. Scott. *The Church Then and Now: Cultivating a Sense of Tradition*. Kansas City: Leaven, 1984.

Shanabruch, Charles. *Chicago's Catholics: The Evolution of an American Identity*. Notre Dame: University of Notre Dame Press, 1981.

Shapiro, Walter. "Politics and the Pulpit." *Newsweek* (17 Sept. 1984): 24–27.

Shaw, Richard. *Dagger John: The Unquiet Life and Times of Archbishop John Hughes of New York*. New York: Paulist, 1977.

Shribman, David. "House Passes Modified Nuclear Freeze Resolution." *New York Times*, 5 May 1983, p. B17.

Shriver, Peggy L. *The Bible Vote: Religion and the New Right*. New York: Pilgrim, 1981.

Smith, Alfred E. "Catholic and Patriot: Governor Smith Responds." *Atlantic Monthly* (May 1927): 721–28.

Steinfels, Peter. "Bishops Warn Politicians on Abortion." *New York Times*, 8 Nov. 1989, p. A18.

———. "Knights Aiding Anti-Abortion Effort." *New York Times*, 13 May 1990, p. A18.

Sundquist, James L. *Dynamics of the Party System: Alignment and Realignment of Political Parties in the United States*. Washington, D.C.: Brookings Institution, 1983.

Tatalovich, Raymond, and Byron W. Daynes. *The Politics of Abortion: A Study of Community Conflict in Public Policy Making*. New York: Praeger, 1981.

"The Bishops and Viet Nam." *Commonweal* (15 Apr. 1966): 94.

"The Bishops Meet." *Commonweal* (2 Dec. 1966): 245.

Tocqueville, Alexis de. *Democracy in America*. Garden City: Anchor, 1969.

"Transcript of the President's News Conference on Foreign and Domestic Matters." *New York Times*, 5 May 1983, p. D22.

United States Catholic Conference (USCC). *Documentation on the Right-to-Life and Abortion*. Washington, D.C.: United States Catholic Conference, 1974.

Verhovek, Sam Howe. "Cleric Assails Cuomo Stand on Abortion." *New York Times*, 24 Jan. 1989, p. B1.

Viguerie, Richard A. *The New Right: We're Ready to Lead*. Falls Church: Viguerie Company, 1980.

Vinovskis, Maris A. "Abortion and the Presidential Election of 1976: A Multivariate Analysis of Voting Behavior." *The Law and Politics of Abortion*. Eds. Carl E. Schneider and Maris A. Vinovskis. Lexington: Lexington Books, 1980, 184–205.

Vorgrimler, Herbert, ed. *Commentary on the Documents of Vatican II*. 5 vols. New York: Herder and Herder, 1967.

Wald, Kenneth D. *Religion and Politics in the United States*. New York: St. Martin's, 1987.

Waller, Douglas. *Congress and the Nuclear Freeze: An Inside Look at the Politics of a Mass Movement*. Amherst: University of Massachusetts Press, 1987.

Walsh, Edward. "Bishops Like Ford's Stand on Abortion." *Washington Post*, 11 Sept. 1976, p. A1.

Weber, Paul J. "Bishops in Politics: The Big Plunge." *America* (20 Mar. 1976): 220–23.

Weigel, George. *Tranquillitus Ordinis: The Present Failure and Future Promise of American Catholic Thought on War and Peace*. Oxford: Oxford University Press, 1987.

Weinraub, Bernard. "Mondale Pledges Immediate Effort for Arms Freeze." *New York Times*, 6 Sept. 1984, p. A1.

———. "Mondale Plans to Focus on Issues Where He Says Reagan Is Weak." *New York Times*, 9 Sept. 1984, p. A1.

———. "Campaign Courtesy: Bush Calls on Bishop." *New York Times*, 3 Oct. 1988, p. A22.

Wills, Garry. *Bare Ruined Choirs*. Garden City: Doubleday, 1972.

Woodward, Kenneth L. "Faith, Hope, and Votes." *Newsweek* (17 Sept. 1984): 34–35.

Life Amendment Political Action Committee
(LAPAC), 88
Lowi, Theodore, 44–45, 47
Lynch, Patrick, 17

McAvoy, Thomas, 20, 22–24, 27, 28
McDevitt, Gerald, 44
McGlynn, Edward, 19–21, 23
McGovern, George, 65, 70, 84, 112, 141
McGrory, Mary, 126
McHugh, James, 57, 59, 68–69
McKeown, Elizabeth, 25
McQuaid, Bernard, 19, 33
McShane, Joseph, 26
Maher, Leo, 139
Manatt, Charles, 113, 125
Manning, Timothy, 58
Markey, Edward, 105, 111
Marshall, Charles, 38
Medeiros, Humberto, 58, 85–86, 143
Menendez, Albert, 88
Model Penal Code, 54
Mondale, Walter, 74, 112–13, 117–18, 124–
25, 141–42, 145
Moral Majority, 89–90
Mundelein, George, 27–28
Murphy, Francis, 92, 98, 105
Murray, John Courtney, 39

National Catholic War Council, 25, 27
National Catholic Welfare Conference, 26–
27, 29–30, 32, 47–49
National Coalition of American Nuns, 83
National Committee for a Human Life Amendment, 58
National Conference of Catholic Bishops
(NCCB), 1976 election, 71–84, 115, 118,
127, 135; 1980 election, 82, 85, 91, 115,
127; 1982 election, 105–6; 1984 election,
107–8, 112–27, 130, 135; 1988 election,
127, 130–35; abortion and, 4–8, 10, 54–
61, 64–65, 67–86, 91, 98–99, 108, 111,
113–16, 118–22, 124–26, 139–40, 143–46;
antiabortion Constitutional amendment
and, 57–58, 68, 71, 75, 77, 85; antiabortion movement and, 4–8, 10, 57–61, 64–
65, 82, 84–85, 91, 98–99, 107; debate
within, 6–7, 59–60, 68–70, 73, 84–86,
107, 114–20, 124–26, 130–31, 136–37;
Democratic party and, 65, 70–82, 85, 107,
112–14, 118–26, 131–34, 138, 140–42,

145; economy and, 4, 128–31, 141–42; establishment of, 49–52; modern political
role of, 56–57, 60, 64–65, 92, 102–3,
129–30; new right and, 86, 91–92, 107; nuclear freeze movement and, 105–7, 108–
12, 145; nuclear weapons and, 4, 7, 10,
68, 91–92, 96–116, 125, 128, 130–31,
138, 140–41, 144–45; Republican party
and, 70–71, 73, 76–83, 106–8, 113–14,
118–19, 123–26, 140, 145; Roe v. Wade,
57–58, 136, 139, 145; Vatican and, 18–22,
27, 39, 54, 137–38; Vietnam War and 94–
96, 104; Webster v. Reproductive Health
Services, 135, 136n.22. See also bishops
National Federation of Priests Council, 82–83
National Opinion Research Center, 35
National Right-to-Life Committee, 58, 88
New Deal, 28–29, 33, 44–45, 129
Nixon, Richard, 63, 65–66, 70, 141
Nofziger, Lyn, 123
Novak, Michael, 131
nuclear freeze, 103–6, 108–13, 130, 145
nuclear weapons, bishops and, 4, 7, 10, 68,
91–92, 96–116, 125, 128, 130–31, 138,
140–41, 144–45; Catholics and, 103–4;
counterforce targeting, 97, 101; countervalue targeting, 97, 100; Democrats and,
111–14, 117–18, 125, 140; deterrence, 92,
97–99, 101; "first use," 100–101; John
XXIII and, 97; John Paul II and, 101; just
war theory and, 97, 99–102; Pius XII and,
96–97; Republicans and, 107–11, 117–18,
125, 140
Nuclear Weapons Freeze Campaign, 105–6

O'Brien, David, 29, 31, 35–36
O'Connell, William, 27
O'Connor, John, 8, 110, 115–24, 126, 134,
143
O'Toole, James, 32–33

Paige, Connie, 88
Pastoral Constitution on the Church in the
Modern World, 39–43, 51, 55, 97
Pastoral Letter of 1837, 15
Pastoral Letter of 1919, 28
Pastoral Plan for Pro-Life Activities, 58–60,
68–69, 71, 78, 80, 83, 116
Paul VI, Pope, 55, 94
Pax Christi, 99, 105, 116
Peace on Earth, 94n.7, 97